D0983620

The indentured labor trade was initiated to replace freed slaves on sugar plantations in British colonies in the 1830s, but expanded to many other locations around the world. This is the first survey of the global flow of indentured migrants that developed after the end of the slave trade from Africa and continued until shortly after World War I. This volume describes the experiences of the two million Asians, Africans, and South Pacific islanders who signed long-term labor contracts in return for free passage overseas, modest wages, and other benefits. The experience of these indentured migrants of different origins and destinations is compared in terms of their motives, conditions of travel, and subsequent creation of permanent overseas settlements. The study considers the perspectives of both recruits and employers, identifies objective and quantifiable data for making comparisons, and relates this new indentured labor trade to other large-scale migrations.

Studies in Comparative World History

Indentured labor in the age of imperialism
1834–1922

Studies in Comparative World History

Editors

Michael Adas, Rutgers University
Edmund Burke III, University of California, Santa Cruz
Philip D. Curtin, The Johns Hopkins University

Other books in the series

Indentured labor in the age of imperialism, 1834–1922

DAVID NORTHRUP

Boston College

Published by the Press Syndicate of the University of Cambridge
The Pitt Building, Trumpington Street, Cambridge CB2 1RP
40 West 20th Street, New York, NY 10011-4211, USA
10 Stamford Road, Oakleigh, Melbourne 3166, Australia

First published 1995

Printed in the United States of America

Library of Congress Cataloging-in-Publication Data
Northrup, David.
    Indentured labor in the age of imperialism, 1834–1922 / David
Northrup.
        p. cm. – (Studies in comparative world history)
    Includes bibliographical references and index.
    ISBN 0-521-48047-7. – ISBN 0-521-48519-3 (pbk.)
    1. Indentured servants – History.   2. Contract labor – History.
I. Title.   II. Series.
    HD4871.N67 1995
 331.5'42'09 – dc20   94-38289
                                                                CIP

A catalog record for this book is available from the British Library.

ISBN 0-521-48047-7 Hardback
ISBN 0-521-487519-3 Paperback

Contents

Maps, figures, and tables

Maps

Figures

Tables

Preface

Despite its importance for the nineteenth century, the indentured labor trade remains little known to most well-informed people, including historians. To most North Americans, indentured labor refers only to the seventeenth- and eighteenth-century migration from Europe to the Americas. The African slave trade of that same era is well known, but not the sizable indentured trade that followed the end of slavery. Yet in its own way this new indentured labor trade from Asia, Africa, and the Pacific islands deserves comparison with the larger, contemporary exodus from Europe to overseas locations in the nineteenth century.

The obscurity of the topic is not a product of its neglect by historians. Indeed, there has been a growing volume of books and articles on indentured labor in recent decades. But most of these works have examined the subject in terms of a single place of origin, a single destination, or, most common of all, the experience of a single migrant people in a single overseas location. Although comparative studies of indentured labor have begun to appear, most works are still intended for other specialists. This is the first book to attempt to tell the global story of the new indentured labor trade for a general audience.

Indeed, I must admit that when I began this research seven years ago, I little suspected how broad the topic was and into how many interesting new corners of world history it would lead me. My interest in indentured labor grew out of a series of projects focused on the organization of labor in precolonial Africa, the export of labor through the Atlantic slave trade, and the tortured transition from slavery to various forms of forced and coerced labor in colonial Africa.[1] Not surprisingly, my initial approach focused on the resemblance of indentured labor to slavery, particularly

[1]David Northrup, *Trade without Rulers: Pre-Colonial Economic Development in South-Eastern Nigeria* (Oxford: Clarendon Press, 1978); *Beyond the Bend in the River: African Labor in Eastern Zaire, 1865–1940* (Athens: Ohio University Press, 1988); ed., *The Atlantic Slave Trade* (Lexington, Mass.: D. C. Heath, 1994).

after reading Hugh Tinker's influential book on Indian indentured labor.[2] In the Preface to that work, Tinker relates how he began his research with a moderate and detached point of view about indentured labor and was gradually led by his reading of the evidence to present a darker picture of it as a new system of slavery. It is ironic that in the course of my research on the subject my views shifted from near Tinker's final outlook back toward a median position, which sees indentured labor overall as having more in common with the experiences of "free" migrants of the same era than with the victims of the slave trade. In part this was due to the influence of a new generation of historical scholarship unavailable to Tinker. In part it resulted from a predisposition, derived from current trends in the study of the slave trade, to pay particular attention to the motives and actions of the migrants themselves. In addition, the methodologies and controversies of slave trade historiography have provided useful models for comparing the literature of indentured labor, notably in the discussion of shipboard mortality in Chapter 4.

As a brazen and belated intruder in this field of study, I am humbly and gratefully aware that I am reaping the fruits of others' labors. Although I have made use of the large body of contemporary records and reports published in the British *Parliamentary Papers*, there can be little herein that is not conscious or unconscious product of others' research and conclusions. Insofar as this work can claim originality, it lies in the breadth of its treatment and in its comparative approach. It is hoped this synthesis proves useful to beginning students wishing an overview of this topic, to more advanced students trying to gain perspective on it, as well as to specialists seeking to place their work in a broader context.

This is the place to acknowledge the fullness of my debts. In addition to the scores of specialized works cited in the following chapters, the quantity, quality, and breadth of scholarship by several individuals has been a profound influence on the field of study. To the extent that I see any farther, it is because I stand on the shoulders of these giants; to them I dedicate this volume. I owe much to a series of thoughtful comparative articles in which Stanley L. Engerman examined the size and significance of contract labor. Though somewhat differently conceived, this study walks in the marvelously straight furrows he has plowed. I have profited immeasurably from the outstanding work by Ralph Shlomowitz, whose writing includes a raft of carefully focused and meticulous examinations of the Pacific islander trade as well as broad comparative essays on the indentured labor trade's global compass. The germ of my interest in this

[2]Hugh Tinker, *A New System of Slavery: The Export of Indian Labour Overseas, 1830–1920* (London: Oxford University Press, 1974). For a critique of this work's weakness in comparative migration and migration theory, see the review by Brian Blouet and Olwyn M. Blouet, *Caribbean Studies* 16.2 (1976): 251–53.

subject was planted by a fortuitous encounter with Arnold J. Meagher in Lisbon more than thirty years ago when he was finishing up his magisterial (but unfortunately never published) dissertation on the Chinese indentured labor trade to Latin America. Wherever he may be, I wish him to know that his work convinced me that a comparative survey of the trade was possible and has been a regular source of information and insight on a wide range of topics.[3]

I also wish to include Hugh Tinker in this dedication. While I am led to disagree with some aspects of his thoughtful, scholarly, and passionate examination of Indian indentured labor, my frequent citation of him in footnotes reveals the extent of my indebtedness to his pioneering research. I could not hope to match the depth of knowledge and insight of his work and am grateful that the broader scope and shorter length of my own make it unnecessary to do so. My own work is more skeletal than Tinker's in two senses: it is very much sparer, a bare-bones outline, and, in using a comparative approach, it pays more attention to the overall structures that underpinned the trade and less to the surface details. This sometimes leads me to quite different emphases.

For their generous criticisms of earlier versions of this work and/or for their kindness in providing me with copies of their own and others' work, I wish to give heartfelt thanks to Professors David Eltis (Queens University, Ontario), Stanley Engerman (University of Rochester), Daniel Headrick (Roosevelt University), Doug Munro (University of the South Pacific, Fiji), Monica Schuler (Wayne State University), Ralph Shlomowitz (The Flinders University of South Australia), Mrinalini Sinha (Boston College), and William Storey. Only the author bears responsibility for the errors and lapses that remain.

[3]For references see the bibliography.

1

Beginnings

In the summer of 1870 Mohamed Sheriff was buying flowers for the table in the bazaar in Lucknow, the capital of Oudh, a state that had been forcibly annexed to British India in 1856. Like many other upper-caste brahmans (priests) and *kshatriyas* (warriors) of Oudh, Sheriff had found employment in the Indian army, in his case as a servant to a British officer in the 13th Native Infantry. Whether because his officer had left India or for other reasons, Sheriff had left his employ, so that when a man approached him in the bazaar to ask if he was looking for work, Sheriff answered "yes." The man told him there was plenty of work in the sugar plantations of Demerara, and Sheriff agreed to go.

The man in the market was the local agent of a labor recruiter, the final link in a chain that extended back to the sugar growers of Demerara in British Guiana on the Caribbean coast of South America. Along with nine others recruited from Lucknow on this occasion, Sheriff was escorted to Calcutta, probably traveling the major portion of the distance on the railway completed just four years earlier. On 25 August 1870, five days after arriving in Calcutta, he boarded on the *Medea*, a large 1,066-ton vessel chartered to carry indentured migrants from Calcutta to British Guiana at the rate of twelve pounds a head. With Sheriff were 446 other Indian recruits, mostly younger males, but including 91 women, 31 children, and 21 infants. During their eighty-seven-day voyage through the Indian Ocean, around southern Africa, and across the Atlantic, five more infants were born. Six persons died during the voyage – a much lower death rate than a few years earlier.

Described as "intelligent looking" and able to speak English, Sheriff had served as a *sirdar* (headman) for the other immigrants in their dealings with the ship's officers. For this he expected to receive a payment of $3, but by the end of the voyage he had abandoned hope of receiving a $19 bonus the Indian recruiter had promised him in Lucknow. Nor, he told British investigators who met the ship in Guiana, had he received from the

1

officials who examined him in Calcutta the required copy of the indentured contract into which he had entered by accepting free passage to
Guiana. That he received the salary of "ten annas to two rupees a day" he
had been promised by the recruiter when he got to Moor Farm, a plantation whose owner purchased his indenture, is also doubtful. According to
the investigators, wages for able-bodied Indian males on sugar plantations
in British Guiana in 1870 were about 28 cents a day, not quite 10 annas and
far less than two rupees (32 annas).

The physical adjustments to the arduous and unfamiliar life of the sugar
plantation would not have been easy for Sheriff, who was not a farmer, a
characteristic he shared with many of his fellow recruits from Lucknow,
whom he described as "not all cultivators – some barbers, coachmen,
porters, and other followings." Still, Sheriff's psychological adjustment to
his new surroundings may have been easier than that of his companions,
since he had traveled abroad before, having accompanied the 14th Regi-
ment during the British invasion of Ethiopia in 1868. No known records
trace his life as an indentured laborer. Nor is it known if he stayed on in
British Guiana (as most Indians did) or if he ever returned to India.

While no single example can hope to capture the enormous range of
individual indentured experiences, in their broad outlines those of Mohamed Sheriff had much in common with those of tens of thousands of
other migrants[1] who left their homes between 1834 and 1914 under indentured contracts to labor in lands far from home. He is exceptional
largely in that his name and some of his life story have survived in
historical records. The lives of most others can be imagined only through
anonymous statistics. Along with the *Medea*, fifteen other chartered ships
left Calcutta for British Guiana during the 1869–70 season, carrying a total
of 6,685 passengers. At the time of his arrival there were 52,598 recent
migrants in British Guiana, mostly Indians, over 70 percent males, more
than three-quarters still under indenture. That same season eight ships
landed 3,811 additional Indians from Calcutta in the British West Indian
colonies of Jamaica and Trinidad.[2] In 1870 thirteen vessels carried 4,076

---

[1] To avoid cumbersome and confusing switches in point of view, this study refers to intercontinental travelers as migrants rather than immigrants and emigrants. It also often follows
the common historical convention of using "nineteenth century" to refer to the historical era
from 1815–1914, rather than to just the years 1801–1900.

[2] Sheriff's interview and the calculation of prevailing wage rates are in the 1871 Report of the
Commissioners Appointed to Enquire into the Treatment of Immigrants into British Guiana,
in Great Britain, *Parliamentary Papers* (hereafter *PP*) 1871 xx [c. 393], pp. 59–60, 97. Details of
the voyage and other immigrants may be found in the 1871 General Report of the Colonial
Land and Emigration Commission (CLEC), pp. 7–10 and appendix 16; *PP* 1871 xx (369). For
Indian railroads, see Daniel R. Headrick, *The Tentacles of Progress: Technology Transfer in the
Age of Imperialism, 1850–1940* (New York: Oxford University Press, 1988), p. 65. Sheriff may
well have journeyed up from Bombay on the even newer rail line that was completed to
Allahabad in 1870.

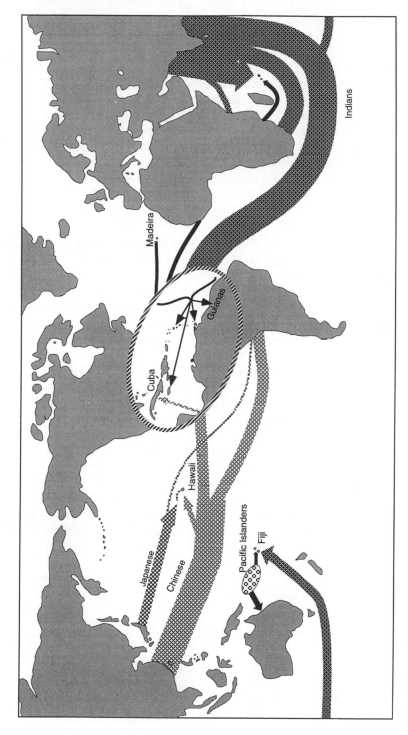

Map 1. Principal overseas indentured migrations, 1834–1919 (routes approximate).

indentured Indians to the British colony of Mauritius, one of the Mascarene islands of the Indian Ocean. Indians were also migrating under indenture by that time to Southeast Asia and to French colonies in the West Indies, but indenture was not a uniquely Indian experience. That same year (1870) 12,383 Chinese indentured laborers set sail for Peru and 1,312 for Cuba; 305 Chinese arrived in Hawaii, and a few Pacific islanders were recruited to Queensland, Australia.[3] Indentured migration from Africa had just ended; the first experiment in such recruitment from Japan had taken place in 1868 and would be resumed on a larger scale in 1885.

Indentured labor, slavery, and free migration

Though he may not have received a copy of its terms, Mohamed Sheriff was aware that he had signed a contract of indenture. The particular contract he signed, stricter than those affecting migrants from India to British Guiana before 1862, bound him to five years of service for whichever employer purchased it and then to a second five-year contract to complete his "industrial residence" in the colony.[4] At that point he was entitled to free passage home, but many accepted a cash "bounty" for signing a new labor contract instead.

Although such serial indentured contracts were a novel feature of the later nineteenth century, indenture had a long history in British colonies in the Americas. More than half of all European migrants to British colonies in the seventeenth and eighteenth centuries are estimated to have been indentured, including three-quarters of those to seventeenth-century Virginia. Impoverished British, Irish, Scottish, and German migrants accepted the conditions of indentured "servitude" in order to begin a better life in the New World colonies. A trickle continued to arrive until shortly before the new, largely Asian, indentured migrants began to arrive in the 1830s.[5]

These new indentured migrants differed from their European predecessors in more ways than their origins. Indentured Asians, Africans, and Pacific islanders of the nineteenth century went to a wider variety of destinations in the Americas, as well as to islands in the Indian and Pacific Oceans, to Australia, and to parts of East and southern Africa, making theirs more global than the European migrations across the North Atlantic.

[3]Colonial Blue Book of Mauritius, 1871; Arnold J. Meagher, "The Introduction of Chinese Laborers to Latin America: The 'Coolie Trade,' 1847–1874" (Ph.D. dissertation, History, University of California, Davis, 1975), tables 13–14; Katharine Coman, The History of Contract Labor in the Hawaiian Islands (New York: Arno Press, 1978), p. 63.

[4]Alan H. Adamson, Sugar without Slaves: The Political Economy of British Guiana, 1838–1904 (New Haven: Yale University Press, 1972), pp. 54–56, 110.

[5]David W. Galenson, "The Rise and Fall of Indentured Servitude in the Americas: An Economic Analysis," Journal of Economic History 44.1 (1984): 1–26.

Unlike the earlier European indentured servants who generally received only their maintenance, the indentured laborers of the nineteenth century received wages along with free housing and medical care, along with clothing and full rations in many cases. Nor were the new indentured laborers direct successors to the old. Indentured Europeans in the West Indies had largely been replaced by enslaved Africans during the second half of the seventeenth century and slaves also displaced most indentured servants in the Chesapeake Bay colonies during the eighteenth century. As Chapter 2 will describe in more detail, the new indentured migrants were first recruited as successors to the slaves freed in the British colonies in the 1830s. When French, Dutch, and Spanish colonies ended slavery, they too turned to indentured labor, as would the owners of plantations and mines in places that had never had slavery.

Some influential commentators have portrayed the new indentured labor not just as a successor to slavery but as a disguised continuation of that abolished institution. The British secretary of state for the colonies in 1840 expressed fears that the still modest Indian indentured labor trade might easily become "a new system of slavery," while the viceroy of India, in urging its termination in 1915, charged that it had indeed become "a system of forced labour . . . differing but little from . . . slavery." Several modern historical analyses also link indentured labor and slavery at least in some sectors of the trade, of which Hugh Tinker's study of indentured Indian labor is the most influential.[6]

There are striking resemblances. Especially in the early years of the trade, many indentured laborers were recruited through kidnapping and coercion or were seriously misled by unscrupulous recruiters about their destinations, duties, and compensation – circumstances that gave rise to unflattering nicknames: "blackbirding" in the South Pacific, the "pig trade" in China, the "coolie trade" in India. Crowded conditions of transport and the high mortality rates in transit have also invited comparison

[6]Quotes from Hugh Tinker, *A New System of Slavery: The Export of Indian Labour Overseas, 1830–1920* (London: Oxford University Press, 1974), pp. vi, 339–40. See also Johnson U. J. Asiegbu, *Slavery and the Politics of Liberation, 1787–1861: A Study of Liberated African Emigration and British Anti-Slavery Policy* (London: Longmans, 1969), p. 119, who states that the African "emigration scheme degenerated into almost open slave trading after 1843." With regard to the labor trade from East Africa to Réunion, François Renault, *Libération d'esclaves et nouvelle servitude: Les rachats de captifs africains pour le compte des colonies françaises après l'abolition de l'esclavage* (Abidjan: Nouvelles Editions Africaines, 1976), p. 71, concludes "le respect du volontariat chez l'engagé se reduisait, en règle générale, à une fiction administrative" [the voluntary aspect of the recruit was reduced, as a general rule, to an administrative fiction]. According to Monica Schuler, "The Recruitment of African Indentured Labourers for European Colonies in the Nineteenth Century," in *Colonialism and Migration: Indentured Labour before and after Slavery*, ed. P. C. Emmer (The Hague: Martinus Nijhoff, 1986), pp. 125–27: "In practice, . . . African indentured labour recruitment cannot be distinguished from either the 'legal' or 'illegal' slave trade."

with the slave trade. Finally, at their destinations indentured laborers performed tasks, lived in dwellings, and endured harsh disciplinary measures that in many cases were identical to those of the slaves they replaced – or very nearly so. In Cuban plantations, slaves and indentured Chinese even worked side by side. On Peruvian desert islands where Chinese mined guano deposits, conditions may have been worse than those associated with slavery.

Despite these similarities, most recent scholarship has questioned whether the indentured labor trade as a whole is best viewed as little more than a modified form of slavery. Researchers have argued that the worst circumstances applied to a distinct minority of indentured migrants, whereas most indentured laborers were recruited, transported, and employed under conditions that were quite distinct from the systems of New World slavery. Using more rigorous methods of comparison and relying less on emotive anecdotal evidence, economic and demographic historians have emphasized the voluntary nature of most indentured migration and the role of epidemiological factors rather than abuse in producing high mortality rates among some emigrant groups during transit and acclimatization to a new environment. For example, with regard to indentured Pacific islanders Ralph Shlomowitz reports, "During the past twenty years, . . . a revisionist interpretation has emerged: after an initial period . . . the labor trade came to be, in the main, a voluntary business arrangement, subject to government supervision, with the islanders being willing participants." More generally, Stanley Engerman argues, "It must be emphasized that the movement of contract labor differed from slavery," at least in being a voluntary bondage of limited duration. The view of indentured labor as "an extension of slavery . . . is not supported" by a recent volume of articles, according to its editors.[7] Paralleling recent debates about systems of slavery, the critical issue is not deciding whether a system was "harsh" or "mild," but which conditions were exceptional and which typical. Another feature of the new historiography is its concern with relating indentured labor to the changing historical circumstances in capital markets, ideas, and technology that shaped the nineteenth century.

In evaluating these conflicting schools of interpretation, it is useful to bear in mind that during the nineteenth century the new indentured migrants were not alone in being described as laboring under a new form of slavery. The campaign to free black slaves in the West Indies had led to protests from industrial Europe's "white slaves," the disenfranchised la-

---

[7]Ralph Shlomowitz, "Epidemiology and the Pacific Labor Trade," *Journal of Interdisciplinary History* 19.4 (1989): 589; Stanley Engerman, "Contract Labor, Sugar, and Technology in the Nineteenth Century," *Journal of Economic History* 43 (1983): 645; E. van den Boogaart and P. C. Emmer, "Colonialism and Migration: An Overview," in Emmer, *Colonialism and Migration*, p. 11.

borers in the satanic mills. In 1838 the Workingmen's Association of North-ampton denounced their "slavery to the rich" and "the shackles which held them in a state of bondage." The next year the liberal French Catholic Felicité de Lamennais wrote a volume on the working class called *Modern Slavery (De l'esclavage moderne)*. The *Communist Manifesto* at midcentury argued that industrial workers were "slaves of the bourgeois class," as well as of the machine and the bourgeois state, and near the end of the century Pope Leo XIII's famous encyclical letter on the condition of the working class echoed the first of these judgments.[8]

While the charge that industrial workers were "slaves" was in part metaphorical and much influenced by the campaign rhetoric of the abo-litionists, it is quite true that the "free" laboring person (like the bonded migrant) was under economic, political, and social constraints that were more than just the common human need to earn one's bread by the sweat of one's brow. The labor law of the period, though stopping short of the provisions of slave codes, could be harsh and unforgiving: workers were bound by contract to set pay and hours, absences and lateness were se-verely penalized, and discipline could be enforced by corporal punish-ment. Even after many reforms, "wage slavery" remained a popular meta-phor. In short, it is important to see the new indentured labor in the context of its times.

Does the fact that both wage and indentured laborers in the nineteenth century were so frequently spoken of as "slaves" suggest they may have shared more in common than is generally acknowledged? Colin Newbury and others have pursued this approach with regard to the contempo-raneous overseas migrations of "free" Europeans and "indentured" non-Europeans. There were differences as well as similarities, but, on the whole, indentured laborers seem to have had much more in common with the masses of Europeans who ventured overseas in this period than with the older European indentured servants or African slaves. In the first place, despite some exceptions, most indentured migrants left their homes vol-untarily, just like most of the fifty million unindentured Europeans (a few convicts aside) who migrated overseas. Both were pushed to leave their families and friends by economic misery, discrimination, and famine at home and pulled to new locations overseas by hopes of better conditions and opportunities. Second, both resulted in permanent settlements as well as cyclical migrations. Newbury also points out that the distinction often drawn between the European "settler" and the non-European "sojourner"

---

[8]See R. J. M. Blackett, *Building an Antislavery Wall* (Ithaca: Cornell University Press, 1989), pp. 23–25; Marcus Cunliffe, *Chattel Slavery and Wage Slavery: The Anglo-American Context, 1830–1860* (Athens: University of Georgia Press, 1979), pp. 10–12. Pope Leo wrote in *Rerum Novarum*, para. 6: "a very few rich and exceedingly rich men have laid a yoke almost of slavery on the unnumbered masses of non-owning workers."

or "laborer" is not justified. Despite the fact that indentured labor contracts usually guaranteed return passage, a great many indentured laborers settled permanently in their new homes after the expiration of their contracts, rather than return to their countries of origin. If the assumption of impermanence on the part of indentured laborers is exaggerated, new studies have shown the proportion of European migrants who returned to their countries of origin was often quite high.[9]

A third factor that free and indentured migrants had in common was the ships and maritime regulations of their transport overseas. The vessels carrying free and indentured migrants in the nineteenth century were much larger and faster than those that carried slaves and indentured migrants in the previous centuries. Such changes in shipping and in the scale of migration reflect the broader changes in the era's economy, which encouraged overseas investment and commercial development of new areas of the world far distant from the high-growth industrial societies.

While sharing these common factors, the two groups of nineteenth-century migrants also differed in important ways. Europeans went overwhelmingly to other temperate areas where they were free from legal bondage, while indentured Asians, Africans, and Pacific islanders went to tropical areas where they faced long years of bondage to repay the debt of their transport. In part, as studies by David Galenson and W. Arthur Lewis have pointed out, nineteenth-century Europeans were willing to migrate only to destinations with wage rates higher than those prevailing in their own region (which were already high by global standards) and most faced only a brief passage to North America, while people from low-wage countries in other parts of the world had to accept the offers of more distant tropical areas that were willing to subsidize their voyages in return for indenture.[10]

However, political manipulation was also an essential part of the differentiating process. In the first place, significant numbers of impoverished Europeans received government-subsidized passages that had no restrictions attached. From 1840 to 1878 the Colonial Land and Emigration Board in Great Britain selected residents of the British Isles for free or assisted

[9]Colin Newbury, "Labour Migration in the Imperial Phase: An Essay in Interpretation," *Journal of Imperial and Commonwealth History* 3.2 (1975): 235; Sucheng Chan, "European and Asian Immigration into the United States in Comparative Perspective, 1820s to 1920s," in *Immigration Reconsidered: History, Sociology, and Politics,* ed. Virginia Yans-McLaughlin (New York: Oxford University Press, 1990), p. 38.

[10]Galenson, "Rise and Fall of Indentured Servitude," pp. 16–26; W. Arthur Lewis, *The Development of the International Economic Order* (Princeton: Princeton University Press, 1978), pp. 14–20. Galenson calculates that the cost of a passage from East Asia to Hawaii, North America, or the West Indies was 3.5 to 10 times the per capita annual income in the region of origin, whereas the cost of a passage across the Atlantic was only half of the per capita annual income of European areas.

passage to colonies in Australia. Over 350,000 Europeans received passages assisted by the governments of Australia, New Zealand, southern Africa, and other British colonies. The governments of underpopulated lands such as Canada also subsidized passages for British citizens and other Europeans, including 200,000 Ukranians. The provincial government of São Paulo, Brazil, similarly underwrote the recruitment of over 800,000 Europeans, mostly from Italy, in the decades before 1907. Overall about 10 percent of European migrants in the nineteenth century traveled under government subsidy, while another 25 percent had their passage funded by relatives and friends.[11]

Governments chose to subsidize the cost of European migration, while requiring non-Europeans to repay their passage in indenture, for reasons that included unconcealed racial preferences and prejudices. For example, the governor of British Guiana justified imposing no indenture on Portuguese whose passage that colony's government paid while simultaneously imposing one on Indian and Chinese migrants on his belief that the Portuguese did not require to be compelled to work.[12] As will be detailed in Chapter 2, many countries and colonies also encouraged European settlement to "whiten" their populations under the guise of maintaining "civilized" standards. As Sidney Mintz has pointed out, a clear corollary of such white preference was the construction of "racist policies" to exclude non-European migrants from temperate areas where higher wages were inherently more attractive.[13] Instances include the Asian exclusion laws in the United States and Canada and the restrictions on the entry and status of Indians and Chinese in southern Africa and of Chinese and Pacific islanders in Australia.

To summarize, comparing indentured laborers with other nineteenth-century migrants reveals both similarities and differences. In form the new indentured trade of the nineteenth century strongly resembled the Eu-

---

[11]D. A. E. Harkness, "Irish Emigration," in *International Migrations*, vol. 2, *Interpretations*, ed. Walter F. Willcox (New York: National Bureau of Economic Research, 1931), pp. 266, 276–77; Dudley Baines, *Emigration from Europe, 1815–1930* (London: Macmillan, 1991), pp. 50–52. Newbury, "Labour Migration," pp. 240–42; he terms (p. 255) indentured the 900 Europeans who signed one-year contracts in return for free passage to Queensland, Australia, in 1906–12.

[12]*PP* 1859 xvi [c.2452], Governor Wodehouse to H. Labouchere, 6 June 1857, p. 232. Brian L. Moore, "The Social Impact of Portuguese Immigration into British Guiana after Emancipation," *Boletín de Estudios Latinoamericanos y del Caribe* 19 (1975): 4–5, argues that since the 41,000 Portuguese, mostly from Madeira, introduced into the British West Indies at government expense between 1841 and 1881, were allowed to pay a monthly tax instead of being held to a contract: "In effect, [their] obligation to labour for a given period on the plantations was waived, or at least treated leniently, in contrast to other immigrants who were introduced at public expense."

[13]Sidney W. Mintz, *Sweetness and Power: The Place of Sugar in Modern History* (New York: Viking Penguin, 1985), p. 72.

ropean indentured labor trade of earlier centuries, but had no direct historical connection. Rather it was created to replace African slavery. That fact and the resemblances in their recruitment methods and labor conditions permit an interpretation of the new indentured labor as an extension of African slavery. But if indentured labor had one foot in slavery, it clearly had the other in the much larger voluntary overseas migrations of that era. As will be argued in more detail in the following chapters, indentured Asian, African, and Pacific island migrants had much in common with the even larger number of European migrants in their motives, conditions of travel, and subsequent creation of permanent overseas settlements. At the same time differences between the two migrant groups stemming from preexisting economic conditions and political manipulations meant that the initial labor experiences and destinations of indentured laborers set them apart from their European counterparts. Though a part of larger population movements, the indentured laborers of the nineteenth century also stand as a distinct group who deserve to be studied on their own.

Focus and scope of this study

There are many studies of indentured migrants from particular regions and into particular territories, but none that treats the labor of the nineteenth century as a whole. This study seeks to compare the different nineteenth-century indentured migrations and to relate their experiences to those of other contemporary migrant groups. Because, as the previous section of this study has shown, there are many areas of partial overlap between the experiences of indentured, enslaved, and free migrants, the first task is to delineate the limits of the study's central focus. In brief, it is concerned with labor migrations that were indentured, were intercontinental, and occurred during the period 1834–1922.

The first characteristic, *indenture*, serves to focus the study very largely on Asian, African, and Pacific islander migrants, since only a small number of Europeans migrated under indenture for reasons discussed earlier. Yet this is not a study of non-Western migration as a whole. This rubric also excludes the enormous numbers of internal labor migrants in these lands as well as the substantial numbers of Asians who ventured overseas free of any bond. The initial Chinese migrations to the Australian and Californian goldfields, for example, were of free migrants, as was most of the Indian migration to Ceylon (Sri Lanka). As Chapter 3 will make clear, these migrations were an important part of the context in which indentured labor operated, but also need to be clearly distinguished from the indentured migrations.

More difficult to classify are some Asian migrants who traveled on borrowed funds. Few would consider the need to repay money owed to family and friends a significant limitation on a migrant's freedom. However, when the debt was owed to a stranger who had also arranged employment at the new destination, a situation quite common among some Chinese and Indians, the difference from a formal contract of indenture becomes tenuous. In the case of recruits from India to Southeast Asian plantations it was known as the *kangany* system in Malaya and the *maistry* system in Burma. A recruiter (kangany, maistry) hired by employers or employer organizations advanced money to each recruit for expenses and passage from India and arranged for a labor contract at destination out of which this debt was repaid in installments.[14]

Another example of formalized debt contract was the "credit ticket" system that had developed between China and parts of Southeast Asia in the nineteenth century. Chinese labor brokers in southern China advanced recruits money for their passages and expenses and upon their arrival in the Straits Settlements (Malaya) sold these "unpaid passengers" for $20–24 to Chinese planters or foreign tin-miners.[15] A similar system organized by private companies was used to recruit Japanese laborers for Peru (1899–1909), Hawaii (1894–1900), and Mexico (1901–7).[16] Many Chinese came to North America (and Australia) under similar terms of debt bondage. According to Persia Campbell, "there is no doubt that the greater part of the Chinese emigration to California was financed or controlled by merchant brokers, acting independently or through the Trading Guilds," who advanced the Chinese the funds and retained control of the debt after their arrival. The Chinese repaid the debt in monthly installments including interest calculated at the rates equivalent to 50 to 100 percent a year. In Canada the brokers sold their lien to the employer who deducted it from wages, preventing the laborer from leaving his employ until the debt and accumulated interest charges were paid. It proved difficult for official investigators in both the United States and Canada to resolve whether

[14]Usha Mahajani, *The Role of Indian Minorities in Burma and Malaya* (Westport, Conn.: Greenwood Press, 1973), p. 97; Michael Adas, *The Burma Delta: Economic Development and Social Change on an Asian Rice Frontier, 1852–1941* (Madison: University of Wisconsin Press, 1974), pp. 91, 98–99. Recruiters were usually experienced Indian workers. Mahajani implies this led to "perpetual indebtedness of the laborer to his Kangany or Maistry"; Adas does not.

[15]Persia Crawford Campbell, *Chinese Coolie Emigration to Countries within the British Empire* (London: P. S. King & Son, 1923), pp. 1–6. She observes that half or more of the Chinese passengers to Malaya from the ports of Amoy, Hong Kong, and Swatow were under such credit ticket terms in 1876 but that by 1887 the number had declined to 27% of the Chinese arriving in Singapore and by 1890 to 8.4%, the rest being free of such debt to agents (though, of course, they may have owed friends and relatives).

[16]Toraje Irie, "History of Japanese Migration to Peru," *Hispanic American Historical Review* 31.3–4 (1951): 443; Dorothy Ochiai Hazama and Jane Okamoto Komeiji, *Okage Sama De: The Japanese in Hawaii, 1885–1985* (Honolulu: Bess Press, 1986), p. 25; Yuji Ichioka, *The Issei: The World of the First Generation Japanese Immigrants, 1885–1924* (New York: Free Press, 1988), p. 69.

these Chinese were being held in an involuntary bond because of the circumstances of their debt.[17]

In the case of Chinese migrants to California, where formal contracts of indenture were illegal, the debate has become quite sharp. The influential older study by Gunther Paul Barth holds that credit ticket passages to California were "made at times under arrangements similar to the thinly veiled slave trade of the coolie system," referring to the indentured Chinese labor trade to the Americas whose voluntariness has itself been the subject of sharply differing interpretations. On the other hand, Shih-shan Henry Tsai argues that "whether they came with their own money or under credit contract, these Chinese were free agents, as were the European immigrants." Most recently, Patricia Cloud and David Galenson have staked out a position between these two, arguing that what began as credit ticket emigration became "a system of effectively indentured labor based for the most part on voluntary bargains," whose details were concealed to evade legal prohibitions against indentured contracts. As such divergent interpretations suggest, hard evidence is very meager, strongly influenced by the political climate of the times, and difficult to interpret.[18]

Where evidence permits, this study includes Asians traveling to the Americas whose passage and subsequent labor obligations were closely linked. The term "contract laborers," often used to describe this expanded category, is avoided here because of the ease with which it can be confused with the many other kinds of labor contracts. Thus, in speaking of "indentured laborers," this study will include a portion of individuals under bonds that are analogous but not identical to legal indenture.

---

[17]Campbell, *Chinese Coolie Emigration*, p. 28.

[18]Gunther Paul Barth, *Bitter Strength: A History of the Chinese in the United States, 1850–1870* (Cambridge, Mass.: Harvard University Press, 1964), p. 67; Shih-shan Henry Tsai, *China and the Overseas Chinese in the United States, 1868–1911* (Fayetteville: University of Arkansas Press, 1983), p. 16; Patricia Cloud and David W. Galenson, "Chinese Immigration and Contract Labor in the Late Nineteenth Century," *Explorations in Economic History* 24.1 (1987): 26, 37–40. See Charles J. McClain, Jr., "Chinese Immigration: A Comment on Cloud and Galenson," *Explorations in Economic History* 27.3 (1990): 363–78, and Patricia Cloud and David W. Galenson, "Chinese Immigration: Reply to Charles McClain," *Explorations in Economic History* 28.2 (1991): 239–47. Galenson, "Rise and Fall of Indentured Servitude," p. 23: "Much remains unknown about the actual operation of the system under which Chinese, and later Japanese, migrants worked in the western United States, but many contemporaries believed these workers were effectively indentured, in being tied to specific employers for fixed terms." Campbell, *Chinese Coolie Emigration*, pp. 28–53: "Counsel for the Chinese declared [to a Canadian commission in 1900] that no evidence could be produced to show that the Chinese emigrated under servile contracts. It was definitely denied by some of the Chinese witnesses that in 1882 any Chinese were under a "contract" of labor. But it was not denied that a great number of them were under bonds of debt" (p. 53). At that time there was strong pressure to block Chinese entry to North America for reasons that had more to do with racism and the complaints of competition by other immigrant groups, so it was in the interest of Chinese to claim their status was similar to that of other immigrants.

Confining the study to *intercontinental* migrations distinguishes long-distance overseas migrations from population movements within single continents, whether overland or by sea voyage, some of which were also under contracts of indenture (as in the case of South Indians to Assam and to some Southeast Asian locations). Although from the perspective of a single region *inter*continental and *intra*continental labor migrations were part of a single continuum, from a global perspective the experiences of intercontinental migrants stand apart. In the first place the ocean voyages, lasting one or more months, were themselves a major distinguishing experience for intercontinental migrants. Moreover, the expense of retracing such a long voyage meant that the typical intercontinental migrant spent much longer under indenture abroad and was much less likely to return home than the typical intracontinental migrant. That fact in turn meant that the intercontinental migrants and their descendants abroad were more likely to develop distinct cultural and social identifies than their counterparts who retained closer ties to their homelands.

In some cases the line between intercontinental and intracontinental migrations is not simply a matter of distance. For example, Indian migrations to the Mascarenes are counted as intercontinental, since Mauritius and Réunion are usually considered as a part of Africa, even though these voyages were not too much longer than some maritime migrant routes between parts of Asia. The rationale for including the Mascarenes is not just a matter of geographical precision but of historical continuity. As Chapter 2 explains, indentured Indian migrations to the Mascarenes were intimately linked with the extension of routes to the West Indies and were counted by contemporary officials as "regulated" (subject to more rigorous inspection and record keeping), whereas those to Ceylon and Southeast Asia were not. The migrations from East Asia and the South Pacific to Hawaii may also be considered intercontinental if one adopts the perspective of the American government, eager to extend the scope of the Monroe Doctrine, that Hawaii was a part of the American continents, in order to make these distant Pacific island groups parts of different continents. The most arbitrary use of "intercontinental" is in the case of the South Pacific islanders' migrations to Australia and Fiji, which may all be considered to be within the "continent" of Oceania. That aside, it can be argued in favor of their inclusion that the circular interisland recruiting routes made their voyages far longer in reality than the distances from any island to its destination, but far stronger reasons for their inclusions are that they are historically linked to the other migrations and the fact that so much fine work has been done on these migrations recently that it would be foolish not to include them. The reader is asked to excuse some measure of arbitrariness in the application of this definition so that the larger experience may be considered as a meaningful whole.

The *temporal* focus of this volume is less open to ambiguity. It begins with the first significant migration from India to Mauritius and ends with the expiration of the last batch of Indian contracts in the Caribbean colonies. What needs to be explained is not the few minor cases that fall outside these temporal limits but the underlying forces that caused the new intercontinental indentured labor trade to rise and fall during these decades. Some discussion of the defining characteristics of this era is thus called for. It was, of course, the age of industrialization, an age of powerful new wealth and new technologies. While the industrial revolution gave rise to new factories and cities, first in Britain and then other areas adjoining the North Atlantic, its effects were soon felt in rural areas in the far corners of the world. As Eric Wolf has pointed out, "industrialization and the introduction of large-scale cash cropping in agriculture went on apace."[19] Cotton plantations, which rarely employed indentured labor, were one well-known example as were sugar plantations, which depended heavily upon it. So too were other plantations employing migrant labor that fall outside the definitions of this study, such as the tea plantations on Ceylon, which employed over 350,000 unindentured Indian migrants by 1917, and the cocoa plantations on the Portuguese islands of São Tomé and Príncipe that imported nearly 100,000 indentured Africans from Angola by the early 1900s.[20]

The nineteenth century was also the golden age of capitalism. Immanuel Wallerstein has called the period of 1730 through the 1840s, "the second era of great expansion of the capitalist world-economy," while Eric Hobsbawm has called the quarter century that followed the "age of capital."[21] Capital was not simply liquid assets, since factories, fields, ships, and even labor itself (especially when enslaved or indentured) can be considered capital. Rather capitalism refers to the integrated system of production, transportation, and markets that drew the world together as never before and with such immense implications for the laboring masses of the world. If the popular image of capitalists as greedy moneybags describes one aspect of their numbers, it is more useful to understanding the global economy to consider them as investors and manipulators, rational actors in an era of rapidly changing prices and demands. The role of capital investment in directing the demand for indentured labor in sugarcane colonies is examined in Chapter 2.

This was also an age of imperialism, a word with almost as many

---

[19]Eric Wolf, *Europe and the People without History* (Berkeley: University of California Press, 1982), p. 355.
[20]Tinker, *New System of Slavery*, pp. 32–33; James Duffy, *A Question of Slavery* (Cambridge, Mass.: Harvard University Press, 1967).
[21]Immanuel Wallerstein, *The Modern World-System III* (San Diego: Academic Press, 1989); the quote is the subtitle. E. J. Hobsbawm, *The Age of Capital, 1848–1875* (New York: New American Library, 1979).

different meanings and controversial interpretations as capitalism. One need not agree with the particular meanings attached to it by the classic works of Hobson or Lenin in order to use the term more generally to describe a phenomenon that was economic at its base and global in its reach. The word imperialism is also a welcome designation for the wave of colony grabbing that swept across parts of Asia and most of Africa in the last third of the nineteenth century.[22] Chronologically this "new imperialism" matches the history of the indentured labor trade poorly and only a tiny number of indentured laborers went to colonies founded in that period, notably the Indian labor for building the East Africa railroad and for the plantations of Fiji.[23] But the "new imperialism" was actually the second stage of a longer process that began with the first round of European colonization and empire building in the sixteenth and seventeenth centuries and which assumed a new form from the growth of industrialization and capitalism. Thus this study uses the term imperialism to refer to both economic and territorial expansion by industrial (and capitalist) nations, an expansion that reached a certain dramatic, if not entirely rational crescendo in the "new imperialism" at the end of the century, just as the longer process of global capital expansion Wallerstein describes reached its culmination in Hobsbawm's "age of capital."

These time limits do not preclude a more cursory examination of related topics. In order to introduce sufficient background to understand these migrations, the scope of the early chapters includes earlier developments. The study also breaches the terminal date to consider the long-term fate of the different migrant groups and the ways in which plantation economies adjusted to the end of the indentured labor trade.

In brief, the goal of this study is to compare the rise and fall of the new indentured labor trades in a broad context but with a clear focus. The emphasis is on highlighting the similarities and differences of the various branches of these population movements. Since the trades were created by the demand for labor, the next chapter takes up the reasons why that demand arose and was sustained for many decades. However, if the full story is to be told, it is vital that the motives of individuals who undertook these migrations be given equal consideration. Despite problems of comparable documentation, that is the subject of Chapter 3.

---

[22]J. A. Hobson, *Imperialism: A study* (London: A. Constable 1902): V. I. Lenin, *Imperialism: The Highest State of Capitalism* (Moscow: Foreign Languages Publishing House, n.d.). A very useful summary of this topic is Harrison M. Wright, ed., *The "New Imperialism": Analysis of Late-Nineteenth-Century Expansion,* 2nd ed. (Lexington, Mass.: D. C. Heath, 1976).

[23]From 1896 to 1901 indentured Indians were recruited on three-year contracts for East Africa, their numbers reaching 19,000 at the peak of activity; Tinker, *New System of Slavery,* p. 277. Brij V. Lal, *Girmitiyas: The Origins of the Fiji Indians* (Canberra: Journal of Pacific History, 1983).

2

Demands

An acquaintance tells me of an odd situation which may present itself of the Slave difficulty: & that comes from a queer quarter, no less than China – that some gangs of Chinese labourers have been imported into Cuba, who do the field-work so well, are healthy & orderly, & work at such a small price, that it is found that crops can be raised at a much less price than by the cumbrous & costly Slave machinery. A score or two of years hence, with the immense multiplication & rapidity of transport . . . now only just beginning to be established; scores of Celestial immigrants may be working in the cotton & tobacco fields here & in the West Indies Islands. Then the African Slave will get his manumission quickly enough.

> – William Makepeace Thackeray to his mother,
> Washington, D.C., 13 February 1853

Thackeray rightly connected the rise of the Chinese indentured laborers with the ending of slavery, though he somewhat exaggerated their cheapness and future geographical distribution. The first ship carrying Chinese laborers to Cuba, the *Oquendo*, had set sail in 1847, fully six years before he wrote, and the first experimental use of Chinese plantation labor in the West Indies had begun in 1806 when two hundred Chinese men were dispatched to Trinidad. That experiment had not ended Trinidad's reliance on slave labor nor did Chinese migration play the role Thackeray predicted in ending slavery in Cuba and the United States. Still, Chinese laborers were a major element in easing the transition from slave labor in Cuba as well as Peru and, on a smaller scale, they played a similar role in some British Caribbean colonies.[1]

[1] Arnold J. Meagher, "The Introduction of Chinese Laborers to Latin America: The 'Coolie Trade,' 1847–1874" (Ph.D. dissertation, History, University of California, Davis, 1975), pp. 40, 399, and passim. Barry W. Higman, "The Chinese in Trinidad, 1806–1838," *Caribbean Studies* 12.3 (1972): 21–28.

However, Chinese were not the principal alternative to African slaves. East Indians were drawn into the indentured labor trade in much greater numbers, along with Africans, South Pacific islanders, Japanese, and some Europeans. Nor was the end of slavery the only force that generated the indentured labor trade. In the decades following the famous novelist's letter, multitudes of indentured laborers traversed the oceans to plantations and mines in lands that had never known slavery. This chapter examines the growing demand for labor that began with the ending of slavery in the Caribbean and Mascarene colonies and quickly spread more widely along with sugarcane plantations and other products of Western economic and territorial imperialism.

From slavery to indentured labor

Despite the existence of a few earlier experiments, it is fair to say that the new indentured labor trade arose in direct response to the abolition of slavery in the colonies of Great Britain in the 1830s and to its subsequent abolition or decline in French, Dutch, and Spanish colonies. Ironically what was conceived as a progressive step toward free labor came to be viewed by some contemporaries and some modern historians as a new form of bondage and a thinly disguised continuation of slavery. A brief survey of the politics and perspectives of that era of reform will help to make the matter clearer.[2]

Since the late eighteenth century British abolitionists had been campaigning against the notorious commerce dominated by their own compatriots. Given slavery's importance to the plantation economy of the British West Indies and the great political power of the planter class and their allies, the abolitionists first directed their efforts to the limited goal of ending the trade in slaves from Africa. This was not just a tactical expedient, for most abolitionists (like Thackeray) accepted the validity of the argument put forth by Adam Smith that free labor would be both cheaper and more efficient than slavery. Deprived of fresh supplies of slaves, the plantation owners would be led by economic self-interest, if not by morality, to ameliorate the conditions of their slaves and eventually transform them into a free labor force.

In 1792 the House of Commons voted in favor of a resolution that, if implemented, would have ended British participation in the Atlantic slave trade in 1796. Britain's actual withdrawal from the slave trade began a

---

[2]Two works have greatly influenced my understanding of these events: William A. Green, *British Slave Emancipation: The Sugar Colonies and the Great Experiment* (Oxford: Clarendon Press, 1976), and David Brion Davis, *Slavery and Human Progress* (New York: Oxford University Press, 1984), especially part 2.

decade later in 1806 when, as a wartime measure against Napoleon's continental domination, Parliament banned British subjects from engaging in the slave trade to foreign colonies. This measure terminating two-thirds of the existing British slave trade, eased the passage a year later of the bill outlawing British participation in the remaining slave trade from Africa.

British abolition turned out to be just the first step in a long and complex process. The Atlantic slave trade continued and even expanded as citizens of other nations quickly stepped into the profitable commerce Britain had abandoned. In the meanwhile British colonies were finding it difficult to adjust to doing without fresh supplies of slaves. Slave populations, whose numbers had been built up by a century and a half of massive imports, started to decline as soon as fresh supplies were cut off. In the twenty-seven years after 1807 the number of enslaved persons in the British Caribbean as a whole decreased 14 percent from about 775,000 to 665,000, with a similar shrinkage probably taking place in the slave population of the British colony of Mauritius in the Indian Ocean. The decline was most marked in the newer sugar-producing colonies of British Guiana and Trinidad, which had the highest proportion of African-born slaves and whose population thus reflected the Atlantic slave trade's gender imbalance of two males for each female. Despite legal imports of slaves from other British West Indian colonies, their slave populations shrank by more than a quarter. Although the effects on sugar production varied widely from colony to colony, the overall sugar exports from the British West Indies stagnated during these decades.[3]

Moreover, these labor shortages failed to promote better treatment for slaves in the British colonies, still less to transform slavery into the freer labor system the abolitionists had expected. Indeed, many observers of this social experiment believed slavery's harshness increased. Abolitionists then launched a second campaign in the reform years of the early 1830s aimed at legal emancipation of the slaves. Though moved by the abolitionists' moral fervor, the practical members of Parliament had no desire to combine social reform with economic disaster. "The great problem to be solved in drawing up any plan for the emancipation of the slaves in our colonies," wrote Lord Howick, a leading abolitionist, at the end of 1832, "is to devise some mode of inducing them when relieved from the fear of the driver and his whip, to undergo the regular and continuous labour which

[3]B. W. Higman, *Slave Populations of the British Caribbean, 1807–1834* (Baltimore: Johns Hopkins University Press, 1984), pp. 72, 135–47. Reliable estimates of the slave population of Mauritius do not exist before 1826 when 69,000 were recorded; at emancipation in 1835 compensation was paid for 56,700, another 4,000 having been manumitted between 1826 and 1835; Sadasivam Reddi, "Aspects of Slavery during the British Administration," in *Slavery in South West Indian Ocean*, ed. U. Bissoondoyal and S. B. C. Servansing (Moka, Mauritius: Mahatma Gandhi Institute Press, 1989), pp. 106–9.

is indispensable in carrying on the production of sugar."[4] Thus the law passed in 1833 freeing slaves in British colonies was combined with two measures aimed at protecting the plantation economies from the shock of complete emancipation: direct financial compensation to the owners of emancipated slaves and a forced apprenticeship of four to six years for freed persons over the age of six and a half. Neither worked as intended.

The vast sum of £20 million paid to planters for the loss of their slaves was intended to reduce their high debt burden and enable them to compete with colonies still using slave labor. Amounting to just under half the market value of the freed slaves, the compensation payments did reduce the planters' massive indebtedness but this increase in their individual credit worthiness failed in most cases to attract new investment because of well-justified doubts about the ability of British sugar plantations to turn a profit without slavery.

The apprenticeship program was also a form of compensation to the planters since it required emancipated field slaves to provide 40.5 hours a week of unpaid labor to their former masters during the six years following emancipation. It was also expected to introduce the freed persons to wage labor since apprentices were paid for any additional labor. In fact, apprenticeship fulfilled neither goal. Many planters used the apprenticeship laws to extract as much unpaid labor as possible while simultaneously reducing some customary distributions of food and clothing to their plantation workers, turning "apprenticeship" into "little more than a mitigated form of slavery" in William Green's judgment. Moreover, the need to pay wages for work done above the 40.5 hours a week drove up the planters' production costs. In the end, planters got less unpaid labor than expected because growing unrest among the apprentices, partly stimulated by the continuing abolitionist criticism of the system, forced the West Indian legislatures to terminate apprenticeship earlier than planned. Complete emancipation in the British West Indies arrived on 1 August 1838 and nine months later in Mauritius.[5]

In most colonies, complete emancipation was even less successful in creating an effective labor force than apprenticeship had been. Staying clear of the hated plantation was a high priority for many persons liberated from a lifetime of forced labor, though not always an achievable one. For example, two months after the end of apprenticeship many Jamaican plantations were operating with only a quarter of their former labor force and only a few had over half, so that much of the 1838 sugar crop rotted

[4]Quoted by Eric Williams, *From Columbus to Castro: The History of the Caribbean, 1492–1969* (New York: Vintage Books, 1984), p. 328.
[5]Green, *British Slave Emancipation*, pp. 131–61, 218–21 (quotation from p. 151); William Law Mathieson, *British Slave Emancipation, 1838–1849* (New York: Octagon Books, 1967), pp. 235–39.

in the fields and only limited planting was done for the 1839 season. Throughout most of the British West Indies, "black labourers were unwilling to remain submissive and disciplined cane workers."[6] The situation was similar in Mauritius: nearly all of the 10,000 purchasing their freedom during the apprenticeship period abandoned the plantations for good; virtually none of the 13,000 female laborers completing apprenticeship ever returned on wages; only 4,000 of the 17,000 men completing apprenticeship agreed to sign one-year labor contracts. By August 1846 only 189 former apprentices were still working as laborers on the plantations.[7] Thus a growing social and economic crisis quickly replaced moral reform as the central issue in the British plantation colonies.

The desertion of the cane fields had little to do with freed persons' dislike of regular and continuous labor. Where land was available, former slaves preferred devoting their energies to scratching out a humble existence on their own farms to resuming their former roles on the plantations. Indeed, many hard-working individuals had used earnings saved during the apprenticeship period to purchase early release from that bondage or to acquire a small parcel of land. By the 1860s a third of the black population of Jamaica was living in independent villages in the island's mountainous interior, often on land purchased with missionary help. Trinidad and British Guiana also had abundant land not under sugar cultivation and faced widespread labor shortages immediately after emancipation. Planters there offered higher wages to attract people back to the plantations and also used their political power to close off alternative livelihoods by passing laws making it more difficult to buy small plots of land, evicting squatters from public land, and enforcing harsh vagrancy laws. However, where land for independent farms was unavailable, such as in Barbados, most laborers had little choice but to return to the plantations. Barbados was also the only place in the British West Indies where the population grew after the end of the slave trade, which served to keep the labor force abundant and cheap and forced many Barbadians to emigrate to other parts of the region in search of work.[8]

Even where planters succeeded in restricting alternative livelihoods for emancipated men, most British plantations saw a sharp falling off in the

[6]Green, *British Slave Emancipation*, p. 170.
[7]M. D. North-Coombes, "From Slavery to Indenture: Forced Labour in the Political Economy of Mauritius, 1834–1867," in *Indentured Labour in the British Empire, 1840–1920*, ed. Kay Saunders (London: Croom Helm, 1984), pp. 81–83, 118–19; Reddi, "Aspects of Slavery," pp. 119–21.
[8]Donald Wood, *Trinidad in Transition: The Years after Slavery* (London: Oxford University Press, 1968), pp. 91–97; Alan H. Adamson, *Sugar without Slaves: The Political Economy of British Guiana, 1838–1904* (New Haven: Yale University Press, 1972), pp. 32–33; J. H. Galloway, *The Sugar Cane Industry: An Historical Geography from Its Origins to 1914* (Cambridge: Cambridge University Press, 1989), pp. 146–54.

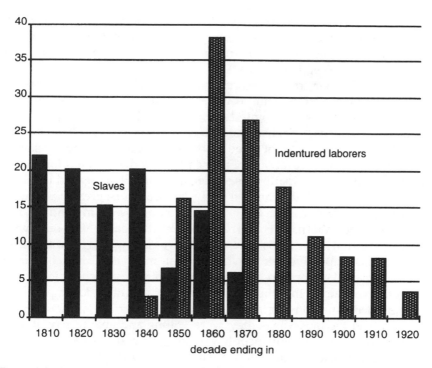

Figure 2.1. Annual average slave and indentured labor imports (by thousands) into the Caribbean and Mascarenes, by decade, 1801–10 to 1911–20. *Sources:* For slaves to the Caribbean, David Eltis, *Economic Growth and the Ending of the Transatlantic Slave Trade* (New York: Oxford University Press, 1987), table A.8. For slaves to the Mascarenes, Paul E. Lovejoy, *Transformations in Slavery: A History of Slavery in Africa* (Cambridge: Cambridge University Press, 1983), pp. 151, 221, and François Renault, *Libération d'esclaves de nouvelle servitude: Les rachats de captifs africains pour le compte des colonies françaises après l'abolition de l'esclavage* (Abidjan: Nouvelles Editions Africaines, 1976), pp. 42, 72. For indentured laborers, Table A.2.

labor of two groups who had been of great importance to the slave gangs – women and children. Women sought out domestic employment, while increasingly numbers of children spent their days in schools promoted by missionary societies. Even more significant was the fact that many men who returned to plantation labor after apprenticeship did so on a less continuous basis. Trinidadian and Jamaican plantation agents told parliamentary investigators that the productivity of the labor force after apprenticeship was only two-thirds of what it had been earlier because of absenteeism. Labor shortages had driven up wage rates somewhat in the months after the end of apprenticeship, but estate managers were convinced that more money would not attract more work because what laborers really wanted was time to cultivate their own lands. Thus they believed that the freed persons would cease working in the cane fields as soon as they had the minimum funds they required to live. In the words of one estate manager in Trinidad, it was "an irrefragable fact; the more money, the less work." This conclusion is open to question but the prevalence of such beliefs served to keep wages low.[9]

Ironically, in their struggle to retain the profitability of the plantation system, the planters found important allies among British abolitionists, who, as Eric Williams has pointed out, were ideological radicals but economic conservatives.[10] Their campaign against slavery had been accompanied by the argument that "free labour could produce tropical staples more cheaply than slave labour." Emancipation in the British colonies was meant to inspire emancipation elsewhere. As Lord Elgin argued to Jamaican legislators in 1842, their region was "the theatre of a great experiment, the issue of which may affect the doom of thousands now in bondage, and of millions yet unborn." Yet at that moment the reality was otherwise: sugar production in the British West Indies was falling and its price rising, reducing its competitiveness in world British markets. Cuban, Brazilian, and American planters were hardly to be inspired by such a model.[11]

Planters concluded that the solution to their mounting labor problems lay in attracting new immigrants from abroad. Given the arduousness of the work and the low wages they were willing and able to pay, it soon became apparent that only people already too poor to pay their own passage to the islands would accept such terms of employment. Though populations around the Atlantic were tapped for the West Indies, the planters' search for an adequate supply of recruits soon turned to the denser populations of Asia.

Many planters' first preference was for European laborers, whose work habits they believed superior and whose presence would "whiten" the population mix that under slavery had become over 90 percent African in most plantation colonies. Although their recruitment efforts coincided with the beginnings of a massive European out-migration, the West Indies secured only a tiny portion of their needs from this source. Private recruiters brought a few hundred poor French and German migrants to Trinidad in 1839–40 and over 4,500 other Europeans were introduced at public expense, mostly to Jamaica, between 1834–45. However, their strong antipathy to plantation labor and the existence of much more at-

[9]Testimony of Robert Henry Church of Trinidad, 5 May 1842, and Thomas MacCornack of Jamaica, 16 June 1842, in *PP* 1842 xiii (479), Report from the Select Committee on West India Colonies, pp. 110–11, 344–46 (quotation from Mr. Church, p. 111). Mary Elizabeth Thomas, *Jamaica and Voluntary Laborers from Africa, 1840–1965* (Gainesville: University Presses of Florida, 1974), p. 9.

[10]Eric Williams, *Capitalism and Slavery* (Charlotte: University of North Carolina Press, 1944), pp. 181–88.

[11]Green, *British Slave Emancipation*, pp. 191 (quotation), 266.

tractive alternatives in North America made Europeans difficult to recruit.[12] The one notable exception was the emigration of some 30,000 Portuguese driven to accept indentured contracts into British Guiana in the 1840s and 1850s after the tragic failure of both the potato and grape harvests in Madeira. But they only partially relieved the labor shortage. New European migrants succumbed to tropical diseases in large numbers and the survivors quickly deserted the plantations for shopkeeping and other less onerous jobs.[13]

Another group planters tried to attract were persons of African descent born in the Americas, whose strength and endurance they had long respected. Densely populated Barbados provided a steady supply of laborers, but efforts to attract recruits from North America yielded limited results despite the growing discrimination free blacks faced in the United States in the years before the Civil War. Trinidad paid for the passage of over 1,200 recruits from New York, Baltimore, and Philadelphia between 1835–40, though when the Jamaican commissioner for emigration toured the same cities in 1842, trying to offset his colony's inferior wage rates by touting Jamaica's superior social and political rights, the results were disappointing. Besides their small numbers, few of those recruited from the United States chose to remain in the Caribbean and few of these who stayed continued as plantation laborers.[14]

Several British colonies also attempted to meet their labor needs by recruiting Africans freed from slave ships apprehended by the British patrols, beginning in the early 1830s with the modest numbers liberated from slavers intercepted in the Caribbean en route to Cuba. In 1835 the governor of Trinidad sought permission to recruit from the much larger body of liberated Africans in the British colony of Sierra Leone on the West African coast. Initially the British government rejected the plan, sensitive to abolitionist arguments that such recruitment would appear to be a thinly disguised revival of the slave trade. However support began to come round from several sources. Abolitionists were worried lest the collapse of British West Indian sugar plantations undermine their conten-

---

[12]Thomas, *Jamaica and Voluntary Laborers*, pp. 19–28. In Limerick the Irish staged a riot against any of their number boarding what was termed a "slave ship" that was recruiting labor for the West Indies.

[13]Wood, *Trinidad in Transition*, pp. 89–91; G. W. Roberts and J. Byrne, "Summary Statistics on Indentured and Associated Migration Affecting the West Indies, 1843–1918," *Population Studies* 20.1 (1966): tables 3 and 7; Brian L. Moore, "The Social Impact of Portuguese Immigration into British Guiana after Emancipation," *Boletín de Estudios Latinamericanos y del Caribe* 19 (1975): 3–5. A few thousand to block the settlement of ex-apprentices in the island's highland interior; see Douglas Hall, "Bountied European Immigration to Jamaica with Special Reference to the German Settlement of Seaford Town up to 1850," *Jamaica Journal* 8.4 (1974): 49–50. For a comprehensive treatment of migration into the British West Indies, see Green, *British Slave Emancipation*, pp. 261–93.

[14]Wood, *Trinidad in Transition*, pp. 67–68; Thomas, *Jamaica and Voluntary Laborers*, pp. 19–20.

tion that free labor was superior to slave labor economically as well as morally. The costs and practical difficulties of maintaining the growing number of African "recaptives" in Sierra Leone and elsewhere led others to see practical merit in an emigration program. Thus, the balance of official opinion tipped in favor of government-sponsored sailings across the Atlantic, which began in 1841 initially under colonial control and from 1843 under the British government.[15] Despite the many problems in initial recruitment detailed in Chapter 3, the British West Indian colonies managed to import some 13,500 liberated Africans from Sierra Leone during 1841–50, plus an equal number from other liberation depots. However, the success of the patrols in bringing the slave trade to an end also reduced the number of recaptives. As Table A.2 shows, in the next decade the number of liberated Africans introduced into the British West Indies fell to just under 5,000, with another 4,300 being introduced after 1860.

Long before liberated African migration ebbed, far larger numbers of laborers were being recruited from British India. Mauritian planters had imported a few indentured Indians (along with some Chinese from Singapore) in 1829[16] and turned to India for labor as soon as slavery came to an end. British Guiana followed suit in 1838. However, reports of abuses in the recruitment of Indians had led the government of India to ban further sailings the next year. After certain reforms and reconsiderations, voyages to Mauritius were permitted to resume in 1843 and to the West Indies in 1845. By 1850 nearly 120,000 Indian laborers had arrived in Mauritius, over 12,000 in British Guiana, and another 10,000 in Trinidad and Jamaica. The very heavy Indian migration to Mauritius during the two decades after 1843 (see Table A.2) provided that colony with enough resident labor to reduce the need for fresh imports during the rest of the century, especially as demand for Mauritian sugar stagnated. As the Mauritian demand waned, Indian migration to the more distant locations rose, satisfying British West Indian labor needs for the rest of the century.

While the numbers of Indian laborers were still modest and their work habits and endurance below expectations, West Indian planters had won British government permission in 1850 to recruit indentured laborers from China. British Guiana initially offered a bounty of £100 for each Chinese migrant delivered to the colony. High mortality and high costs caused by competition from California, Australia, and Peru led to the suspension of Chinese imports. A new, better regulated trade landed 12,178 Chinese to the British West Indies between 1859 and 1866, with a few more later. Though highly regarded, Chinese labor was a luxury the colonial planters

[15]Green, *British Slave Emancipation*, pp. 265–76.
[16]Huguette Ly-Tio-Fane Pineo, *Lured Away: The Life History of Cane Workers in Mauritius* (Moka, Mauritius: Mahatma Gandhi Institute, 1984), p. 17.

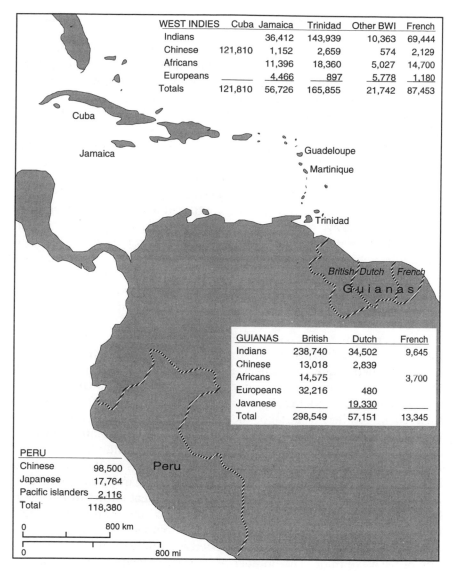

WEST INDIES	Cuba	Jamaica	Trinidad	Other BWI	French
Indians		36,412	143,939	10,363	69,444
Chinese	121,810	1,152	2,659	574	2,129
Africans		11,396	18,360	5,027	14,700
Europeans	___	4,466	897	5,778	1,180
Totals	121,810	56,726	165,855	21,742	87,453

GUIANAS	British	Dutch	French
Indians	238,740	34,502	9,645
Chinese	13,018	2,839	
Africans	14,575		3,700
Europeans	32,216	480	
Javanese	___	19,330	___
Total	298,549	57,151	13,345

PERU	
Chinese	98,500
Japanese	17,764
Pacific islanders	2,116
Total	118,380

Map 2. Principal indentured labor imports into the Americas. *Source:* Appendix b

could afford only intermittently, since the costs of recruitment were double those from India.[17]

Emancipation in the French and Dutch plantation colonies occurred later than in the British colonies, producing similar labor shortages. Both sought to alleviate these shortages by importing indentured labor, primarily from British India along with modest numbers from China. Both also drew extensively on their own overseas empires, the French bringing substantial numbers of laborers from their outposts in Africa and India, while nearly half of the labor the Dutch brought to the West Indies came from Java.

Although France lost its most important plantation colony, Saint-Domingue (Haiti), as a result of the massive slave revolt of the 1790s, the remaining French plantation colonies continued to depend on slave labor until 1848. On the eve of their emancipation most slaves in France's Indian Ocean colony of Réunion had been induced to sign two-year labor contracts, which most subsequently refused to renew, preferring casual labor in town or subsistence farming in the interior plateaus to further labor on the plantations. French West Indian colonies also experienced a massive exodus from the plantations, the labor force in Martinique, for example, falling from 72,000 in 1848 to 20,000 in 1851.[18]

To meet the labor shortage in Réunion French planters sought to imitate the example of their British neighbors in Mauritius by bringing labor from India, but their request for direct access in 1851 was put off by British Indian authorities who expressed doubts about French sincerity in protecting their British Indian subjects' rights. While negotiations dragged on, the French recruited what labor they could from their coastal enclave of Pondicherry in southeastern India. From there Réunion obtained an average of 5,400 Indians a year in 1849–55, but the average number of recruits fell to 1,750 a year during 1856–60, due to restrictions on the recruitment of British Indians through that port. Nearly a thousand indentured Chinese were recruited in 1859. More active recruitment efforts in Zanzibar, Mozambique, Madagascar, and other eastern African locations were able to make up some of the shortfall, but under circumstances that both contemporary and modern observers regarded as a thinly disguised continuation of the slave trade. The number of Africans stayed under a thousand a year in the early 1850s, averaged 4,150 a year in the middle 1850s, but then, as Indian laborers became harder to obtain, shot up to 10,000 in 1858.

[17]Meagher, "Introduction of Chinese Laborers," pp. 270–77; Walton Look Lai, *Indentured Labor, Caribbean Sugar: Chinese and Indian Migrants to the British West Indies, 1838–1918* (Baltimore: Johns Hopkins University Press, 1993), pp. 87–91, table 23.

[18]François Renault, *Libération d'esclaves et nouvelle servitude: Les rachats des captifs africains pour le compte des colonies françaises après l'abolition de l'esclavage* (Abidjan: Nouvelles Editions Africaines, 1976), pp. 11–13.

In all at least 34,200 Africans were recruited from the Comoro Islands, Madagascar, and the East African mainland, mostly for Réunion.[19]

Meanwhile, the planters of the French Caribbean were also struggling to supplement their labor supply. Subsidized voyages supplied a few hundred French and Madeiran migrants but with no better long-term benefits than in the British West Indies.[20] Much more labor came from recruitment from the Atlantic side of Africa under circumstances as legally dubious as that from eastern Africa. The French had experimented with the repurchase (*rachat préalable*) of slaves in their West African colony of Senegal in 1839–40 to secure labor on fourteen-year contracts for public works in that colony. In 1853 the practice was resumed in Senegal and extended in 1854 to French coastal enclaves further south. The same year repurchased Africans began to be transported to the French Caribbean colonies of Cayenne (French Guiana), Martinique, and Guadeloupe in 1854 on six-year contracts. During the eight years of its operation some 18,400 African contract laborers were received in these colonies. Contemporaries and most modern historians agree that only legal niceties distinguished this recruitment from the slave trade.[21]

The mounting scandals associated with this recruitment in Africa moved British authorities to relent and grant the French access to the better-regulated Indian labor market in return for terminating their labor imports from Africa. The French imported indentured Indians from Calcutta to Réunion beginning with 5,333 in 1862 and a ship from Madras reached Guadeloupe with 330 in 1864. Regulations permitted indenture for five-years (longer than in British colonies at that time) but entitled Indians to free return passage at the end of that period, in contrast to the

---

[19]Hubert Gerbeau, "Engagées and Coolies on Réunion Island: Slavery's Masks and Freedom's Constraints," in *Colonialism and Migration: Industrial Labour before and after Slavery,* ed. P. C. Emmer (The Hague: Martinus Nijhoff, 1986), pp. 223–24; Meagher, "Introduction of Chinese Laborers," p. 290.

[20]Renault, *Libération d'esclaves,* p. 16, says there were about 500 subsidized French migrants from 1845 to 1850 plus 680 indentured Madeirans.

[21]Renault, *Libération d'esclaves,* pp. 18–91, 158; Monica Schuler, "African Immigration to French Guiana: The *Cinq Frère* Group, 1854–1860," *Bulletin of the African Studies Association of the West Indies,* 4 (1971): 64–72, and "Kru Emigration to British and French Guiana, 1841–1857," in *Africans in Bondage: Studies in Slavery and the Slave Trade,* ed. Paul E. Lovejoy (Madison: African Studies Program, University of Wisconsin, 1986), pp. 174–78. Renault says (p. 29) that in the effort to reconcile freedom and labor, the former was the loser. Schuler, "Kru Emigration," p. 125, is more circumspect, noting that a principal recruiter was a former slave trader but stressing the difficulty of determining how willing the recruits may have been. Gerbeau, "Engagées and Coolies," pp. 221–23, gives numerous examples of forced recruitment. Paul Lovejoy, *Transformations in Slavery: A History of Slavery in Africa* (Cambridge: Cambridge University Press, 1983), p. 146, refers to this as a "disguised trade in slaves." David Eltis, *Economic Growth and the Ending of the Transatlantic Slave Trade* (New York: Oxford University Press, 1987), p. 246, counts all African recruits to the French Caribbean as slaves.

ten years then required in British colonies. In addition to the 49,000 Indians brought to Réunion between 1844 and 1860, the island recruited 35,000 other laborers by 1883 and a total of 79,000 Indians sailed for the French Caribbean between 1853 and 1888. By the mid-1880s British officials had sufficient evidence of the ill-treatment of indentured Indians in the French colonies to warrant their refusing to sanction any more shipments.[22]

The slave trade to Dutch Guiana (Surinam) had ended in 1807, at a time when the colony was under British occupation. The Dutch regained control in 1814 but did not emancipate their slaves until 1863, even then imposing an apprenticeship that lasted another ten years. As in the British colonies, Surinam's slave population had declined after being cut off from new supplies from Africa, falling from about 50,000 in 1800 to some 30,000 in 1863 and acute labor shortages after emancipation caused Surinam's sugar production to drop sharply. To meet the labor needs on its own plantations the government of Surinam had brought 18 Chinese laborers from Java in 1853 and another 500 directly from China in 1858, the Chinese being regarded as the most industrious and dependable workers available. Between 1865 and 1869 a private Surinam Immigration Corporation brought 2,015 more Chinese from Hong Kong, far below the planters' wants and at a very high cost. Experiments with small numbers of European laborers imported from Madeira and the Netherlands and of Javanese from the Dutch East Indies, as well as 1,500 free blacks from Barbados during these years also proved unsatisfactory as a long-term solution to the colony's labor problems.

By the time apprenticeship came to an end in 1873 China had banned further indentured labor emigration, so the Dutch planters turned to indentured labor from India. Although viewed as less reliable than the Chinese, Indian laborers could be obtained in steady lots at predictable prices through arrangement worked out with the British authorities. Some 34,500 Indians were introduced over the next forty-four years with the right of a free return passage after the end of a single five-year contract. (In comparison, Indians in British Guiana had to work two five-year terms before being entitled to free passage home.) Surinam planters also imported 19,000 indentured laborers from Java between 1853 and 1920.[23]

---

[22]Hugh Tinker, *A New System of Slavery: The Export of Indian Labour Overseas, 1830–1920* (London: Oxford University Press, 1974), pp. 95–96, 99–100, 109, 240, 259, 265, 276–78; see map 3.

[23]Meagher, "Introduction of Chinese Laborers," pp. 287–89; J. Ankum-Houwink, "Chinese Contract Migrants in Surinam between 1853 and 1870," *Boletín de Estudios Latinoamericanos y del Caribe* 17 (1974): 49, 56–59; K. O. Laurence, *Immigration into the West Indies in the Nineteenth Century* (Kingston, Jamaica: Caribbean University Press, 1971), pp. 43–45; Craig A. Lockhard, "Repatriation Movements among the Javanese in Surinam: A Comparative Analysis," *Caribbean Studies* 18.1–2 (1978): 85–86; Pieter Emmer, "The Importation of British

Though these details about Surinam have taken the story into the twentieth century, the main thrust of the argument so far has been that it was the end of slavery, first in the British colonies and subsequently in the French and Dutch colonies, that precipitated the growth of the indentured labor trade. Unable to sustain its numbers once the Atlantic slave trade was cut off, the enslaved population began to decline and after their emancipation freed persons were disinclined to continue plantation labor at the former levels of intensity – or at all. New labor supplies were needed, but the wages the planters believed they could offer were such that only persons too poor to pay their own way could be attracted. Through metropolitan subsidy, colonial taxation, and, in some cases, the use of highly irregular methods of recruitment, laborers were brought from the Atlantic islands, North America, Africa, and China, but the most enduring source for the Caribbean and Mascarene colonies was India.

The new imperial economy

The intercontinental indentured labor trade had arisen to remedy the labor shortages caused by slave emancipation, but its endurance and growth were governed by much broader changes. Spreading Western political and economic empires not only facilitated the recruitment of labor from India, China, Pacific islands, and other places – points that will be examined in the next two chapters, but also led to the establishment of new colonies that sought indentured labor. The most significant part of this new labor demand stemmed from the rapid expansion of sugarcane plantations in the second half of the century, in these new colonies as well as in older producing areas. As this section will detail, new technology and new capital investment also played vital roles in sustaining the demand for indentured labor.

During the century before Western imperialism reached its crescendo in the late nineteenth century, there had been a steady expansion of economic and territorial empires (especially by Great Britain). During and after the Napoleonic Wars, Britain took possession of several older colonies that soon became major importers of indentured labor: Trinidad acquired from Spain in 1797, Mauritius (Ile de France) taken from France in 1810, British Guiana annexed from Holland in 1814. Other colonies, first developed as European settler areas, acquired an appetite for indentured labor only later in the century. From the Cape Colony in southern Africa, taken from Holland in 1806, new settler colonies were founded in midcentury that

Indians into Surinam (Dutch Guiana), 1873–1916," in *International Labour Migration: Historical Perspectives,* ed. Shula Marks and Peter Richardson (Hounslow, Middlesex: M. Temple Smith, 1984), pp. 94–97.

later imported indentured labor: Natal used Indian labor for sugar plantations and the Transvaal's gold mines employed Chinese labor. Other new
colonial foundations pertinent to the growth of the indentured labor trade
included the British settlements in Australia and Britain's progressive
annexation of the Straits Settlements around Singapore from 1786 to 1824,
which led to protectorates over Malaya from 1874 to 1896. The imperial
ventures of the United States in Hawaii and Cuba also opened up important destinations for the East Asian labor trade.

The indentured labor trade depended as much on the West's "informal"
empire of financial and commercial networks as it did on the formal
empire of colonies. As the cost of ocean travel fell and its speed increased
in the nineteenth century, more distant parts of the world became important to the Western industrial giants. By one calculation, the volume of
world trade rose tenfold between 1850 and 1913.[24] The spectacular growth
of world sugar production in the nineteenth century was an important part
of this phenomenon.

Amid the turbulence of slave emancipation the one bright spot for sugar
producers was that the market for their product was increasing rapidly. In
industrial societies a growing urban proletariat joined the middle classes
in consuming vast quantities of candy, jams, and sugared pastries, while
spooning still more sugar into their tea, coffee, and chocolate – themselves
newly popular beverages for the masses. In Britain sugar consumption per
capital increased fivefold during the century. Growing urbanization and
rising living standards promoted a rapid increase in consumption in continental Europe and North America as well. To meet this rising demand
global production of cane sugar rose from 300,000 tons in 1790 to 10 million
tons in 1914.[25]

The dark side of these changes for the cane sugar producers was a steep
and steady fall in sugar prices during the century before World War I. Indeed, rising consumption was strongly stimulated by falling prices. In British Guiana, which may serve as an example of global trends, the downward
slide had begun even before the end of slavery, the prices received by producers falling by over 50 percent between 1800 and 1829, from £40.45 a ton
to a low of £18 including the imperial preference of £3.75. The sugar market
recovered briefly when production dropped in the 1830s as slavery and apprenticeship were ended, but declined again as West Indian production
picked up. The fall in sugar prices continued as the imperial preference was
phased out beginning in 1846 and competition grew from new sugarcane

[24]W. W. Rostow cited by Paul Kennedy, *The Rise and Fall of the Great Powers* (New York:
Random House, 1989), p. 414.
[25]This treatment of the sugar economy is heavily indebted to Galloway, *Sugar Cane Industry*,
chaps. 6–9. See also Mintz, *Sweetness and Power*, pp. 73ff.

plantations in other parts of the world as well as from sugar beet cultivation in France. By the 1870s producer prices were down to around £22 a ton and, as the glut grew in the 1890s, they fell by another £10 on average, reaching a low of £9.60 in 1896, then recovering slowly.[26]

In this competitive environment the successful growers needed more than access to a steady supply of cheap labor. To remain profitable while the unit price of sugar tumbled they had to invest heavily in better land, fertilizer, and new machinery that could increase their productivity. Such investments required borrowing large amounts of capital from lenders, who favored regions richest in natural resources and with the best access to large markets. It is fair to say that access to a regular supply of low-wage labor, though very important to sustaining the scale of production, was less decisive in the long-run profitability of individual sugar plantations and particular colonies than was the quality of land and the quantity of capital available. Some additional consideration of land, capital, and technology, therefore, is in order before returning to the role of indentured labor.

Since the seventeenth century the West Indies had witnessed the rise and fall of individual sugar colonies whose fertile lands were first exploited, then depleted. Barbados had given way to Jamaica, which in turn had lost out to Saint-Domingue, until revolution undid that colony in the 1790s. During the first part of the nineteenth century fresh and fertile fields enabled British Guiana and Trinidad to grow faster than the older French and British colonies, but by midcentury the large Spanish colony of Cuba took over the lead.

The nineteenth century also saw the rapid extension of sugar production outside the West Indies. By midcentury Mauritius had become Britain's premier sugar producer, having expanded from 27,000 acres under sugarcane cultivation in the 1820s to 129,000 in the 1860s. During the second half of the century the quest for virgin tropical soils led to the establishment of new sugar plantations in Southeast Asia, Australia, Hawaii, and southern Africa. Indeed, by 1900 the sugar from these new producers surpassed that from the West Indies and Mascarenes combined.

Virgin lands outproduced those depleted by decades of sugarcane production, but equally important was investment in new technology that increased the yields from the milling and curing operations. Beginning in midcentury the traditional vertical three-roller crushers driven by animals or waterpower were replaced by heavier horizontal rollers, powered by

[26]Dwarka Nath, *A History of Indians in British Guiana* (London: Thomas Nelson & Sons, 1950), table 32. According William Woodruff, *Impact of Western Man: A Study of Europe's Role in the World Economy, 1750–1960* (New York: St. Martin's Press, 1967), table VII/2, the British West Indian share of the U.K. sugar market fell from 37% in 1850 to 4% in 1900, while European beet sugar climbed from 1% to 80%. Galloway, *Sugar Cane Industry*, p. 133, says beet sugar had two-thirds of the world market at end of the century.

steam engines. Such roller units arranged in series in Hawaii raised the quantity of juice extracted from about 65 percent to over 95 percent by the early twentieth century, a level that soon became the industry standard. Once the juice was extracted, it had to be boiled down to a heavy syrup (massecuite), traditionally a long, fuel-consuming process, then allowed to cure in smaller containers where the sugar crystals formed and the waste molasses drained away. A new vacuum-pan process permitted the boiling to be done at lower temperatures and thus with greater fuel efficiency. Another new device, the centrifugal, used high-speed spinning to extract the molasses in much less time, producing a dryer sugar in the process.

The need to make large investments in new equipment produced two different successful strategies in the sugarcane colonies, both of which spelled the end of traditional planter society. Especially in the newer producing regions of Hawaii, Java, and Natal, there was a consolidation of ownership of the fields and, during the last quarter of the century, the growth of corporate ownership of both the cane fields and mills. In other places, the traditional self-contained plantation declined as cane growing and milling became separate operations, permitting many independent growers to supply cane to independently owned central mills. The latter system was most characteristic of Australia, but small producers also became a major factor in the survival of sugar mills in the Mascarenes, in Cuba (where they grew a third or more of the sugar in 1887), and in Trinidad (where they raised a third of the sugar in 1906).

The expansion of land, capital, and technology on the sugarcane plantations affected the use of labor in many different ways. In some cases the availability of cheap labor enabled the old plantation system to survive into the twentieth century, delaying the introduction of new technology. For example, a continuing surplus of labor in Barbados, despite the departure of 100,000 persons, kept wage costs so low that the island lagged behind other producers in technological changes before 1900. Brazil and Louisiana were also able to draw upon the impoverished local population, thus avoiding the expense of importing and training new labor. By a successful marriage of land and local labor, Java expanded its sugar production rapidly in the second half of the century, surpassing Mauritius as the Indian Ocean region's major sugar producer in the 1870s and, during the Spanish-American War, eclipsing Cuba as the world's greatest producer.[27]

Other sugar-producing areas, such as Hawaii and Fiji, outgrew their local labor supply after 1850 and turned to imported indentured labor. Yet, in many cases, the decision to import indentured laborers from afar was not just a matter of demographics. As Eric Williams has pointed out, many

---

[27]Galloway, *Sugar Cane Industry*, pp. 134–41, 152, 165–79, 211–13.

more West Indians migrated within or from the Caribbean region in the early twentieth century than entered British Guiana and Trinidad under indentured contracts.[28] Thus the key issue in the West Indies, as in Peru and southern Africa, was why an intercontinental labor migration took place when a regional one might have sufficed (and later did so). The answer is not indentured laborers' greater productivity. Indeed, most planters were convinced that their indentured Indian laborers were less productive than the Creole Africans they supplanted. Nor was indentured labor necessarily cheaper once the considerable recruitment costs were taken into consideration. The key factor may have been that the terms of the indentured contract allowed for much greater control of the labor force, a point that will be developed in Chapter 5.

Because these changes in the sugar industry produced highly varied responses, it is useful to look in more detail at how the demand for indentured labor was connected to developments in different cane-growing areas. This overview will include Peru and southern Africa where the labor was also used for mining.

Jamaica's sugarcane industry illustrates an unsuccessful adjustment to these new circumstances. Although it had been Britain's premier sugar colony in the eighteenth century, Jamaica's decline had begun even before emancipation. The underlying problem was that the soil's fertility had been exhausted by decades of sugarcane production. The nearly six million pounds paid to the island's planters in compensation for their slaves did little to reverse the inexorable decline, since slipping production restricted the ability of most Jamaican planters to finance more efficient production methods themselves and to borrow more funds. Some plantations survived but many more went under. Despite the arrival of 57,000 indentured laborers, Jamaican sugar exports declined rapidly during the last quarter of the century. Access to labor was not sufficient to save Jamaica's sugar industry.

In contrast, the greatest sugar producers and the greatest importers of indentured labor in the British Caribbean were British Guiana and Trinidad, whose virgin fertile lands attracted ample new capital. Guiana's sugar exports grew 270 percent between 1852 and 1908, most of the increase before 1870 being attributable to a 142 percent expansion of acreage (31,000 to 76,000); most of that after 1870 was due to technological innovations that increased yields per acre by 55 percent. Trinidad's development was similar, with sugar exports increasing 270 percent between 1850 and 1880.[29] The colonies' increased production was greatly facilitated by large

[28]Williams, From Columbus, pp. 359.
[29]Adamson, Sugar without Slaves, pp. 106, 179; Nath, Indians in British Guiana, tables 29–30; Bridget Brereton, A History of Modern Trinidad, 1783–1962 (Kingston, Jamaica: Heinemann Educational Books, 1981), p. 84.

indentured labor imports, the two accounting for over 85 percent of all the indentured labor entering the British Caribbean, 299,000 into British Guiana and 166,000 into Trinidad.

Britain's Indian Ocean sugar colony, Mauritius, also greatly increased production. Sugar exports rose from an annual average of 33,443 tons in the 1830s, to 100,000 tons in the 1850s and 1860s (at which time the colony was producing nearly 8 percent of the world's cane sugar). That growth depended heavily on the easy access to indentured laborers from India, 375,000 of whom had arrived by 1870, two-thirds since midcentury. But growth slowed considerably after that. Capital necessary for modernization became hard to attract, both because Mauritius lay far from the major sugar markets in Europe and North America and because the opening of the Suez canal in 1869 diverted shipping between India and Europe north of the island. Under those circumstances the colony labor needs came to be largely satisfied by the resident population of Indians no longer under indenture and by the older African residents. As a partial alternative to capital investment the planters from the 1870s engaged in a *grand morcellement* of their estates, the selling off of the less profitable lands in small parcels to Indians no longer under indenture, whose continued cultivation of sugarcane did much to sustain the colony's production and caused a modest boom in the early twentieth century.[30]

On the whole France's plantation colonies faced an even harder transition from slavery. The French West Indies, cut off from adequate supplies of new labor and facing direct competition in their traditional French market from domestic sugar beet growers, registered only modest gains in production during the second half of the century. A severe earthquake on Guadeloupe in 1843, which destroyed many of the old mills, had the unexpected benefit of speeding the transition to more efficient central factories. Réunion went through a cycle of boom similar to that of Mauritius in the earlier nineteenth century with sugar production peaking at 73,000 tons in 1860. During the crisis after 1860 its production fell by two-thirds, and even during the recovery from 1890 to 1914 annual production remained at between 35,000 and 40,000 tons. J. H. Galloway attributes Réunion's decline to France's greater commercial interest in neighboring Madagascar and to the competition from domestic sugar beets.[31]

The revival of Peru illustrates another working of the international economy in a country attempting economic development.[32] Native and

[30]Larry W. Bowman, *Mauritius: Democracy and Development in the Indian Ocean* (Boulder, Colo.: Westview Press, 1991), pp. 20–26.

[31]André Scherer, *La Réunion* (Paris: Presses Univérsitaires de France, 1980), pp. 52–58, 74–75; Galloway, *Sugar Cane Industry*, pp. 221–22.

[32]Woodruff, *Impact of Western Man*, p. 171; Jonathon V. Levin, *The Export Economies: Their*

colonial Peruvians had long enriched their fields from the mountains of
guano (bird droppings) that had accumulated over many centuries on the
rainless islands adjacent to the rich feeding grounds of the Humboldt
Current off Peru's Pacific coast, but it was not until the development of
scientific soil analysis in Europe during the early nineteenth century that
the commercial value of these nitrogen-rich deposits came to be more
widely recognized. Guano shipment began in the 1840s to the United
States (where it revitalized the tobacco fields of the upper South), to the
West Indies (where it helped to avert the complete collapse of sugar
production in Jamaica), as well as to Australia and Europe. By 1860 Peruvian guano had become one of Latin America's most important exports.
The capital was largely British, partly French, but the labor force was
primarily indentured Chinese.

Peru's participation in the growing market for sugar was held back by
several factors in the first half of the nineteenth century: the disruptions of
the wars of independence; a labor shortage due to British abolitionist
policies, which virtually ended the flow of slaves into Peru after 1810,
causing the slave population to decline from over 40,000 in 1792 to 25,500
at midcentury; and high interest rates in the 1830s along with problems of
entry into the Chilean market. The plantations' revival came from the
capital generated by the growth of guano mining, some of which was
channeled to plantation owners by the government's payment of seven
million pesos compensation when slavery was abolished in 1854. By then
improved sea transportation gave Peruvian planters better access to distant markets, but the greatest constraint on sugar's expansion remained
finding sufficient labor. Indigenous population densities were low and free
immigration small. Not until the late nineteenth century would rising
population pressures and civil unrest drive a significant number of Peruvian Indians into the labor market to sustain the plantation systems. Until
then plantation owners relied on indentured Asian labor, importing nearly
100,000 Chinese between 1849 and 1874 and 18,000 Japanese between 1898
and 1923.[33]

Southern Africa was another nexus of new European settlement, capital,
and labor. During the century older settlers expanding out of the Cape Colony founded new settlements. Between 1849 and 1851 about 5,000 British
settlers were attracted to the fertile Indian Ocean colony of Natal by subsi-

Pattern of Development in Historical Perspective (Cambridge, Mass.: Harvard University Press,
1960), pp. 27–31, 49–63, 73–74, also tells the story of international capital.
[33]Michael J. Gonzales, *Plantation Agriculture and Social Control in Northern Peru, 1875–1933*
(Austin: University of Texas Press, 1985), pp. 18–21, 84–95, 118–36; Watt Stewart, *Chinese
Bondage in Peru: A History of the Chinese Coolie in Peru, 1849–1874* (Durham, N.C.: Duke
University Press, 1951), pp. 20, 100.

dized passage and free land, even though the land was generally not of the best sort. Initial plans for small cotton plantations using labor from local Zulu villages did not succeed, since the African population of about 100,000 found little attraction in plantation work for wages. Instead, the Zulu were able to satisfy their wants by farming the substantial tracts reserved to them, selling cash crops to the towns, hunting for ivory, or renting surplus land in the areas designed for European settlers. As cotton gave way to sugar cultivation in the early 1860s, under the leadership of experienced planters from Mauritius and the British West Indies, it was natural to bring in indentured Indian labor. Once the Indian government's initial resistance had been overcome, some 6,450 Indians were brought on three-year contracts between 1861 and 1867. Following a lull during the sugar depression from 1866 to 1872, sugarcane came to be the dominant crop in the subtropical coastal lowlands, with large company-owned estates becoming the norm. Under the supervision of an official protector of Indian immigrants, another 146,000 indentured Indian laborers were introduced between 1875 and 1911, mostly for work on the sugar plantations.[34]

The discovery of gold in the neighboring independent colony of Transvaal set off a mining boom in the 1880s that attracted large numbers of young English-speaking males. For two decades most unskilled labor was obtained from nearby African communities, the number of African miners attracted by the high wages rising above 100,000 in 1899. The destruction and dislocation caused by the long South African War (1899–1902) virtually halted gold mining. When peace returned, the mineowners faced declining ore quality and shrinking access to cheap labor, since Africans were turning to safer and better-paying jobs in towns, which also afforded them much more personal freedom than the prisonlike mining compounds. Until the recruitment of large numbers of contract laborers from much poorer neighboring colonies (notably Portuguese Mozambique) could be built up, a temporary solution was the importation of 64,000 indentured Chinese laborers in 1904–6. Although such labor was costly to recruit (about twenty pounds each), part of the cost was offset by the fact that the Chinese worked at much lower wage rates than local Africans.[35]

[34]Leonard Thompson, "Co-operation and Conflict: The Zulu Kingdom and Natal," in *The Oxford History of South Africa*, ed. Monica Wilson and Leonard Thompson (Oxford: Oxford University Press, 1969), 1:334–390; Henry Slater, "The Changing Pattern of Economic Relationships in Rural Natal, 1838–1914," in *Economy and Society in Pre-Industrial South Africa*, ed. Shula Marks and Anthony Atmore (London: Longman, 1980), pp. 148–61; Peter Richardson, "The Natal Sugar Industry, 1849–1905: An Interpretative Essay," *Journal of African History* 23.4 (1982): 515–27. Tinker, *New System of Slavery*, pp. 30, 113, 258, 272, 280–83.
[35]Peter Richardson, *Chinese Mine Labour in the Transvaal* (London: Macmillan, 1982); Ching-Hwang Yen, *Coolies and Mandarins: China's Protection of Overseas Chinese during the Late Ch'ing Period (1851–1911)* (Singapore: Singapore University Press, 1985), pp. 335–47.

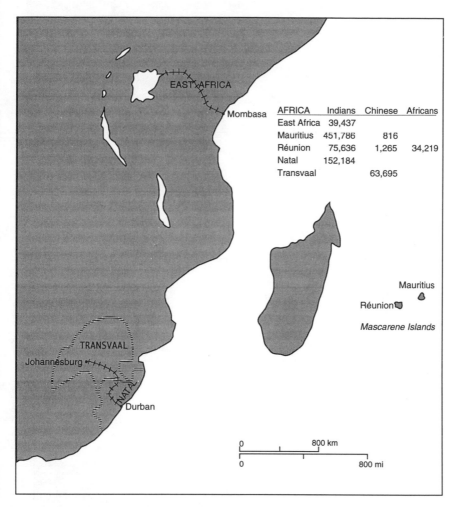

AFRICA	Indians	Chinese	Africans
East Africa	39,437		
Mauritius	451,786	816	
Réunion	75,636	1,265	34,219
Natal	152,184		
Transvaal		63,695	

Map 3. Principal indentured labor imports into Africa. *Source:* Table A.2.

Queensland in northeastern Australia also became a significant importer of indentured labor in this period. As in Natal, colonists had moved into Queensland to grow cotton but turned to sugar after the bottom fell out of the cotton market following the U.S. Civil War. Separated from New South Wales in 1859, the new Queensland government first sought to bring labor from India but, before that could be arranged, private recruiters began securing laborers from the South Pacific islands to the northeast. Between 1863 and 1904 some 62,500 indentured laborers from the Solomons, the

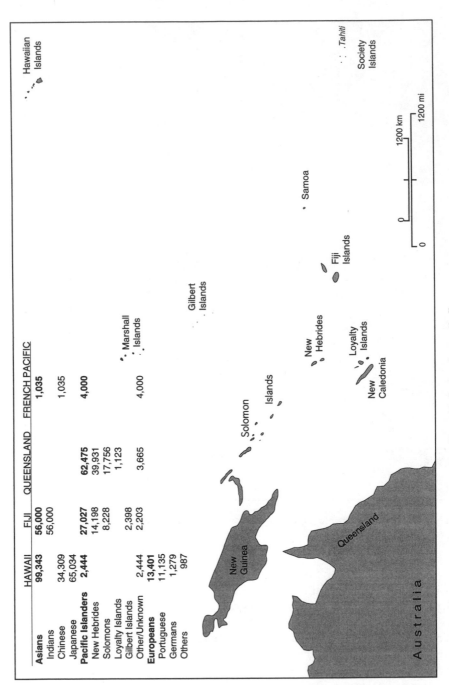

	HAWAII	FIJI	QUEENSLAND	FRENCH PACIFIC
Asians	**99,343**	**56,000**		**1,035**
Indians	34,309	56,000		
Chinese	65,034			1,035
Japanese				
Pacific Islanders	**2,444**	**27,027**	**62,475**	**4,000**
New Hebrides		14,198	39,931	
Solomons		8,228	17,756	
Loyalty Islands			1,123	
Gilbert Islands		2,398		
Other/Unknown	2,444	2,203	3,665	4,000
Europeans	**13,401**			
Portuguese	11,135			
Germans	1,279			
Others	987			

Map 4. Principal indentured labor imports into Oceania. *Source:* Appendix B.

New Hebrides, and other island chains were brought to the Queensland plantations.[36]

A contrast to the Queensland approach to labor was to be found in Fiji, acquired as a British colony in 1874, where the Colonial Sugar Refining Company of Sydney (which had a virtual monopoly on refining sugar in Queensland) expanded in 1874 and began operations to serve the sugar estates. Like their counterparts in Natal, the indigenous people of Fiji were not pushed by land shortage to seek wage labor for Europeans, especially since their numbers tumbled due to the introduction of new diseases (as in Hawaii), nor were the colonial authorities willing to impose a forced labor system when voluntary migrants could be brought so much more easily. Between 1864 and 1916, 26,000 Pacific islanders and 56,000 indentured Indians were introduced to Fiji. Their labor brought Fiji's sugar exports to 46,400 tons in 1893 and double that by 1914.[37]

The nineteenth century also saw rapid transcontinental and overseas expansion of the United States, whose vast domestic markets and imperial thrusts also helped generate a demand for indentured labor. As the previous chapter has argued, the effect of Chinese migration to California and other parts of the American West starting in the mid-nineteenth century has been the subject of differing interpretations but there is no ambiguity about the vital role Chinese and other contract labor played in the expansion of sugar plantations in Hawaii and Cuba.

American interest in the Hawaiian islands began with the New England whalers and missionaries, who arrived in 1819–20. After President John Tyler staked out the tropical islands as part of the American economic sphere of interest in 1842 by invoking the Monroe Doctrine, the Hawaiian government altered its laws to permit the establishment of American-owned sugar plantations. Hawaiian sugar interests enjoyed a brief period of prosperity before 1850, when California's annexation to the United States cut them out of the protected American market. Better marketing conditions during the American Civil War attracted new investment to Hawaii that made the fledgling sugar industry more competitive and, after ten years of negotiation, a reciprocal treaty between Hawaii and the United States was signed in 1876, giving Hawaiian sugar duty-free access to the

---

[36]Galloway, *Sugar Cane Industry*, pp. 228–33; Peter Corris, *Passage, Port and Plantation: A History of Solomon Islands Labour Migration, 1870–1914* (Carlton: Melbourne University Press, 1973), pp. 25–59; Charles A. Price, with Elizabeth Baker, "Origins of Pacific Island Labourers in Queensland, 1863–1904: A Research Note," *Journal of Pacific History* 11.2 (1976): 110–11, for the statistics. Another 85,000 or more islanders were recruited to plantations in German New Guinea from 1884 to 1914; Stewart Firth, "The Transformation of the Labour Trade in German New Guinea, 1899–1914," *Journal of Pacific History* 11.1–2 (1976): 51.

[37]Tinker, *New System of Slavery*, p. 30; Galloway, *Sugar Cane Industry*, pp. 222–23; Newbury, "Melanesian Labor Reserve," p. 12; Ralph Shlomowitz, "The Fiji Labor Trade in Comparative Perspective, 1864–1914," *Pacific Studies* 9.3 (1986): 107–52.

American market. This set off a period of very rapid expansion fed by heavy investment in land, irrigation, and technology.[38]

Although labor shortages caused by demographic collapse of the indigenous population had begun to appear before 1850, in the early 1870s the native Hawaiians supplied still nearly 80 percent of the plantation labor force, even though that required employing half of all Hawaiian men. However, the expansion of sugarcane plantations after the reciprocal treaty could only be accomplished by importing new labor. Chinese immigration, which had rarely amounted to more than a hundred a year between 1852 and 1875, jumped to an average of 2,600 a year in the decade after 1876. Most of those after 1876 signed contracts only after arriving in Hawaii but owed debts to recruiting companies for their passage. As the demand for labor increased efforts were made to tap other immigrant sources. A very costly effort that brought 2,500 Polynesians to Hawaii between 1879 and 1885 suffered from high mortality. Smaller numbers of German and Norwegian migrants and 11,000 Portuguese migrants were also attracted in this period.[39]

An annual average of 2,000 Chinese continued to arrive in Hawaii between 1886 and 1899, but their numbers were surpassed, first by nearly 30,000 indentured Japanese laborers who were brought between 1885 and 1894 under government-sponsored contracts, and then by 36,000 laborers recruited by private companies, who had to reimburse the costs of their passage from their wages. Another 70,000 Japanese emigrated to Hawaii from 1900 to 1908. This Hawaiian sugar growth exemplified the ability of heavy investment of capital and technology both to produce sugar with great efficiency and to dominate social and environmental factors.[40]

The spectacular development of the Spanish colony of Cuba was also heavily dependent on American capital and markets and, to a lesser extent than Hawaii, on Asian indentured labor. Though the largest of the West Indian islands, Cuba had been of minor economic importance until it received an infusion of expertise and capital from French planters fleeing the Haitian revolution who began the development of the island's extensive and cheap fertile land for sugar cultivation. Government, private

---

[38]Despite its age, there is a great deal of useful information in John W. Vandercook's *King Cane: The Story of Sugar in Hawaii* (New York: Harper & Brothers, 1939).

[39]Edward D. Beechert, *Working in Hawaii: A Labor History* (Honolulu: University of Hawaii Press, 1985), pp. 58–63, 81, 90–91; Clarence Glick, *Sojourners and Settlers: Chinese Migrants in Hawaii* (Honolulu: Hawaiian Chinese History Center and the University Press of Hawaii, 1980), pp. 6–11; Judith A. Bennett, "Immigration, 'Blackbirding,' Labour Recruiting? The Hawaiian Experience, 1877–1887," *Journal of Pacific History* 11.1–2 (1976): 16–24.

[40]Yuji Ichioka, *The Issei: The World of the First Generation Japanese Immigrants, 1885–1924* (New York: Free Press, 1988), pp. 40ff.; Yukiko Kimura, *Issei: Japanese Immigrants in Hawaii* (Honolulu: University of Hawaii Press, 1988), pp. 3–13; Dorothy Ochiai Hazama and Jane Okamoto Komeiji, *Okage Sama De: The Japanese in Hawaii'i, 1885–1985* (Honolulu: Bess Press, 1986), pp. 23–25. Galloway, *Sugar Cane Industry*, pp. 226–28.

Cuban, and British capital (for railroads) promoted the development of the industry in the middle decades of the century but the later growth of Cuba's sugar was tied to its proximity to the growing American market, which by 1865 bought 65 percent of the Cuban crop. North American merchants also became increasingly important to the financing of the Cuban sugar producers, and in the final decades of the century the investment of large amounts of North American capital for new mills and railroads sustained the industry's modernization and continued growth. American investment in Cuba amounted to $50 million at the end of the century and rose to $1.3 billion in the 1920s. Despite temporary pauses caused by the Ten Years' War of 1868–78 and the Spanish-American War of 1898–1900, Cuba's sugar production rose rapidly from next to nothing in 1800 to 300,000 tons in 1850 and then to 3 million tons in 1914.

Much of the labor to clear and operate the sugar plantations came from massive imports of slaves, half a million between 1801 and 1850 and another 200,000 between 1851 and the early 1860s, when the intervention of Union forces during the American Civil War finally forced an end to the slave trade.[41] In response to long-standing external and internal abolitionist pressures, an 1870 law declared free all slaves over sixty years of age and those subsequently born of slave parents. Slavery itself was reduced to a sort of apprenticeship (*patronato*) in 1880, the final liberation coming in 1886. As slave labor became scarcer, Cuban planters had sought other sources of labor. A small number of Mayan Indian prisoners were obtained from Mexico on ten-year bonds in 1849 and another 1,800 more from 1854 to 1861. More important were the 122,000 indentured Chinese imported to work in the cane fields from 1847 until China halted shipments in 1873 due to their mistreatment.[42]

Conclusion

This chapter has argued that the reemergence of an overseas indentured labor trade in the nineteenth century was the result of two separate but overlapping factors. One was the chronic labor shortage that developed in the wake of slave emancipation, first in the British plantation colonies in the 1830s and subsequently in French, Dutch, and Spanish colonies. The growth and expansion of this demand were also intimately linked with a new phase of imperialism in the nineteenth century, in which Western capital, settlers, and new technology penetrated a world open to their awesome power and skills. The development of sugar plantations in lands

[41]Eltis, *Economic Growth*, p. 245.
[42]Laurence, *Immigration into the West Indies*, pp. 27–35; Franklin W. Knight, *Slave Society in Cuba during the Nineteenth Century* (Madison: University of Wisconsin Press, 1970), pp. 43–45, 154–78; Galloway, *Sugar Cane Industry*, pp. 162–69.

that had never known slavery was an aspect of this imperial expansion, which drew heavily on indentured labor, as was the opening of some mining operations. Not surprisingly, its industrial strength, colonial empire, and global trading interests made Great Britain the key player in this process, but important contributions were also made by the United States and France, as well as Spain, the Netherlands, Peru, and Hawaii.

A quite different form of Western expansion in this period was the massive migration of impoverished Europeans to North America and in lesser proportions other continents. Yet the indentured labor trade was very largely made up of persons from Asia, Africa, and the Pacific islands, although it did include small numbers of Europeans. How this phenomenon was tied to demographic and economic conditions in their countries of origin, political circumstances, and prevailing racial attitudes is the subject of the next chapter.

3

Supplies

Born in India, we are prepared to go to Fiji,
Or, if you please, to Natal to dig in the mines.
We are prepared to suffer there,
But brothers! Don't make us labourers here.[1]

The growing demand for plantation labor coincided with a growing willingness – often bordering on desperation – by individuals in many parts of the world to accept long-distance migration as a way to improve their lives. In the language of migration studies, the *push* of undesirable circumstances at home was joined to the *pull* of opportunities overseas. This chapter looks at how the new indentured labor was connected to changing economic and political circumstances in the migrants' homelands and to local and regional patterns of labor migration. A third factor, the *politics* of imperial expansion, completed the legal and logistical connections between the labor-short employers and the distant reservoirs of distressed potential migrants.

The mix of circumstances was different in each part of the world. For Africa, the new trade was closely linked to the ending of the long-standing slave trade. For China and India, indentured labor overseas was an extension of much larger patterns of local and regional labor migration. For Japan and the South Pacific, overseas migration was intimately connected to the end of centuries of isolation from the outside world. The scale and scope of nineteenth-century indentured migrations (see Figure 3.1) were also shaped by new factors. Most areas of supply were experiencing a rising tide of population and impoverishment. All were affected by the expanding network of Western political and economic imperialism.

---

[1]Poetry of Indo-Fiji and from northwest provinces of India, quoted by Brij V. Lal, *Girmitiyas: The Origins of the Fiji Indians* (Canberra: Journal of Pacific History, 1983), p. 88.

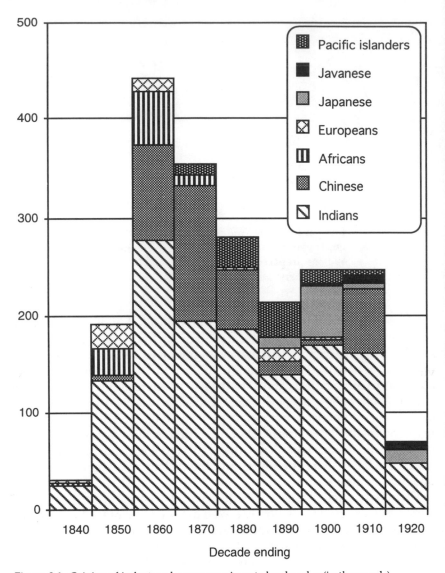

Figure 3.1. Origins of indentured overseas migrants by decades (in thousands).
Source: Table A.1.

Africa

In contrast to the dominant importance of the African slave trade in global labor migrations before the early nineteenth century, the number of Africans in the new indentured migrations was modest. Nevertheless, it is useful to begin this overview of supply conditions in Africa since that was where some of the earliest cases of indentured labor recruitment began. In addition, the failure of Africa to meet the expectations of labor recruiters underlines the importance of an adequate push factor in ensuring the success of the overseas labor trade.

Indentured African labor began as a by-product of Britain's suppression of the Atlantic slave trade. Believing Africans rescued from slave ships could not return to their homes or fend for themselves in the colonies where they might be freed, the Privy Council issued regulations in 1808 for placing such liberated Africans under the care of others. Able-bodied men were to be inducted into Britain's West India Regiments or into the Royal Africa Corps of the British Navy, which had the additional advantage of reducing the need for British personnel in the unhealthy tropics. Other liberated Africans were to be apprenticed to "respectable persons" in British colonies. Some 3,250 Africans liberated by Vice-Admiralty Courts in the British West Indies between 1807 and 1819 were inducted into the military for life or apprenticed to individuals under fourteen-year contracts of indenture. Several thousand of the 20,571 Africans liberated at Sierra Leone between 1808 and the end of 1825 were also made to enlist in British military forces and most of the rest were indentured as apprentices to Sierra Leone residents for terms ranging from three to nine years. According to Christopher Fyfe, some of these apprentices learned a trade, others ran away or were resold as slaves, and "many remained drudges, virtual domestic slaves, to masters and mistresses who treated them badly, even cruelly."[2]

These early patterns foreshadowed many aspects of the later overseas indentured labor migrations, but, except for military recruits, Britain resisted shipping liberated persons out of Sierra Leone for several decades lest such migrations be seen by Africans and by European humanitarians as a disguised revival of the slave trade. Meanwhile, efforts were made to correct other shortcomings of the anti-slave trade campaign. By the 1830s African adults newly liberated at Sierra Leone no longer faced long terms of apprenticeship, but were maintained at government expense for six months and allotted free land and tools, while missionaries provided further support and comfort. Food and land were in abundant supply and the colony developed a series of village communities, complete with churches

---

[2]Johnson U. A. Asiegbu, *Slavery and the Politics of Liberation, 1787–1861* (London: Longmans, 1969), pp. 27–31; Roger Norman Buckley, *Slaves in Red Coats: The British West India Regiments, 1795–1815* (New Haven: Yale University Press, 1979), pp. 131–37; *PP* 1821 xxiii (61), Annual Returns by the Collectors of Customs of Negroes that have been apprenticed [1807–19]; *PP* 1826–27 vii (312), Report of the Commissioners of Inquiry into the State of the Colony of Sierra Leone, 9 May 1827, pp. 52–53; Christopher Fyfe, *A History of Sierra Leone* (London: Oxford University Press, 1962), pp. 105–7, 114 (quotation from pp. 182–83). Asiegbu (p. 31) estimates the total number of liberated Africans recruited for military service up to 1840 was at least 12,000.

and schools. However, the end of slavery in the British Caribbean colonies led to considerable pressure to transform a policy that had been designed to find suitable and inexpensive accommodation for liberated Africans into one that was more responsive to planters' needs for more African labor. By ending the recruiting ban the government could, at one stroke, stem the costs of maintaining the rising population of liberated Africans in Sierra Leone, alleviate the labor crisis in the West Indies, and satisfy the concerns of British abolitionists and officials who were eager to demonstrate that there was a practical alternative to slavery in plantation colonies.

In 1840 restrictions on the recruitment of liberated Africans in Sierra Leone for overseas employment were lifted, although the first agents from Jamaica, Trinidad, and British Guiana who tried recruiting in Sierra Leone in mid 1841 could persuade only a few persons to leave. When the British government took direct control of the operations in 1843, providing government transport vessels and simplifying the recruitment regulations, the results were still disappointing. Few Africans liberated from slave vessels were in sufficiently distressed circumstances to want to undertake the perils of a second sea voyage. Even those who might have benefited from leaving were held back by fears of reenslavement and harsh treatment – fears actively promoted both by Sierra Leone landowners not wanting to lose their source of cheap labor and by missionaries dreaming of sending out bands of Christian recaptives from Sierra Leone to win the African continent to the Gospel.

The lack of volunteers from among liberated Africans caused recruiters to examine the potential of neighboring populations, particularly a group of related peoples just to the south, largely in what became Liberia, known to Europeans as the Kru, whose men had long hired themselves out as auxiliary laborers on European vessels trading in coastal West Africa. The Kru had become indispensable to the burgeoning palm oil trade and also served regularly on the Royal Navy's antislavery patrols. Kru laborers helped establish the brief British outpost on Fernando Po Island in 1827 and accompanied the British explorations of the Niger River in 1833 and 1841. They seemed the perfect candidates for services in the Caribbean colonies. Unlike most of the Africans, the Kru were eager to work for Europeans and their employers were unstinting in their praise of Kru laborers' hard work, loyalty, and thrift. In 1844 a British commissioner reported that the Kru might well furnish "many thousands" of hardworking and willing laborers a year for the West Indies. However, determined efforts first by British recruiters and then by the French succeeded in recruiting only about 2,400 Kru for the Caribbean colonies between 1841 and 1857.[3]

---

[3]*PP* 1847–48 xliv (732), Emigration from Sierra Leone to the West Indies, Report of R. Guppy to the Governor of Trinidad, 18 October 1844, p. 7. The best overview of the Kru is George E. Brooks, Jr., *The Kru Mariner in the Nineteenth Century: An Historical Compendium* (Newark,

Particular issues stymied the recruitment of Kru laborers: most resisted signing long-term contracts and refused to bring their wives with them (which might have made long-term contracts more palatable); they disliked plantation work and found the wages offered in the Caribbean colonies unattractive; those who went reported instances of mistreatment and difficulties in returning home. Even if some of these issues could have been resolved, the number of recruits that the modest Kru population could have yielded would never have been large. Nor were the prospects promising for voluntary labor recruitment elsewhere in the continent that had supplied slaves to the Americas and the Islamic world during many previous centuries. Communal labor was abundant and slave labor was growing rapidly in mid-nineteenth-century sub-Saharan Africa, but laborers like the Kru who regularly hired themselves out at some distance from their homes were decidedly exceptional. Most Africans had access to all the land and other productive resources they needed. Indeed, the abundance of land in relation to population was a principal reason for the absence of labor markets and a principal motive for the spread of domestic slavery. In addition, the arduousness and insecurity of travel throughout the continent severely limited the mobility of those who might have wished to leave home.[4]

The failure to find sufficient voluntary laborers did not end recruitment efforts from Africa. Instead, it accentuated the shift to ethically ambivalent schemes that tapped the victims of the Atlantic slave trade and of indigenous African slavery. To diminish the appeal of staying in Sierra Leone, the colony's government discontinued settling-in allowances in 1844, forcing newly arrived recaptives to emigrate, enlist in the military, or fend for themselves. In addition, Africans freshly released from captured slave ships were kept in quarantine so as to insolate them from stories about hard conditions in the West Indies. Before the recaptives were released, they were given a talk on the merits of life in the Caribbean colonies

Del.: Liberian Studies Association in America, 1972), and the definitive examination of their recruitment to the Guianas is Monica Schuler, "Kru Emigration to British and French Guiana, 1841–1857," in *Africans in Bondage*, ed. Paul E. Lovejoy (Madison: African Studies Program, University of Wisconsin, 1986), pp. 155–201.
[4] A. G. Hopkins, *An Economic History of West Africa* (New York: Columbia University Press, 1973), pp. 11–27; Colin W. Newbury, "Historical Aspects of Manpower and Migration in African South of the Sahara," in *Colonialism in Africa 1870–1960*, vol. 4, ed. Peter Duignan and L. H. Gann (Cambridge: Cambridge University Press, 1975), pp. 523–27; Paul E. Lovejoy, *Transformations in Slavery: A History of Slavery in Africa* (Cambridge: Cambridge University Press, 1983), pp. 153–58 and passim. On the basis of considerable research, Paul Lovejoy concludes, "there were certainly more slaves in Africa in the nineteenth century than there were in the Americas at any time"; foreward to Claude Meillassoux, *The Anthropology of Slavery: The Womb of Iron and Gold* (Chicago: University of Chicago Press, 1991), p. 7. Cf. Patrick Manning, *Slavery and African Life: Occidental, Oriental, and African Slave Trades* (Cambridge: Cambridge University Press, 1990), p. 23, "After about 1850, there were more slaves in Africa than in the New World."

and those who signed up were loaded directly onto migrant ships.[5] Under these circumstances, the number of migrants from Sierra Leone rose to an annual average of 1,500 in the late 1840s. Even more Africans were recruited from the liberation depot on the small mid-Atlantic island of St. Helena, whose limited resources virtually precluded permanent settlement by more than a few.

However, the supply of recaptives was finite. After midcentury their numbers fell off rapidly as the Atlantic slave trade was brought to an end. In all, about 37,000 liberated Africans were recruited for the British Caribbean from 1834 to 1867, including some from New World liberation depots.[6] Although liberated Africans were an inevitable by-product of Britain's commendable actions in suppressing the slave trade, their diversion to colonial plantations still had many shortcomings as a program for recruiting free labor. Asiegbu's charge that under the new policies of the mid-1840s labor recruitment "degenerated into almost open slave trading" may be an exaggeration, but it would be equally hard to extol such policies as a model for free-labor recruitment.[7] The options were sorely limited by practical and budgetary constraints and, while it does not reduce these faults, it may be noted that the French and Portuguese, who did not take an active role in suppressing the slave trade and thus had no supply of recaptives under their control, were doing far worse.

In order to secure labor for public works in their West African colony of Senegal the French in 1839–40 had begun purchasing the freedom of slaves held by other Africans and then binding them to fourteen-year contracts to work off the cost of their freedom. In 1853 the practice of monetary redemption (*rachat préalable*) of slaves was resumed in Senegal and the next year extended to French coastal enclaves further south. From recruitment within a colony it was only a small step in 1854 to transporting redeemed West Africans on six-year contracts across the ocean to the French Caribbean colonies of Cayenne (French Guiana), Martinique, and Guadeloupe. Many of the Senegalese recruits, who left from the notorious slave depot of Gorée, protested upon their arrival in French Guiana that they were not volunteers or had been misled about the wages and conditions of work

[5] Asiegbu, *Slavery and the Politics of Liberation*, pp. 44–83; Monica Schuler, "*Alas, Alas, Kongo*": *A Social History of Indentured African Immigration into Jamaica, 1841–1865* (Baltimore: Johns Hopkins University Press, 1980), pp. 6–26; William A. Green, "The West Indies and Indentured Labour Migration: The Jamaican Experience," in *Indentured Labour in the British Empire, 1840–1920*, ed. Kay Saunders (London: Croom Helm, 1984), pp. 6–17.

[6] See Table A.1 and Map 5. In addition to the liberated Africans from St. Helena, Sierra Leone, Rio, Havana, and other depots, by an order of 1844 slaves captured in East Africa could be taken directly to Mauritius for liberation. This assured the colony "a cheap supply of African labour without the expense of emigration offices and agents," according to Asiegbu, *Slavery and the Politics of Liberation*, p. 57, although in fact few recaptives appear to have been taken there.

[7] Asiegbu, *Slavery and the Politics of Liberation*, p. 119; cf. Schuler, "*Alas, Alas, Kongo*," p. 6.

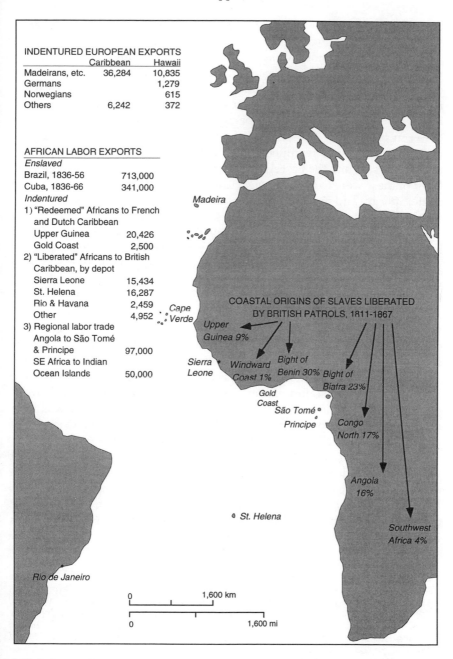

INDENTURED EUROPEAN EXPORTS

	Caribbean	Hawaii
Madeirans, etc.	36,284	10,835
Germans		1,279
Norwegians		615
Others	6,242	372

AFRICAN LABOR EXPORTS

Enslaved

Brazil, 1836-56	713,000
Cuba, 1836-66	341,000

Indentured

1) "Redeemed" Africans to French
   and Dutch Caribbean

Upper Guinea	20,426
Gold Coast	2,500

2) "Liberated" Africans to British
   Caribbean, by depot

Sierra Leone	15,434
St. Helena	16,287
Rio & Havana	2,459
Other	4,952

3) Regional labor trade

Angola to São Tomé & Principe	97,000
SE Africa to Indian Ocean Islands	50,000

COASTAL ORIGINS OF SLAVES LIBERATED
BY BRITISH PATROLS, 1811-1867

Madeira

Cape Verde

Upper Guinea 9%

Sierra Leone

Windward Coast 1%

Bight of Benin 30%

Bight of Biafra 23%

Gold Coast

São Tomé

Principe

Congo North 17%

Angola 16%

Southwest Africa 4%

St. Helena

Rio de Janeiro

0 ——— 1,600 km

0 ——— 1,600 mi

Map 5. Principal indentured labor exports from Africa and Europe. *Source:* Appendix B.

there. During the eight years of its operation some 20,426 African laborers were sent to the French Caribbean (including about 1,200 Kru and other Africans who were not the produce of such ransoming). An even larger recruitment took place from eastern Africa for the French Indian Ocean colonies under similar circumstances. From a trickle of 574 in 1850 the redeemed African migration there rose to a peak of 10,000 in 1858. Assuming a mortality in transit of 25 percent, François Renault estimates that between 1848, when slavery was officially abolished, and 1861 as many as 60,000 Africans were recruited from the Comoro Islands, the large island of Madagascar, and the East African mainland, most destined for Réunion. Most of these were technically *engagés à temps*, that is, contract laborers, but contemporary and modern observers have found little to distinguish them (or those sent to the French West Indies) from slaves.[8]

In their west-central African colony of Angola, the Portuguese had begun using enslaved Africans on local plantations in the 1850s, when it was no longer possible to send them overseas. Forced by foreign pressure to abolish slavery in 1858, the government "apprenticed" the freed slaves to their former masters until 1875. Next came a system of contract labor in Angola under which "nonproductive" Africans (in effect, anyone not already working for the Portuguese) could be forced to sign a five-year labor contract at very low pay. The growing "pacification" of the colony's hinterland provided captives who were also forced to sign contracts. Between 1876 and 1915 some 97,000 contract laborers were shipped from Angola to Portugal's island colonies of São Tomé and Príncipe under five-year indentures that provided for free return passage. Charging this was little more than slavery under a new name, investigators could find evidence of only thirteen ever having been returned to Angola by the end of 1908.[9]

Even if one were willing to overlook all its serious shortcomings, the fact remains that indentured labor recruitment in Africa failed to satisfy the demand resulting from the ending of slavery. Indeed, more than five times as many enslaved Africans were brought to Cuba between 1840 and 1867 as entered all Caribbean colonies under indenture. Of over 60,000 overseas indentured recruits from Africa, less than 10 percent were completely

---

[8]Schuler, "Kru Emigration," pp. 174–83; François Renault, *Libération d'esclaves et nouvelle sérvitude* (Abidjan: Nouvelle Éditions Africaines, 1976), pp. 34–39, 158. Renault (p. 29) says that in the effort to reconcile freedom and labor, the former was the loser. David Eltis, *Economic Growth and the Ending of the Transatlantic Slave Trade* (New York: Oxford University Press, 1987), p. 246, counts all of these as slaves. Hubert Gerbeau, "Engagées and Coolies on Réunion Island: Slavery's Masks and Freedom's Constraints," in Emmer, *Colonialism and Migration*, pp. 221–23, gives numerous examples of forced recruitment. Lovejoy, *Transformations in Slavery*, p. 146, refers to this as a "disguised trade in slaves."
[9]James Duffy, *A Question of Slavery* (Cambridge, Mass.: Harvard University Press, 1967), pp. 98, 209, 211. William A. Cadbury, *Labour in Portuguese West Africa*, 2nd ed. (New York: Negro Universities Press, 1969), pp. 59, 81, 85.

voluntary (about 2,400 Kru and perhaps as many liberated Africans re-cruited from among the established population in Sierra Leone). Those Africans rescued from slave ships by the British between 1844 and 1867 (about 60 percent of the total) had little choice but to migrate overseas under indentured contracts, but the constraint of their migration, resulting as it did from their status as displaced persons and the absence of realistic viable circumstances, can clearly be distinguished from the still existing slave trade from which they had been rescued. It is far more difficult to make such a distinction in the case of slaves redeemed in Africa by the French (and, on a much smaller scale, by the Dutch) for the purpose of being shipped overseas to Caribbean colonies. Like the indentured labor trades to offshore African islands in the Atlantic and Indian Oceans, this was forced labor largely devoid of any voluntary component.

The African labor trade illustrates two points of general significance to supply conditions in the global indentured labor trade. First, the absence of an adequate number of voluntary migrants did not prevent recruiters from using more questionable recruiting methods. Second, short of reviving the methods of the slave trade, it was impossible for recruiters to obtain large numbers of migrant laborers in the absence of social and economic circumstances that made people willing recruits. The slave trade had been the classic example of labor recruitment by pull alone, offering a sufficient price to draw people to enslave others. Offering a much lower inducement, the indentured labor trade's success depended on there being a com-plementary push from within areas of labor supply. Few Africans felt such a push in the nineteenth century and few of those were sufficiently des-perate to migrate overseas. Indeed, well into the colonial period, colonial officials in Africa found recruiting sufficient labor extremely difficult un-less it was done by force.

China

The circumstances of Chinese overseas labor migration resembled those in Africa in two significant ways: Western recruiters of different nations were confined to a few coastal enclaves and a large component of the recruits were involuntary. The division of political authority made regulation of the trade difficult, though separate efforts by Britain and China eventually improved the conduct of the trade. This absence of effective regulation permitted both Western and Chinese recruiters to use coercive and de-ceptive methods especially in the early years. China differed notably from Africa in the much larger number of persons who were sent overseas under contracts of indenture. This difference can be explained partly in terms of China's much larger population (about times five that of the entire African continent in these decades), but must ultimately be attributed to the fact that many more Chinese were voluntary migrants. Not only was Chinese labor migration already well established, but worsening conditions in nineteenth-century China drove many more people to make use of China's superior internal transport to reach the coastal ports and to seek work abroad.

Labor migration from China has a long history. For several centuries before the 1800s some Chinese had ventured overseas to escape their miseries and make their fortunes, establishing colonies in many parts of Southeast Asia. Although from the early Qing (Ch'ing or Manchu) dynasty onward such departures had been declared treasonous activity punishable by death, since officials considered emigrating Chinese to be malcontents who might easily be recruited into the armies of foreign enemies, this law, which remained on the books until 1893, was poorly enforced and appears to have had little effect on voluntary emigration before or during the nineteenth century. This tradition of overseas migration was not only a model for the new indentured voyages; some of the earliest Western recruitment took place among Chinese already resident in Southeast Asia.

Burgeoning Chinese emigration in the nineteenth century was closely related to deteriorating economic and social conditions. One general factor was a population explosion from 150 million in 1700 to 430 million in 1850 that led to overcrowding on rural lands and fed price inflation. Periodic natural disasters, particularly floods and droughts, along with growing political instability, war, and rebellion, drove many to leave home in search of better opportunities. A series of internal conflicts and wars against foreigners seeking access to the vast Chinese markets added to the disruptions. For example, the massive Taiping rebellion of 1850–64 resulted in a large exodus from the lower Yangzi.[10]

Only a small percentage of Chinese migrants went overseas, even though East Asia offered no close counterpart to the settlement frontiers of nineteenth-century North America. The warm southern provinces of China and its Southeast Asian neighbors were already densely settled. Vast deserts made northwestern Xinjiang province, incorporated in 1884, "forbidding territory" in Jonathan Spence's words, and it attracted few new settlers. Only the northern frontier across which China's invaders had often come was welcoming. Despite government prohibitions, millions of

[10]Ta Chen, *Chinese Migrations, with Special Reference to Labor Conditions* (Washington, D.C.: Government Printing Office, 1923), pp. 4, 51–56, 75; Robert L. Irick, *Ch'ing Policy toward the Coolie Trade, 1847–1878* (Taipei: Chinese Materials Center, 1982), pp. 11–14; Ching-Hwang Yen, *Coolies and Mandarins: China's Protection of Overseas Chinese during the Late Ch'ing Period (1851–1911)* (Singapore: Singapore University Press, 1985), pp. 33–36; Marianne Bastid-Bruguiere, "Currents of Social Change," in *The Cambridge History of China*, vol 11, *Late Ch'ing, 1800–1911*, part 2, ed. John K. Fairbank and Kwang-Ching Liu (Cambridge: Cambridge University Press, 1980), pp. 582–84.

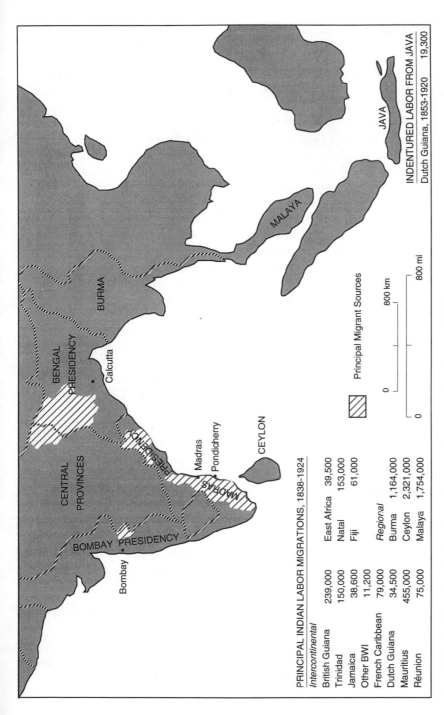

PRINCIPAL INDIAN LABOR MIGRATIONS, 1838-1924

Intercontinental			
British Guiana	239,000	East Africa	39,500
Trinidad	150,000	Natal	153,000
Jamaica	38,600	Fiji	61,000
Other BWI	11,200		
French Caribbean	79,000	*Regional*	
Dutch Guiana	34,500	Burma	1,164,000
Mauritius	455,000	Ceylon	2,321,000
Réunion	75,000	Malaya	1,754,000

INDENTURED LABOR FROM JAVA

Dutch Guiana, 1853-1920	19,300

Principal Migrant Sources

Map 6. Principal indentured labor exports f om southern Asia. *Source:* Appendix B.

Chinese migrated deeper and deeper into the cold but arable northern plains. By the early twentieth century the Chinese settlement in Manchuria was advancing at the rate of 300,000 to 400,000 a year.[11]

A second internal migration was to the coastal cities, which swelled with impoverished people desperately seeking low-paid jobs on the docks and in the factories. For some cities became stepping-stones to areas of earlier Chinese overseas settlement: from Fuzhou to Taiwan, which became a full province of China in 1885, from Canton and Macao to Southeast Asia and the East Indies, which absorbed millions and drew some of China's first diplomatic outposts after them. These ports of southern China also became staging areas for longer voyages to new lands across the Pacific, Indian, and Atlantic Oceans.

Many emigrants, perhaps most, financed their voyages with money advanced by families or future employers, though the origins of a formal system of employer-subsidized Chinese emigration are obscure. At least from 1823 there was a Chinese-run "credit ticket" system, which advanced money for passage and expenses to Chinese migrating to Southeast Asia. Up to 1842 emigration to the Malayan Straits, the Dutch East Indies, and the Philippines was largely conveyed in Chinese junks, but Chinese agents subsequently hired superior European vessels for the voyage to the straits, putting in place another essential piece of the long-distance contract labor trade. As Meagher has observed, "With the involvement of Western shipping in Chinese emigration to Southeast Asia, it was a comparatively easy step to expand the movement to North and South America and Australia."[12]

Easy technically, that is, but it was still a large step psychologically. According to Spence, "Most [migrants] were men who often married just before they left China and dreamed of returning someday to their native villages, loaded with riches, so they could buy more land and expand their families' waning fortunes."[13] For this reason recruiting even destitute Chinese to remote overseas locations from which return would be difficult or into work that held little hope of riches was not easy. In addition, Chinese had long held an unflattering image of Western "barbarians" (an image that Western action in the Opium Wars did nothing to improve), in whose domains they were reluctant to reside.[14] However, when Chinese who had

---

[11]Jonathan D. Spence, *The Search for Modern China* (New York: W. W. Norton, 1990), p. 210; Bastid-Bruguiere, "Currents of Social Change," pp. 583–84.

[12]Persia Crawford Campbell, *Chinese Coolie Emigration to Countries within the British Empire* (London: King & Sons, 1923), pp. 1–3; Arnold J. Meagher, "The Introduction of Chinese Laborers to Latin America: The 'Coolie Trade,' 1847–1874" (Ph.D. dissertation, History, University of California, Davis, 1975), p. 141 (quotation from p. 147).

[13]Spence, *Search for Modern China*, pp. 210–12.

[14]Meagher, "Introduction of Chinese Laborers," p. 148.

been drawn to the gold rushes in California, British Columbia, and Australia began to return with evidence and stories of riches, the sinister world of the barbarians was cast in a more favorable light.

Meanwhile, Western presence on the China coast had grown rapidly. The oldest European base on the Chinese coast, the Portuguese enclave of Macao dated from the 1550s, but the establishment of British control over neighboring Hong Kong and the opening up of five other Chinese port cities in the wake of the First Opium War (1839–41) put in place another link essential for the great overseas migrations to the lands of the Western barbarians. Though labor recruitment was but a small part of imperial expansion, through these treaty ports would come the Chinese laborers whose fabled capacity for hard work at low cost had attracted British interest. Shortly after Britain's exodus from the Atlantic slave trade in 1808, a parliamentary committee examined the practicality of bringing Chinese to the West Indies, noting in its favor the disposition of Chinese to emigrate and their orderly work habits, but on the debit side their intention to return to China, the near impossibility of getting Chinese women to emigrate, the problem of the Chinese government's reaction to what was technically illegal under Chinese law, and the potential opposition of West Indian legislatures to the introduction of a new racial group into their already divided societies. For these and other reasons the European-organized transport of indentured Chinese labor overseas did not begin until the 1840s.[15]

The first experiment involved the transport of 582 indentured Chinese from Singapore to Mauritius in 1843. Impressed by its success and in response to requests from planters in British Guiana, the British secretary of state, Lord Stanley, approved recruiting Chinese in the Straits Settlement for the West Indies, though Indian laborers were recruited instead.[16] Between 1847 and 1852 the trade in indentured laborers grew rapidly, initially from the treaty port of Amoy (Xiamen), and then from Canton and Hong Kong. The trade was largely in the hands of two British firms, Tait and Company and Syme, Muir and Company. "The latter built a special barracoon or 'pig pen' (*chu-tsai kuan*), as the Chinese called it, in front of their firm," where the potential emigrants were stripped naked, examined for defects, and, if approved, made to put their mark on labor contracts and then stamped or painted with the letter of their destination: C for Cuba, P for Peru, S for the Sandwich (Hawaiian) Islands.[17]

---

[15]*PP* 1810–11 ii (225), Report from the Select Committee appointed to consider the practicality and expediency of supplying the West India Colonies with Free Labourers from the East; Irick, *Ch'ing Policy*, pp. 7–8, says "several hundred" Chinese had gone to Brazil from 1810 onward, some had gone to Hawaii from 1820 onward, and that fourteen had made their way to California (presumably from Hawaii) before 1848.

[16]Meagher, "Introduction of Chinese Laborers," pp. 147–48; Irick, *Ch'ing Policy*, p. 82.

[17]Irick, *Ch'ing Policy*, pp. 26–27.

The recruits were delivered to the European firms by Chinese brokers (*kheh-tau*) and their subordinate agents. As befitted the fact that recruiting was illegal under Chinese law, these "crimps" were rough types who, to earn the lucrative "capitation" fees that rose rapidly with the demand for Chinese labor, regularly deceived recruits with unrealistic expectations of riches, concealed the distance of the actual destination, bought up debtors and prisoners of clan wars, and sometimes resorted to kidnapping. Chinese officials were powerless to regulate an illegal trade and the Western shippers, besides ensuring that the recruits could meet minimum health standards, imposed screening procedures that were uneven at best.[18]

The situation quickly became explosive. A major riot in Amoy in 1852 disrupted the trade and led to investigations that revealed the grave abuses. That year also saw the first "mutinies" by unwilling Chinese en route to unknown destinations, including one on the American ship *Robert Bowne* nine days out from the port of Amoy with 410 Chinese migrants. The vessel returned to Amoy where 17 Chinese were charged with mutiny. According to one of them, who stuck to his account under torture:

They were beguiled on board the barbarian ship as contract laborers by emigration agents and confined in the hold. . . . After the ship sailed, the said barbarians gave each man in the hold a contract of servitude. If he did not accept he was flogged. [Then] the said barbarians suddenly seized all of them, brought them on deck and cut off their cues [queues]. More than ten who were sick in bed and could not walk were immediately killed and thrown into the ocean.[19]

Such shocking disclosures attracted great notoriety in the press and led to investigations that uncovered still more abuses. Reforms were implemented both by countries involved in the transport and recruitment of coolies and, after some delay, by the government of China. The American Congress effectively banned participation in the trade by its citizens in 1863, though with little effect until after the Civil War. Other Western nations increased regulation of the trade during the 1850s, but the British occupation of Canton during the Second Opium War (1858–60) also increased the number of refugees and unemployed Chinese who became fair game for the crimps.

As scandals continued, Europeans blamed the Chinese government for inaction and corruption, the British blamed the Portuguese (whose port of Macao became home to most of the trade fleeing stricter British regulation

---

[18]Meagher, "Introduction of Chinese Laborers," pp. 68–81.
[19]Irick, *Ch'ing Policy*, pp. 33–35. Of the Chinese all but one were acquitted, but the American officers were charged with piracy and murder. Meagher finds no evidence to support Irick's suggestion that the ship had a Latin American port as its ultimate destination.

in Hong Kong), and Canton residents attacked both crimps and foreigners associated with the trade. Though enough scandals continued to surface to perpetuate the image of Chinese contract labor as a new slave trade, real reforms were also being implemented. Irick has effectively argued from Chinese documents that, while Chinese officials were impeded by administrative glitches and disputes over how to regulate a trade that was, by Chinese law, entirely illegal, they had far more concern for the welfare of the migrants than contemporary westerners believed. They began to negotiate a series of treaties with westerners in the 1860s and sent investigative commissions to Cuba and Peru in the 1870s. Western governments, including the Portuguese in Macao, also made regular efforts to eliminate the worse abuses. The greatest blame was put on the crimps, whom the governor of Macao maintained "so brainwashed the emigrants into doing and saying as they dictated, so as to deceive the hated foreigner, that even three separate examinations before emigration officials were unable to detect all the victims of coercion."[20]

Because kidnapped, deceived, and willing migrants were all mixed together, it is virtually impossible to distinguish among them as was done earlier for the African migrants. The Chinese commissioners in Cuba in 1874 reported that 80 percent of the Chinese they interviewed declared themselves to have been "kidnapped or decoyed," but this proportion seems improbably high. It is likely that the Chinese laborers, who were very discontented with their conditions in Cuba, gave the commissioners the answer they thought most likely to obtain their release. The reliability of those interviewed was also brought into question by the commissioners' indirect suggestion that few Chinese migrants in Cuba were "industrious men, who emigrate willing to better themselves," some being "bad characters" emigrating "to escape the results of gambling and crime" and many others "stupid fellows" easily ensnared by crimps.[21]

For all the very real abuses associated with their recruitment, more Chinese contract laborers may have been victims of economic and social misery than of deceit and kidnapping. Those who were recruited by deceit may well have been matched by others who did everything in their power to deceive recruiters about their qualifications. An eyewitness at Amoy in 1852 wrote of "the care with which the poor fellows take to conceal any little physical defect[:] men of advanced years pick out their grey hairs . . . ; boys try to appear [as] men . . . and no one is under 19 or over 33 according

[20]Irick, Ch'ing Policy, pp. 67, 95–96, 137; Meagher, "Introduction of Chinese Laborers," pp. 131–37, 311–12.
[21]Ch'en Lanpin, A. Macpherson, and A. Huber, Report of the Commission Sent by China to Ascertain the Condition of Chinese Coolies in Cuba (Taipei: Ch'eng Wen Publishing Company, 1970), pp. 3, 39–40. Meagher, "Introduction of Chinese Laborers," pp. 227–28, casts doubt on the commission's objectivity.

to their own account."[22] The line between voluntary and involuntary is further blurred by the fact that the migrants' desperation and ignorance made them easy to cheat and deceive. As Irick concludes:

Many hoping to better their family fortunes . . . agreed to go abroad under false pretenses and willingly accompanied the crimps to Macao. Some accepted employment in the belief that they would be working in Macao. Others, hearing of the good fortune of clansmen or other villagers in California, undoubtedly offered themselves for employment, not knowing the difference between Peru and California. Still others were easy prey for the crimps because of poor family circumstances. The prisoners of clan wars, especially prevalent in this period of disruption in southern China, were another source of bodies. Macao itself, with its gambling dens, could also be expected to fill a part of the quota; perspective coolies were lured into rigged games and had to forfeit themselves or a member of the family to clear their debts.[23]

While efforts to regulate the trade surely decreased the number of forced migrants, revelations of continuing abuses fed efforts to solve the problem by abolishing the Chinese coolie trade. When bad weather and unrest among the Chinese passengers of the *Maria Luz* out of Macao forced the Peruvian ship to seek refuge in Yokohama in 1872, Japanese investigators determined that all of the 230 Chinese on board were unwilling immigrants to Peru and returned them to China. Influential Chinese residents of Hong Kong added their voices to the protests, as did the crown colony's chief justice, John Smale. A British Foreign Office inquiry led to new regulations in 1873 banning the outfitting or financing of coolie ships in Hong Kong. Along with Chinese actions stemming the flow of potential emigrants into Macao and threatening open hostilities, these British measures finally led Portuguese authorities to ban the trade.[24] The last ships for the Americas left Macao in 1874.

This was not the end of overseas Chinese migration. The push of misery continued to send large numbers of persons abroad, including many who could not pay their own passage. Passengers arriving in Singapore on the credit ticket system had their debt sold to an employer; in California the migrant's debt was separate from the employer's contract and repaid by the individual migrant from his wages. Most migrants to Hawaii, British Columbia, and Australia were under a system similar to California's. The

---

[22]Meagher, "Introduction of Chinese Laborers," p. 71, quoting *The Friend of China*, 25 December 1852, which also reported that a quarter of Amoy's population had perished of hunger and disease in 1851.
[23]Irick, *Ch'ing Policy*, p. 205.
[24]*ibid.*, pp. 206–72. Pressures by American consuls in Amoy and Swatow were effective in forcing the Canton governor to adopt the "get tough" policy against the Macao trade, as Western opposition to the scandals there solidified.

legal distinctions are clear enough but some researchers argue that the practical difference for the Chinese migrant could be very small.[25]

In the early twentieth century the Chinese indentured labor trade was revived under more rigorous regulation, most significantly to southern Africa and to France.[26] An Anglo-Chinese Labor Convention brought 63,695 recruits to the gold mines of the Transvaal in 1904–7; at their peak, they constituted 35 percent of the work force. In contrast to the earlier migrants from southern China, these recruits were nearly all from the provinces of northern China, where a series of disastrous floods of the Yellow River and the disruptions of the Boxer Rebellion had created millions of refugees. Agreements between China and the European Allies also brought at least 140,000 Chinese contract laborers to France in the last years of World War I, where they were largely used in burying the dead and in other support roles.[27]

In summary, indentured labor recruitment in China attracted more people and a greater proportion of willing migrants than in Africa, but remained a very flawed system. The numerous scandals over kidnapping, deception, and other abuses were the signs of deeper structural failings promoted by the absence of a unified system of control, which eventually forced a three-decade suspension of most recruitment. The early-twentieth-century indentured recruitment, based on bilateral agreements strictly regulated at both ends, demonstrated that large numbers of Chinese could be recruited without raising issues of freedom. It also demonstrated the strong push to migrate that social and economic conditions in China promoted, since many more Chinese applied for southern Africa than could be accommodated, even though the work was difficult and dangerous and the wages were far below what local Africans would accept.

India

Although China contributed mightily to the overseas labor trade and to its ill repute, India provided the greatest number of indentured migrants and

---

[25]Credit ticket migrants were 27% of the Chinese arriving in Singapore in 1887, but only 8.4% in 1890. See the discussion of this topic in Chapter 1.

[26]German planters recruited a few thousand Chinese for plantation labor in Western Samoa from 1902 to 1914, and some 1,100 Chinese were recruited to Cuba in 1919. See Campbell, *Chinese Coolie Emigration*, pp. 219–20; Duvon Clough Corbitt, *A Study of the Chinese in Cuba, 1847–1947* (Wilmore, Ky.: Asbury College, 1971), p. 109.

[27]Peter Richardson, "Chinese Indentured Labour in the Transvaal Gold Mining Industry, 1904–1910," in Saunders, *Indentured Labour*, pp. 267, 272; Peter Richardson, "Coolies, Peasants, and Proletarians: The Origins of Chinese Indentured Labour in South Africa, 1904–1907," in *International Labour Migration: Historical Perspectives*, ed. Shula Marks and Peter Richardson (Hounslow: M. Temple Smith, 1984), pp. 167–85; Ta Chen, *Chinese Migration*, pp. 142–44; Thomas E. LaFargue, *China and the World War* (Stanford: Stanford University Press, 1937), pp. 151–52, says Chinese "coolies" were first used in Siberia and that from 1916 to 1918 190,000 served in France.

the clearest test of the system as an acceptable alternative to slave labor. The size of the exodus from India reflected the push of rising distress in that territory and still more its close integration into the British empire. Europeans had only toeholds in Africa and China, but by the mid-nineteenth century virtually all of India was directly or indirectly under British control. Most of the 1.3 million Indian migrants who ventured overseas were processed through British depots, traveled on British ships, and worked in British colonies, with the whole operation coordinated and regulated by the British officials in Westminster and New Delhi. Even those who went to French and Dutch colonies were largely subject to conditions of travel and labor set down in treaties and other agreements with Britain. Was such unified control also more instrumental in removing abuses from the system or in subordinating the welfare of Indians to the interests of colonial planters? It is clear that, in comparison to the China labor trade, Indian migration was more effectively regulated from an earlier stage, had fewer serious lapses and abuses, and achieved a higher level of voluntariness while ensuring a lower level of mortality in transit.

Like the Chinese, the indentured Indian voyages of the nineteenth century had precursors in earlier external Indian migrations. "Indians have never been a stay-at-home people," begins one survey of Indian migrant labor; from the early Middle Ages Indian traders sailed far and wide in the ocean that bore their name, turning much of Southeast Asia and the East Indies into an "Indic World." The traders were joined by itinerant laborers, widely known in sixteenth-century eastern Asia as "coolies" (which may derive from the Tamil word *kuli*, meaning "wages"). At the end of the eighteenth century Indian laborers and traders were a common sight in Southeast Asian ports, Ceylon, and East Africa. Not all these laborers were voluntary migrants: there were also several thousand Indian slaves in the French colonies of Mauritius and Réunion. During the early nineteenth century British officials endeavored to stop the slave trade from South India, while also contributing to the flow of unfree labor by sending Indian convict labor to Sumatra, Penang, Singapore, and Mauritius (British from 1810).[28]

As Chapter 2 has outlined, the new "coolie" migrations had their beginning in the second quarter of the nineteenth century. The first French recruiting efforts between 1826 and 1830, from their coastal enclaves of Pondicherry and Karikal, provided the island of Réunion with about 3,000 laborers and servants. In response to the 1834 law ending slavery in the British Empire, the planters on the neighboring British island of Mauritius also turned to India for labor. By the time the apprenticeship system that

---

[28]Tinker, *New System of Slavery*, pp. 44–45. Quotation from S. B. Mookherji, *The Indenture System in Mauritius, 1837–1915* (Calcutta: Firma K. L. Mukhopadhyay, 1962), p. 5.

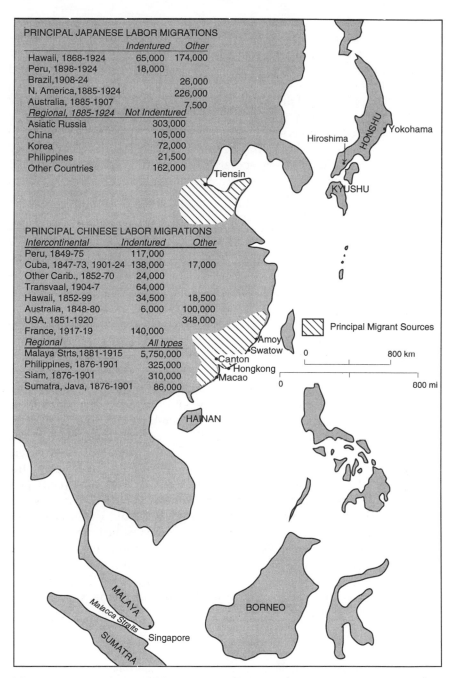

PRINCIPAL JAPANESE LABOR MIGRATIONS

	Indentured	Other
Hawaii, 1868-1924	65,000	174,000
Peru, 1898-1924	18,000	
Brazil,1908-24		26,000
N. America,1885-1924		226,000
Australia, 1885-1907		7,500
Regional, 1885-1924	Not Indentured	
Asiatic Russia	303,000	
China	105,000	
Korea	72,000	
Philippines	21,500	
Other Countries	162,000	

PRINCIPAL CHINESE LABOR MIGRATIONS

Intercontinental	Indentured	Other
Peru, 1849-75	117,000	
Cuba, 1847-73, 1901-24	138,000	17,000
Other Carib., 1852-70	24,000	
Transvaal, 1904-7	64,000	
Hawaii, 1852-99	34,500	18,500
Australia, 1848-80	6,000	100,000
USA, 1851-1920		348,000
France, 1917-19	140,000	
Regional	All types	
Malaya Strts,1881-1915	5,750,000	
Philippines, 1876-1901	325,000	
Siam, 1876-1901	310,000	
Sumatra, Java, 1876-1901	86,000	

Principal Migrant Sources

0   800 km

0   800 mi

Tiensin

Hiroshima   HONSHU   Yokohama

KYUSHU

Amoy
Swatow
Canton
Hongkong
Macao

HAINAN

BORNEO

MALAYA
Malacca Straits
SUMATRA   Singapore

Map 7. Principal indentured labor exports from East Asia. *Source:* Appendix B.

had replaced slavery came to an end in 1839, there were already some 25,000 Indians on Mauritius, including several hundred women. Mauritian planters confidently expected to expand their sugar production by recruiting unlimited supplies of indentured Indian laborers who would work for less than the resident African freedmen.[29] Planters in the British West Indian colonies got the same idea, as their efforts to recruit adequate numbers of free laborers from Africa and elsewhere fizzled.

However, as the prospects for a great expansion of the Indian labor trade loomed, so too did opposition from reform-minded British officials, many with connections to antislavery societies and concerns about the revival of a new forced labor trade. An investigation of the Mauritian labor trade in 1838–39 uncovered sufficient instances of misrepresentation and coercion in the recruitment of laborers and of their exploitation and abuse on some plantations that the Indian government suspended all overseas labor migration in May 1839. Some concern was directed at five-year contracts of indenture, which most of these Indian migrants to British and French colonies had had to sign. However, the most intense debate was not about the flow of laborers to destinations within the Indian Ocean, which seemed unstoppable despite the ban, but whether migrations should again be allowed to the more distant Caribbean colonies. Lord John Russell, the British secretary for the colonies, in February 1840 expressed deep reservations about future migrations: "I should be unwilling to adopt any measure to favour the transfer of labourers from British India to Guiana . . . which may lead to a dreadful loss of life on the one hand, or on the other, to a new system of slavery." The majority report of the investigators of the Mauritius trade, released in October 1840, similarly concluded, "We are convinced . . . if West Indian voyages be permitted, the waste of human life and misery that will fall on the Coolies under the name of free labourers will approach to those inflicted on the negro in the middle passage by the slave trade." Russell's successor, William Gladstone, was also greatly perturbed by the circumstances of a growing exodus of Indian laborers which he conceded was voluntary, writing to the governor of Mauritius in 1846, "if, on the one hand, it is not to be doubted that the Coolie immigration has been advantageous to the material interests of the immigrants themselves, and has also served the purpose of effectually relieving a severe pressure of the demand for labour upon its supply, at and after the moment of emancipation, on the other hand, I think it impossible to deny that serious objections *prima facie* lie against the scheme on almost every other ground."[30]

---

[29]Tinker, *New System of Slavery*, pp. 44–46, 61–63; Mookherji, *Indenture System*, pp. 14–17.
[30]Russell is quoted in Tinker, *New System of Slavery*, p. vi; *PP* 1841 xvi (45), Report of the Committee appointed . . . to inquire into the Abuses alleged to exist in exporting from

Yet humanitarian opposition to indentured labor migration from India was undermined by other practical and moral considerations. Withholding such labor endangered the livelihood of the British plantation colonies and thereby undermined the pragmatic moral lesson emancipation was supposed to demonstrate to French and American authorities: that ending plantation slavery was not inevitably followed by the economic collapse. In addition, it was difficult to champion the virtues of free labor while denying Indians the right to sell their labor overseas. At the end of 1842 the ban on emigration to Mauritius was lifted, releasing a flood of some 45,000 Indians into that colony during 1843 and early 1844. New regulations limited these migrants to one-year contracts that were signed only after their arrival in the colony under the supervision of the colony's new protector of immigrants. Once Indian labor emigration was allowed to Mauritius, its extension to the West Indies could not be denied in principle. Coinciding with the new policy regarding liberated African recruitment in the Atlantic, a law of 16 November 1844 legalized Indian emigration to Jamaica, Trinidad, and British Guiana, with the first shipload sailing from Calcutta in January 1845. Like the Indians to Mauritius and the early African migrants, they were not made to sign a contract of indenture in advance or even on arrival in the West Indies, permitting some, in Green's words, "to exploit their freedom by wandering aimlessly throughout the countryside."[31]

Naturally, pressure mounted to prevent such expensive lapses. Earl Grey, colonial secretary from 1846 to 1852, though also leary of any revival of slave labor, was brought round to permitting the indenturing of laborers prior to sailing by his adherence to two other principles. First, he believed in the right of colonial legislatures to be controlled by the settler population, which in the case of the West Indian colonies meant by the planters, who strongly supported indentured migration. Second, he supported the right of colonial subjects to emigrate, which logically included the right of impoverished Indians to accept subsidized passage in return for a work obligation. Mauritius was allowed to require a one-year prior indenture in 1847, followed by Guiana early the next year and then by other colonies.

Once prior indenture was accepted in principle, the term of the indenture quickly lengthened. Mauritius made three-year contracts the minimum in 1849 with the West Indian colonies quickly falling in line.

Bengal Hill Coolies and Indian Labourers, of various Castes . . . , p. 295; *PP* 1846 xxxv (530), no. 36, Gladstone to Governor W. M. Gomm, 14 May 1846, pp. 216–17.
[31]David Brion Davis, *Slavery and Human Progress* (New York: Oxford University Press, 1984), p. 210; Tinker, *New System of Slavery*, pp. 71–81; *PP* 1867 xlviii [3812], 114, Blue Book of Mauritius, 1865; William A. Green, *British Slave Emancipation: The Sugar Colonies and the Great Experiment* (Oxford: Clarendon Press, 1976), p. 277.

Mauritius and British Guiana provided a free return passage for migrants completing a minimum of five years under contract. From 1862 a minimum five-year initial contract became the norm in all the British sugar colonies and remained so until the end of the system.[32] Destinations also multiplied. Legal bans on emigration to Natal and Réunion were lifted in 1860 and to the French West Indies in 1865. Indentured Indian migration to Dutch Guiana began in 1873, to Fiji in 1879, and to East Africa in 1895.

The multiplication of the scope of the trade depended on the existence of an adequate supply of Indians willing to leave. They were not a simple extension of the maritime tradition mentioned earlier, for in fact overseas migration went against the grain of most Indian communities. For the new overseas migrants, who came from the inland villages rather than the seaports of India, departing from the close-knit rural communities was an act of singular courage or desperation. Venturing across the "Black Water" of the Indian Ocean was also deemed to be a violation of caste for most Hindus. A half century after indentured migration began, an emigration agent in Calcutta could still describe it as "most unpopular," declaring, "The Indian peasant will not emigrate excepting he is actually compelled by stress of circumstances: he prefers to struggle on in his native village, a victim of ever-present poverty, varied by seasons of actual want."[33]

Nevertheless, it is clear that such stressful circumstances led large numbers of Indians to desert their ancestral villages during the nineteenth century. As in China, the overseas labor migration was only a fraction of a much larger movement of people set in motion by overcrowding, ecological disasters, political upheavals, and changing economic conditions. There was considerable migration from rural areas to the cities, short-term migrations within British India for seasonal work, and indentured migration to Assam in northeast India for work on the new tea gardens from about 1840. Indian labor also moved to other British colonies in southern Asia in great numbers. It has been estimated that labor migration from South India to Ceylon for tea plantations (1843–1938) totaled 1.5 million and to Burma for the rice harvest (1852–1938) may have been 2.6 million, though these figures are inflated by the inclusion of large numbers of persons who migrated several times. Between 1844 and 1910, another quarter of a million Indians went to labor in the colonies that became British Malaya. During the last quarter of the nineteenth century total departures from India, both indentured and nonindentured, rose from an

---

[32]Tinker, New System of Slavery, pp. 81–85; Alan Adamson, Sugar without Slaves: The Political Economy of British Guiana, 1838–1904 (New Haven: Yale University Press, 1972), pp. 50–53; Green, British Slave Emancipation, p. 277.

[33]As late as 1931 only 3.6% of Indians lived outside the province or state of their birth; Kingsley Davis, The Population of India and Pakistan (Princeton: Princeton University Press, 1951), p. 107. The quotation is from Fiji Emigration in Calcutta, 1896, cited by K. L. Gillion, "The Sources of Indian Emigration to Fiji," Population Studies 10 (November 1956): 141.

average of 300,000 a year to over 425,000, of which the overseas indentured component was less than a tenth.[34]

One fundamental cause of this rising labor movement was growth of population. India's population of 185 million in 1800 may have increased by 100 million people over the course of the century. The population of the Madras Presidency alone tripled.[35] Rising densities put great pressure on rural resources, lowering living standards for those at the bottom of the social order and adding to the severity of periodic famines to which India had long been prone. Along with massive starvation locally (which did little to slow the overall rise in population), such famines produced large numbers of refugees, whose numbers can be correlated to peak departures from Madras and Calcutta in the second half of the century.[36]

The push to migrate has also been attributed to the effects of British rule, both negative and positive. Reforms in land tenure and taxation led to widespread changes in rural communities, as did the abolition of various forms of rural servitude. The expansion of agricultural plantations and manufacturing created new jobs, while British imports caused structural unemployment in crafts such as the handloom weaving. The suppression of warfare among Indian territories ended disruptions to local commerce and cultivation, whereas the suppression of rebellion against British rule had the opposite effect. This is not the place to try to sort out the controversies over the magnitude and direction of the effects of British rule on India.[37] Although not all would agree, it seems likely that Britain's direct

---

[34]Davis, *Population of India and Pakistan*, pp. 99–101.

[35]The source of the global estimate is Colin McEvedy and Richard Jones, *Atlas of World Population History* (New York: Penguin Books, 1978), pp. 184–85, but Leela Visaria and Pravin Visaria, "Population (1857–1947)," in *The Cambridge Economic History of India*, ed. Dharma Kumar with Meghnad Desai (Cambridge: Cambridge University Press, 1982–83), 2:487, argue that growth was slow until the 1880s or even the 1920s. For Madras see Dharma Kumar, *Land and Caste in South India: Agricultural Labour in the Madras Presidency during the Nineteenth Century* (Cambridge: At the University Press, 1965), pp. 120–24.

[36]A. J. H. Latham, "South-East Asia: A Preliminary Survey, 1800–1914," in *Migration across Time and Nations: Population Mobility in Historical Contexts*, ed. Ira Glazier and Luigi de Rosa (New York: Holmes and Meier, 1986), pp. 20–22, correlates food, famine, disease, and cyclones with peak migrations from Madras to Burma and Ceylon. For other references, see Tinker, *New System of Slavery*, pp. 97, 118–19, and P. C. Emmer, "The Meek Hindu: The Recruitment of Indian Indentured Labourers for Service Overseas, 1870–1916," in Emmer, *Colonialism and Migration*, pp. 194–99, who stresses that Indian indentured migration was based on the push of epidemics and famines.

[37]Lal, *Girmitiyas*, p. 2, ties migration to the "unprecedented changes brought about by British penetration of Indian agrarian society." A spectrum of opposing views are presented in M. D. Morris, T. Matsui, B. Chandra, and T. Raychaudhuri, *The Indian Economy in the Nineteenth Century: A Symposium* (New Delhi: Indian Economic and Social History Association, 1969). The broader debate about the economic impact is neatly summarized by Neil Charlesworth, *British Rule and the Indian Economy, 1800–1914* (London: Macmillan, 1982), while Frank Perlin's review of *The Cambridge Economic History of India*, ed. Tapan Raychaudhuri and Irfan Habib (Cambridge: Cambridge University Press, 1982–83), in *Comparative Studies in Society and History* 30 (1988): 379–81, effectively points out the limitations of that work in addressing the issues.

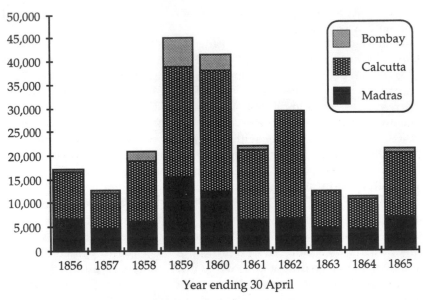

Figure 3.2. Emigration from British India, 1855–65, suggesting the impact of the 1857 Rebellion.
Source: Table A.3.

economic impact on Indians became pronounced only from the middle of the century and that British presence was only one of several factors contributing to the desire to emigrate. Even if people's decisions were determined largely by their personal circumstances and conditions in their locality, the influence of the Raj was certainly pervasive. The strongest case for British rule pushing people to emigrate can be seen in the correspondence between the peak in migration overseas at the end of the 1850s and the widespread disruptions associated with the Indian Rebellion of 1857 and its suppression (see Figure 3.2). As was evident in the example cited at the beginning of Chapter 1, the construction of railroads and other lines of communication also greatly facilitated the movement of would-be migrants to the coastal ports.

Modern studies have clarified some of the connections between internal and external labor migration in the hinterlands of the principal ports. Dharma Kumar has effectively surveyed changing labor migrations in the Madras Presidency of South India which supplied most of the Indian migrants to the Mascarenes and Natal, along with most of the very much larger unregulated labor migrations to Ceylon, Burma, and Malaya. Anand Yang has shown that individuals who were veterans of the growing seasonal migrations in the Bihar province of northeastern India were commonly found in longer-term migrations, including those from Calcutta to the sugar islands of Mauritius and the West Indies. In contrast, the Bombay Presidency in the northwest furnished few overseas indentured migrants, except for the large number of Punjabis to East Africa at the turn of the century, in large part because Bombay's growing textile and other industries absorbed most of the rural migration of west-central India.[38]

Overseas migration was a part of these larger population movements of nineteenth-century India, but it was a very selective part. Perhaps one person in ten who left a natal village in search of new opportunities ventured abroad. Of those who did, only about one in ten became an indentured migrant to a distant overseas colony. In examining those who became overseas indentured migrants, it is thus necessary to consider both how they reflected the larger patterns of migration and how the complex process of self-selection and official selection limited their representativeness.

Not surprisingly, many came from the social and economic margins of Indian society, even if they were not simply the poorest of the poor. In midcentury the port of Calcutta, through which two-thirds of overseas migrants left, drew heavily on the impoverished and hardworking Dhangars and other "hill-people" of the northeast, so-called "tribals" lying outside the Hindu caste system.[39] Already accustomed to migrant work on Bengal indigo plantations, many risked the journey to Mauritius, for example, to take advantage of wages that were easily three times higher in the 1840s. Their recruitment was made even easier by the fact that, like the Chinese, early recruits to Mauritius received "advances" or "gratuities" equivalent to two months' wages before sailing that enabled them to buy themselves out of debt and provide for family members left behind.[40] Other recruits from the bottom of Indian society included landless Tamils

---

[38]Kumar, *Land and Caste*, especially chap. 8; Anand A. Yang, "Peasants on the Move: A Study of Internal Migration in India," *Journal of Interdisciplinary History* 10 (summer 1979): 37–58; Morris David Morris, *The Emergence of an Industrial Labor Force in India: A Study of the Bombay Cotton Mills, 1854–1947* (Berkeley: University of California Press, 1965); Gill M. Yamin, "The Character and Origins of Labour Migration from Ratnagiri District, 1840–1920," *South Asian Research* 9 (1989): 33–53.

[39]Tinker, *New System of Slavery*, pp. 46–55. Dhangars and other "Hill Tribes" formed 30% of the migrants to Mauritius in 1837–38; Report . . . Bengal Hill Coolies, appendix 2A; Tinker (p. 49) estimates they accounted for 40% to 50% of overseas migrants from Calcutta in the 1840s and 1850s.

[40]*PP* 1844 xxxv (530), Emigration to the West Indies and Mauritius, pp. 211–15; *PP* 1846 xxviii (691-II), no. 13, Governor Gomm to Lord Stanley, Mauritius, 2 July 1845 and enclosures. Mr. Robert Neave, Civil and Sessions Judge of Azimgurh, Northwest Province, Bengal, reported that on Bengal plantations Dhangar laborers received wages of three rupees a month, out of which they had to pay for food, clothing, medicine, and fees owed to the crimp who recruited them, whereas those who went to Mauritius started at wages of five or even six rupees a month, in addition to full rations, a clothing allotment, and medical care, and owed nothing to the labor recruiter.

of South India, especially the Pariah (Untouchables) who formed 20 percent or more of Tamil population. A study of the ship records of migrants
from the Madras Presidency to Natal from 1860 to 1902 shows that the two
largest social castes were the Pariah (14.6 percent) and the Vanniah, another agricultural caste (14.3 percent), but that their share of the total
migrants was higher at the end of the period than at the beginning.[41]

As these figures suggest, migrants were not only from the lowest strata
of society. Throughout the period knowledgeable officials reported that
migrants represented a cross-section of rural India. For example, one
well-informed senior civil servant in India who had interviewed several
bands of laborers traveling from Bengal to Mauritius in the early 1840s
reported migrants included "not merely the lowest and most indigent
class of people, but a large number of people of high caste and respecta-
bility," the greater part of whom had left home due to economic distress.[42]
Modern studies have confirmed these conclusions. In the 1870s and 1880s
just over a third of the Hindus leaving North India for overseas destinations belonged to the lowest castes, a third were members of agricultural
castes, and the rest belonged to artisan castes and high castes. Migrants
to Fiji, for example, came from 260 identifiable social groups (Hindu
castes and subcastes, Muslims, and other categories). Such figures raise
the question of whether the Indian migrants were simply the most distressed individuals within these groups or whether the prospect of a new
start overseas attracted the most ambitious among those feeling the pinch
of personal, social, and economic circumstances. Higher than average
personal ambition was characteristic of European migrants in this period
and some contemporary observers believed this to be true of most Indian
migrants as well, but the Indian records contain too little information to
be sure.[43]

A closer look at the process of recruitment suggests that while ambition

[41]Surendra Bhana, *Indentured Indian Emigrants to Natal, 1860–1902: A Study Based on Ships'
Lists* (New Delhi: Promilla, 1991), table 15.

[42]Statement of Mr. Robert Neave, 3 June 1845, enclosed in Gomm to Stanley, Mauritius, 2 July
1845.

[43]Tinker, *New System of Slavery*, pp. 55–56; Lal, *Girmitiyas*, passim, working from the emigration passes of over 45,000 individuals leaving from North India from 1879 to 1916; see also
Bhana, *Indentured Indian Emigrants to Natal* and Ralph Shlomowitz's cautionary review of
the latter in the *Journal of Natal and Zulu History*, 14 (1992): 113–21. Scholars at Flinders
University (South Australia) have confirmed a similar social mix among migrants from
South India; personal communication by Ralph Shlomowitz. Lal, p. 89, quotes British
observers near the end of the indentured migration period in support of migrants rep-
resenting the more highly motivated, whereas Ralph Shlomowitz, "Coerced and Free
Migration from the United Kingdom to Australia, and Indentured Labour Migration from
India and the Pacific Islands to Various Destinations: Issues, Debates, and New Evidence,"
paper prepared for International Institute of Social History Conference, Amsterdam, September 1993, pp. 7–8, is more cautious about reading too much about motivation into the
evidence about Indians.

may have motivated some, other migrants were driven by desperation. Overseas migration was not spontaneous; an army of labor recruiters persuaded Indians to leave home and escorted them to the coastal depots. At the base of the process was the Indian recruiter or *arkatia*, who watched the markets, caravanserais, railway stations, bazaars, temples, and urban centers for likely candidates. The "most villainous part of the whole operation," according to Tinker, the arkatia "knew who was in trouble, who had fallen out with his family, who was in disgrace, who was wild or wanton. If a big man wanted to get rid of a troublemaker, the arkatia was in contact. If the police were making things hot for anyone, he was in the know."[44]

The arkatia made the first contacts, often encouraging unrealistic expectations, and then, pocketing his fee, handed his recruits on to the licensed official recruiters, whose job it was to make sure the recruits were fit, informed, and willing to serve overseas. The inland recruiter screened the candidates for health defects, had their understanding and agreement to the terms of the contract certified by a registering officer (usually a magistrate), and sent those who made it through the process on to Calcutta or Madras. There they were reexamined by a medical officer for fitness and questioned again about their agreement to the terms of the indenture before they could sign the contract and be shipped abroad.

Even though a third of those who registered in a subdepot were eliminated as unfit or changed their minds before sailing from Calcutta, this double screening did not in fact ensure that all recruits were suitable and voluntary. Many seem to have gotten through the process with only the vaguest notion of what they were embarking upon. One weakness in the system was that the official recruiters, a job which did not attract those of the highest character, had a financial incentive to provide as many recruits as possible. Examining magistrates, protectors, and medical personnel were under pressure to process large numbers of recruits quickly and could not always maintain the highest standards. Yet, as in China, the fault also lay with the recruits, who concealed illnesses and claimed to understand what they did not. Despite subsequent information to the contrary, many recruits seem to have clung to the distorted or exaggerated terms sketched for them by the arkatia. When reality dawned, accepting one's fate may have seemed easier than retracing the steps already taken. There was in some, according to one official, a "sense of helplessness, like that of an animal who has been caught in a trap and has given up the useless struggle to escape."[45]

[44]Tinker, *New System of Slavery*, pp. 121–23.
[45]Emmer, "The Meek Hindu," table II; Lal, *Girmitiyas*, tables 4 and 5; quotation from Tinker, *New System of Slavery*, pp. 129–30.

The trap may be an odd symbol for a process that was intended to guarantee Indians the right to emigrate freely, but it is not an entirely inappropriate one. Migrants were certainly caught by the poverty and misfortune of their lives and could easily have found the circumstances associated with recruitment disorienting and intimidating. As with a fish trap, the deeper they entered, the harder it was to wriggle free. Yet many other Indians would have seen overseas recruitment as liberation, not entrapment. Within the spectrum of options open to Indians motivated by ambition or desperation to leave their rural homes, indentured migration overseas promised higher wages and greater chances for savings. Compared with the kidnapping that was rife in the China trade or the highly constrained circumstances of liberated and ransomed Africans, the Indian trade was constructed and run to maximize consent and understanding. The management of the system was not perfect, the arkatia sometimes lured Indians with exaggerated promises, and eager recruits were often incapable of imagining the actual distances and circumstances they would face halfway around the world, but in the judgment of Pieter Emmer, "little evidence exists indicating that fraud, deception and even kidnapping were widely used."[46]

Was it the push of domestic circumstances or the pull of overseas opportunities that most shaped the departures from India? The views of researchers have been remarkably polarized.[47] Most of the disagreement seems to be the result of imprecision in defining the terms of the question. It is clear that in the nineteenth century overpopulation, crop failure, and widespread social and economic change pushed many Indians into some form of labor migration – long and short term, internal and external, regulated and unregulated. It is equally clear that the tiny percentage of that total that was deflected into the overseas indentured trade was very largely a product of the demand for labor in the colonies and the process of recruitment and screening, the pull factors. As in most other cases of migration, the two went hand in hand.

Pacific islands

By the last third of the century few parts of the middle latitudes remained untouched by the new labor trade. Ironically, the peoples of the South Pacific, whose ancient ancestors had explored and settled these far-flung islands in their outriggers, were themselves drawn into new migrations by the expansion of Western shipping and plantation economies. The recruitment began with early whaling ships, which sometimes recruited extra

[46]Emmer, "The Meek Hindu," p. 187.
[47]See Latham, "South-East Asia," for a summary.

crew members from among the islanders, not always under voluntary conditions. There was also some recruitment of island women, many of whom may have been taken against their wills in more than one sense. From the early 1860s islanders were recruited to serve new plantation economies.

Efforts to recruit laborers from Easter Island, Polynesia, and Micronesia for Peru (1862–63) and Hawaii (1879–85) had proved too costly both in lives and in money to continue. The greatest sustained trade was within the southwest Pacific basin (see map 4), with some 90,000 island people going to British colonies in Queensland and Fiji. Sixty percent of these were from the New Hebrides (modern Vanuatu) and 29 percent from the Solomons. Another 16,000 Pacific islanders were recruited to German Samoa and to French Polynesia and New Caledonia. Unlike mainland Asia, recruitment from the smaller islands of the South Pacific was not the extension of any local system of wage labor or seasonal migration. However, in parallel with the external migration to Queensland and Fiji, there developed an internal system of labor recruitment for European plantations on the large island of New Guinea, involving 85,000 indentured laborers on the German half of the island (1884–1915) and 80,000 contract and casual laborers on the British half (1890–1914).[48]

The details of the Pacific island labor trade have received careful examination in recent years, notably by historians at Australian universities.[49] It is now generally accepted that, like the China trade, Pacific island recruitment included widespread kidnapping and deception by private recruiters in its early years, gaining it the nefarious nickname "blackbirding." However, as demand grew, the largest segment of this labor trade came under the careful supervision of the British government officials in Queensland (Australia) and Fiji, thus taking on the general characteristics of the Indian indentured migrations. One major difference from the Indian trade was that most Indians sailed from recruitment centers in a few ports (indeed, very largely from Calcutta and Madras), while the dispersed nature of the Pacific islands required ships to ply a regular circuit of dozens of calling places to obtain a single cargo of laborers.

---

[48]Grant McCall, "European Impact on Easter Island: Response, Recruitment and the Polynesian Experience in Peru," *Journal of Pacific History* 11.1–2 (1976): 90; Henry Evans Maude, *Slavers in Paradise: The Peruvian Slave Trade in Polynesia, 1862–64* (Stanford: Stanford University Press, 1981); Colin Newbury, "The Melanesian Labor Reserve: Some Reflections on Pacific Markets in the Nineteenth Century," *Pacific Studies* 4.1 (1980): 6.

[49]Recent reviews of the literature are Clive Moore, "Revising the Revisionists: The Historiography of Immigrant Melanesians in Australia," *Pacific Studies* 15.2 (June 1992): 61–86; Ralph Shlomowitz, "Marx and the Queensland Labour Trade," *Journal de la Société des Océanistes* 96.1 (1993): 11–17; and Doug Munro, "The Pacific Islands Labour Trade: Approaches, Methodologies, Debates," *Slavery and Abolition* 14 (1993): 87–108.

Despite the attention paid to this trade, the motives of the migrants are difficult to assess precisely. In contrast to the situation among mainland Asian migrants, Pacific islanders seem to have felt little push of economic privation, except for occasional famines. Instead, it appears that the trade goods brought back by the early migrants enticed others to follow them, especially from islands that produced no cash crops that would have provided an alternative source of cash. While the new labor migrations assumed the characteristics of an adventure or rite of passage for young men (in part replacing interethnic warfare), Adrian Graves rightly cautions against a simplistic vision of the migrant as "a Pacific Sambo, mindlessly lusting for the bright lights of civilization." The islanders' decisions to migrate took place in a more complex context of local cultural expectations and ecological crises, as well as evolving regional economic and cultural patterns.[50]

Japan

Widespread squalor and rapid change were characteristic of Japan during the decades after it had been forced to end its long self-imposed isolation by Commodore Matthew Perry's squadron in 1853. One study notes, "by the early 1860's, Yokohama had become rather like a boom town of the Wild West – flimsy, raffish, jaunty and harsh, and populated largely by Jacks-of-all-trades, rootless, incurably optimistic men who made up laws to fit their own particular needs as they bowled along from one adventure to the next."[51] Such was central Yokohama with its elite Western community of diplomats and merchants, but the city's surrounding slums overflowed with Japanese displaced and impoverished by the rapid social changes of this period who had far less reason for optimism. The slum dwellers' lives were further disrupted by the great fire that destroyed much of the city in November 1866. Less than two years later Yokohama sent forth Japan's first small band of 149 overseas contract laborers to Hawaii. After a pause, others followed from Yokohama and other south-

---

[50]Adrian Graves, "The Nature and Origins of Pacific Labour Migration to Queensland, 1863–1906," in *International Labour Migration*, Marks and Richardson, p. 114; Clive Moore, *Kanaka: A History of Melanesian Mackay* (Port Moresby: Institute of Papua New Guinea Studies and University of Papua New Guinea Press, 1985), pp. 45, 337, while accepting that fewer than 5% of migrants to Queensland were physically kidnapped, suggests that many more were "culturally kidnapped," i.e., unintentionally exploited by the disparity between their world and that of the powerful Europeans. Cultural kidnapping may be a useful concept for the context in which Moore is working, but it is not useful comparatively since virtually all migrants were motivated by their belief in a better world overseas.

[51]Pat Barr, *The Coming of the Barbarians: A Story of Western Settlement in Japan, 1853–1870* (New York: Viking Penguin, 1988), p. 144.

ern Japanese cities and from the island of Okinawa, then a Japanese possession.

In contrast to neighboring China, Japanese migrations were distinguished from the beginning by the decisive role played by the new reformist Meiji government in directing and regulating the recruitment of its citizens. Japan also differed from China and India in having scarcely any history of labor migration outside the country before entering the overseas labor migrations of the nineteenth century. However, there was a tradition of short-term internal labor migrancy by destitute young men who left home with the universal hope of returning wealthy. Known as *dekasegi*, this same term came to be used for the overseas migrations that began in 1868. The half century before World War I was also one of heightened internal migration among rural communities and to Japan's growing cities.[52]

Those destitute migrants of 1868 were a product of that urban influx, selected from those who, in the words of the American recruiter, had been "picked out of the streets of Yokohama, sick, exhausted, and filthy and without clothing to cover their nakedness." Despite abuses that resulted in a Japanese investigator taking forty back to Japan with him the next year, seven out of every eight of those who completed their three-year contracts chose not to return to Japan. When the Japanese government organized further emigration to Hawaii in 1885, some 28,000 impoverished Japanese, mostly from the Hiroshima area of southwest Honchu, applied for fewer than 1,000 places. Of the nearly 30,000 who emigrated to Hawaii on three-year contracts during the next decade, more than half decided to stay on (or venture further afield to the United States or elsewhere) at the end of their indenture. With the establishment of private emigrant shipping companies in the 1894, the scale of emigration increased, though the migrants' debts for passage were owed to the emmigration companies, not part of the labor contract signed in Hawaii.[53] By 1907 some 125,000 more Japanese laborers had arrived in Hawaii. By then official Japanese views of overseas settlement had been greatly transformed, with the growing Japanese communities overseas being regarded as a source and symbol of national power.[54] In 1908 U.S. restriction of new Japanese immigrants helped divert

---

[52]Yuji Ichioka, *The Issei: The World of the First Generation Japanese Immigrants, 1885–1924* (New York: Free Press, 1988), pp. 3–4; Gilbert Rozman, "Social Change," in *The Cambridge History of Japan*, vol. 5, *The Nineteenth Century*, ed. Maurius B. Jansen (Cambridge: Cambridge University Press, 1989), pp. 556–58.

[53]Edward D. Beechert, *Working in Hawaii: A Labor History* (Honolulu: University of Hawaii Press, 1985), pp. 65–69; Ichioka, *The Issei*, pp. 40–46; Yukiko Kimura, *Issei: Japanese Immigrants in Hawaii* (Honolulu: University of Hawaii Press, 1988), pp. 3–10; Dorothy Ochai Hazama and Jane Okamoto Komeiji, *Okage Sama De: The Japanese in Hawai'i, 1885–1985* (Honolulu: Bess Press, 1986), pp. 23–25.

[54]Akira Iriye, "Japan's Drive to Great-Power Status," in *Cambridge History of Japan*, 5:759–62.

the flow to South America: by 1924 nearly 26,000 Japanese had arrived in Brazil and 21,000 in Peru.[55]

By no means all of the overseas Japanese were indentured laborers; growing numbers of students, merchants, and unindentured labor migrants also joined in the outflow from Japan. Those to Hawaii before 1894 were mostly under prior contract, as were those to Peru. Though indentured contracts were illegal in the United States from 1885, many Japanese who entered the United States were under a debt to the contracting companies and, like their Chinese counterparts, were closer in status to indentured laborers than to free immigrants. Japanese-run labor contracting companies paid commissions to their agents in Japanese ports, arranged reduced group rates on regular steamship lines or even chartered entire ships, "advanced passage fares and sometimes the thirty dollars steerage passengers needed to avoid being deported as paupers," sometimes provided false passports to gain entry, and brokered the contracts immigrants signed on their arrival in San Francisco. In return they extracted significant levies from the immigrants. Many collected ten cents a day from each recruit's wages along with other fees.[56]

Female migrants

In 1840 a British commission looking into whether a more balanced ratio of men and women might be recruited into the emerging Indian indentured labor trade came to a pessimistic conclusion: "no regulation . . . would . . . , in practice, suffice to secure the emigration or export of a due proportion of women, or an emigration of families" because of the opposition of "all classes of private persons concerned as exporters or importers," the "jealousy and prejudices of Asiatics," the "want of due accommodation" on ships, and "the extreme poverty of the immigrants." In support of its views the commission noted the virtually total absence of women among the substantial numbers of Chinese migrants in Southeast Asia and the East Indies.[57] The commission's pessimism proved exaggerated. Concerted efforts by British agents showed that it was possible to

---

[55]Magnus Mörner, Race Mixing in the History of Latin America (Boston: Little, Brown and Company, 1967), p. 132; Yamamoto Ichihashi, "International Migrations of the Japanese," in International Labor Migrations, vol. 2, Interpretations, ed. Walter F. Willcox (New York: National Bureau of Economic Research, 1931), p. 621.

[56]Ichioka, The Issei, pp. 57–75. Other limits on a laborer's freedom practiced in the Alaska canneries included salary advances, high-priced company stores, and the encouragement of gambling (ibid., p. 78). See also Yuzo Murayama, "Information and Emigrants: Interprefectural Differences of Japanese Emigration to the Pacific Northwest, 1800–1915," Journal of Economic History 51.1 (1991): 127–28, and Masaoka Kodama, "Japanese Emigration to U.S.A. in the Meiji Era," Shakai Keizai Shigaku 47.4 (1981): 6–7.

[57]Report . . . Bengal Hill Coolies, p. 295. The commission, which was opposed to emigration, endorsed a recommendation that a third of future Indian migrants should be women.

Table 3.1. *Female portion of selected overseas migrations, 1843-1919*

Origin	Destination	Date	Women as % of Adults
China	United States	1848-68	3.5[a]
	Peru	1849-75	<0.1[b]
	Cuba	1847-68	<0.1[c]
	British Guiana	1859-74	16.6[c]
	Dutch Guiana	1865-69	14.7[c]
	Hawaii	1879-83	<2.0[d]
Sierra Leone	West Indies	1848-49	34.0[e]
India	Mauritius	1843-45	12.4[f]
	Mauritius	1862-65	26.4[g]
	British Guiana	1851-55	16.1[e]
	British Guiana	1868-1917	30.6[h]
	All destinations	1891-1919	27.8[i]
Japan	Hawaii	1885-94	19.2[j]
	Peru	1899-1909	3.6[k]

Sources: (a) Shih-shan Henry Tsai, *China and the Overseas Chinese in the United States, 1868-1911* (Fayetteville: University of Arkansas Press, 1983), p. 22. (b) Michael J. Gonzales, *Plantation Agriculture and Social Control in Northern Peru, 1875-1933* (Austin: University of Texas Press, 1985), p. 99. (c) Arnold J. Meagher, "Introduction of Chinese Laborers to Latin America: The 'Coolie Trade,' 1847-1874" (Ph.D. dissertation, History, University of California, Davis, 1975), pp. 93-95. (d) Clarence E. Glick, *Sojourners and Settlers: Chinese Migrants in Hawaii* (Honolulu: University Press of Hawaii, 1980), p. 15. (e) Calculated from the records of the Colonial Land and Emigration Commission. (f) Bluebook of Mauritius, 1846, p. 202. (g) Bluebook of Mauritius, 1865, p. 119. (h) Dwarka Nath, *A History of Indians in British Guiana* (London: Thomas Nelson & Sons, 1950), table 19. (i) Great Britain, *Statistical Abstract Concerning British India.* (j) Hilary Conroy, *The Japanese Frontier in Hawaii* (New York: Arno Press, 1978), appendix E. (k) Toraje Irie, "History of Japanese Migration to Peru," *Hispanic American Historical Review* 31.4 (1951): 651-52.

raise the proportion of women to nearly 17 per 100 men among Chinese recruited for British Guiana.[58] Women also constituted a substantial proportion of indentured Indian and African migrants, though not of East Asian and Pacific island migrants. These variations resulted from circumstances in the lands supplying recruits, from the preferences of those who employed such labor, as well as from policies adopted by some recruiters (see Table 3.1).

[58]Meagher, "Introduction of Chinese Laborers," pp. 83–93. Cuban censuses counted 1.6 Chinese women in Cuba for every thousand Chinese men in 1861 and 0.6 per thousand in 1899.

The role of supply conditions is most clear in the case of African migrants. Because females were a third of the slaves traded across the Atlantic, that proportion was also true of the liberated Africans who were subsequently indentured in the Caribbean. In contrast, among Africans who were not preselected by the slave trade, notably the Kru of Liberia, there were only a handful of women. Elsewhere, the departure of women was also subject to greater social and political constraints than was the departure of men. Melanesian chiefs opposed the departure of island women and Melanesian male recruits disliked having women on the ships because of the impossibility of enforcing taboos requiring the seclusion of women who were menstruating or giving birth. Under these circumstances it is remarkable that women still constituted nearly 6 percent of Pacific island recruits to Queensland and Fiji. The number of East Asian women migrants, who were even more likely than men to feel the push of economic and social conditions, also remained small. The male predominance among migrants from China noted by the British commission in 1840 remained characteristic of the later indentured Chinese to Peru or Cuba. To some extent, the paucity of East Asian and Pacific women recruits also reflected the preferences of employers, who had little interest in women as laborers. But even more it reflected the gender roles expected of Asian women. A great deal about Asian patriarchy may be inferred from this explanation of the paucity of Japanese women migrants in an older study: "Japanese women by instinct and training are not adventurous."[59]

India proved the greatest exception to this rule, but not from the beginning. So long as Indians were regarded as temporary recruits who would return home at the end of their indenture, there was no particular effort to recruit women, though some were permitted to accompany their husbands. However, as interest grew in establishing Indians overseas as a long-term labor force, in some cases halfway around the world from their homes, the issue of including women and families among the migrants came to the fore. In 1846 Colonial Secretary Gladstone had written the governor of Mauritius, musing at length on the "difficulties in the moral order of things" resulting from the "thin sprinkling of [Indian] women, whom it has been found practicable to introduce with the large mass of males; the yet rarer occurrence of cases of immigration in families; ... the separation of the men from every natural and domestic relation of life."[60] The issue was practical as well as humanitarian. While men might leave their wives or postpone marriages for a few years in the hope of returning with sufficient savings to better their circumstances, it seemed unrealistic

[59]Moore, *Kanaka*, pp. 64–68; Ralph Shlomowitz, personal communication. Quotation from Yamamoto, "International Migration of the Japanese," p. 622.
[60]*PP* 1846 xxviii (530), no. 36, Gladstone to Gomm, 14 May 1846, pp. 216–17.

to suppose that single men would be content to live abroad for a decade, still less settle there permanently. In 1853, at the instigation of the British Colonial Office, a minimum of one female for every three males was required among Indian migrants to Mauritius. Three years later that proportion was extended to British Guiana. From 1868 the proportion of female migrants was raised to 40 per 100 males (except for Mauritius) and was strictly enforced.

Despite much grumbling from recruiters that Indian women migrants could not be found, these quotas were not only met but exceeded. For example, women had been fewer than 4 percent of the migrants to Mauritius from 1834 to 1842 but between 1862 and 1865 an average of nearly 36 females accompanied every 100 male migrants from India to Mauritius and females formed 32 percent of the immigrant population resident on the island. Similarly, among Indians departing for British Guiana the proportion of women to men rose from 19 per 100 (1851–55) to 44 per 100 (1868–1917). Until the end of the indentured trade, Indian women constituted in excess of 40 per 100 men going to the West Indies, Fiji, and Natal (33:100 to Mauritius).[61]

The morality and motives of female migrants is a subject widely discussed by contemporary observers and modern researchers. In some destinations a high percentage of East Asian women migrants were prostitutes, intended for communal brothels, and in the case of the Chinese sometimes subjected to conditions of virtual slavery.[62] Contemporary British observers were also inclined to characterize migrating Indian women as prostitutes or of low moral character. In the larger context of women migrants, these explanations are inadequate. Two knowledgeable early twentieth-century observers cited by Tinker reported that only a small percentage of departing Indian women were prostitutes, while a third were wives accompanying their husbands and the rest were women seeking to escape social and economic oppression: "mostly widows and women who have run away from their husbands" as well as "women who have got into trouble and apparently emigrate to escape from the life of promiscuous prostitution which seems to be the alternative to emigration." Emmer notes that about half of the Indian women migrating to Surinam were unmarried and suggests that overseas migration may have been "a

[61]Huguette Ly-Tio-Fane Pineo, *Lured Away: The Life History of Cane Workers in Mauritius* (Moka, Mauritius: Mahatma Gandhi Institute, 1984), table 1A; for the other figures, see Table 3.1 of this chapter and Lal, *Girmitiyas*, pp. 97–103.

[62]Ichioka, *The Issei*, pp. 28–30; Meagher, "Introduction of Chinese Laborers," pp. 83–91. Lucie Cheng Hirita, "Free, Indentured, Enslaved: Chinese Prostitutes in Nineteenth Century America," *Signs* 5.1 (1979): 3–29, estimates that 85% of Chinese women in San Francisco in 1860 may have been prostitutes and cites contracts from later in the century that bound women to work off the debt of their passage by years of prostitution and examples of Chinese prostitutes who were virtual slaves.

vehicle for female emancipation" for the unwed and "an escape from a culture which was hostile to single women." Brij V. Lal's study of those going to Fiji demonstrates that half of Indian women migrants came from higher or middling castes, though the proportion from low castes was higher than among males.[63] Existing evidence provides only a slender basis for speculation, but it does seem clear that for women, as for men, emigration provided a means to escape oppressive circumstances and held out hope of a better life, even if domestic cultural norms and social institutions made it much harder for women to join the emigrant flow.

Conclusion

This examination of the sources of indentured laborers reveals that the circumstances that pushed, pulled, or coerced populations – and even single individuals – into the trade were complex and varied. Many individuals were kidnapped, coerced, or deceived, but it would seem that most had at least a partial understanding of what they were entering into and had chosen migration in hopes of improving their individual circumstances or aiding their relatives who remained at home. The indentured labor trade in the nineteenth century thus depended on matching the motives of the migrating laborers with the demands of employers. Rarely can the motives of individual migrants be known, but it has been possible to distinguish among the circumstances of larger groups. The trade from Africa was closely connected to the Atlantic slave trade, both as a byproduct of its suppression and as a disguised continuation of it. In the case of India and China the new indentured migration was built on an older tradition of labor migration and was accompanied by growing internal and regional labor migration. It is not possible to measure the force of this outward push, but it is clear that where it was generally lacking, as in Africa, only by highly coercive measures could a labor supply be produced. Inevitably the outward push was tied to the pull of real or imagined attractions in the destination. In the case of most Pacific island migrants, the attraction of trade goods and adventure was the dominant factor.

Most indentured laborers came from the dense populations of China and India, but sheer size was not the only factor. India's contribution to the trade was much greater than China's. As a proportion of their total population Japan and the Pacific islands also furnished more overseas migrants than did China. Effective regulation and management were very impor-

---

[63]Tinker, *New System of Slavery,* p. 205; Pieter Emmer, "The Great Escape: The Migration of Female Indentured Servants from British India to Surinam," in *Abolition and Its Aftermath: The Historical Context, 1790–1916,* ed. David Richardson (London: Frank Cass, 1985), pp. 248, 250; Lal, *Girmitiyas,* pp. 104–6.

tant in the yield and efficiency of the recruitment process. In midcentury China, where many carriers and destinations competed for labor and where local authority was weak, recruitment was accompanied by high levels of coercion that led to most recruitment being suspended during the last quarter of the century. Although not without flaws, Great Britain's regulations maintained a high-volume flow of labor migration from India and the Pacific islands to other colonies, interrupted only by temporary suspensions to enforce standards or limit the spread of disease.

While most recruitment was controlled by Western governments, this was not the only possibility. The Japanese government effectively oversaw the recruitment, screening, and transport of its citizens overseas. Through bilateral agreements, China restored a more acceptable system of contract labor in the early twentieth century. No amount of control and efficiency, however, could make the system of indentured labor better than the dynamics that underpinned it. Migrants' desires to escape from problems at home and to better themselves abroad played into the hands of recruiters seeking persons willing to enter into long-term contracts for modest wages. No amount of reform could make that conjunction less hard.

Another factor that facilitated recruitment from some locations was transportation. Island dwellers had little difficulty in reaching the ships that called at their shores, whereas the mechanical and political difficulties of moving populations cheaply to the shores of the giant African continent further restricted recruitment there. Indian migrants (and to a lesser extent the Chinese) reached the coast on railroads built in the nineteenth century. The essential role played by parallel improvements in the scale and speed of maritime transportation is explored in the next chapter.

4

Voyages

Man is of all sorts of luggage the most difficult to be transported.
Adam Smith, *Wealth of Nations*

An efficient, low-cost transportation was necessary to connect the demand for labor and the distant supplies of would-be recruits. This chapter looks at the changes in passenger ships and the regulation of ocean travel that made indentured migrations possible. It demonstrates that the vessels of the new indentured labor trade were generally far larger and much less crowded than those in the middle passage of the Atlantic slave trade. Special note is taken of how conditions varied by source and over time, from the sometimes horrific early voyages of the poorly regulated Chinese trade to the speedy passages of the last decades of the trade. The chapter examines the reasons why mortality rates on indentured migrant vessels, though in aggregate distinctly lower than on slave ships, were still distressingly higher than on ships carrying nonindentured passengers, and why these rates declined. It concludes that the voyages of most indentured laborers, while distinct in some ways, had much in common with those of contemporary unbonded migrants who left Europe in record numbers during the same period.

In common with other migration studies, the chapter uses statistical records to identify trends and make comparisons among different types of voyages. It relies heavily on the manipulation of two existing compilations of ship records: the records of African and Indian indentured laborers published annually by the British Colonial Land and Emigration Commission (CLEC) from 1841 to 1873 and the lists of ships carrying Chinese indentured laborers to Latin America and the Caribbean painstakingly combed from a wide range of sources by Arnold J. Meagher.[1] The ex-

---

[1] The CLEC reports have been conveniently reissued by the Irish Universities Press in the Emigration series of their British *Parliamentary Papers* reprint series. Arnold J. Meagher, "The

amination of the second half of the indentured migration period is greatly indebted to research in other unpublished series. Within the limits imposed by the historical records, the impersonality of this approach is mediated by considerations of the individual experiences.

Ships and regulations

Maritime transportation in the nineteenth century underwent a rapid transformation. The number, size, and speed of oceangoing vessels expanded and these changes, along with the growth of government regulation, transformed the conditions of passenger travel. While ocean voyages in this era may seem far removed from the conditions of intercontinental transport in the late twentieth century,[2] they were equally distant from the conditions endured by overseas migrants, whether slave or free, in the seventeenth and eighteenth centuries.

One major change was the great increase in the size of sailing ships. By the middle of the century increased use of iron fastenings permitted vessels to grow far beyond the limits formerly set by the size of available timbers. Their average size increased steadily thereafter, culminating in the construction of all-iron hulls at the end of the century.[3] Though promoted mostly by the rising volume of cargo shipments, these changes had tremendous implications for passenger travel. As Figure 4.1 shows, African slaves in the first half of the century had been crammed onto ships averaging under 200 tons. In the early 1850s European migrants were crossing the Atlantic on vessels averaging 450 tons. Ships carrying Chinese migrants to the British West Indies from 1852 to 1873 averaged 870 tons and those transporting Indian indentured laborers to that destination from 1858 to 1873 had a mean size of 968 tons. The smallest ship from India in that period measured 435 tons, the largest 2,017 tons.[4]

Introduction of Chinese Laborers to Latin America: The 'Coolie Trade,' 1847–1874" (Ph.D. dissertation, History, University of California, Davis, 1975). Working independently from the same sources, John McDonald and Ralph Shlomowitz have arrived at similar results; see their "Mortality on Chinese and Indian Voyages to the West Indies and South America, 1847–1874," *Social and Economic Studies* 41.2 (1992): 203–40.

[2]Though David Eltis, *Economic Growth and the Ending of the Transatlantic Slave Trade* (New York: Oxford University Press, 1987), p. 136, has pointed out that coach passengers in jumbo jets have no more room than did most nineteenth-century steerage passengers.

[3]Gerald S. Graham, "The Ascendancy of the Sailing Ship, 1850–85," *Economic History Review* 9 (1956): 74–88; Joel Mokyr, *The Lever of Riches: Technological Creativity and Economic Progress* (New York: Oxford University Press, 1990), pp. 129–30.

[4]In comparison, ships carrying slaves from western Africa to the Americas in the period 1790 to 1830 averaged between 150 and 200 tons, whereas those carrying slaves from southeast Africa to Cuba after 1850 averaged about 470 tons; Eltis, *Economic Growth*, p. 128. Vessels carrying Chinese to Latin America averaged somewhat smaller than those to the British West Indies because of the use of a number of undersized vessels in the latter years of the trade to Cuba.

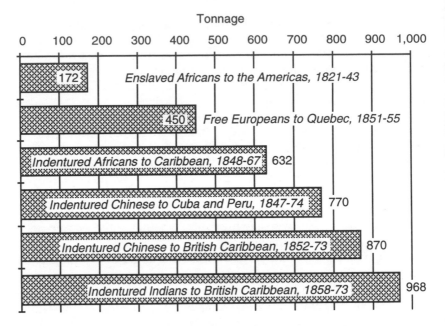

Figure 4.1. Ship size on selected nineteenth-century overseas migration routes. *Source:* Table A.4.

These ships' cleaner lines and more efficiently distributed sails also made them much faster, culminating in the famous clipper ships of the 1860s. It had taken the better part of six months to sail from India to Europe in the early eighteenth century; indentured laborers made the similar voyage from India to the Caribbean in an average of three months between 1851 and 1873. Sailing ships cut the voyage time from China across the Indian and Atlantic Oceans to Cuba from an average of 125 days between 1856 and 1860 to 110 days in the early 1870s. By the latter period some steam-powered ships were making the China–Cuba run in only 85 days.

This development of steamers was another radical change in nineteenth-century shipping, though their use in transporting indentured labor was limited until late in the period. Coal-fired steamships had been experimented with in the early years of the African, Indian, and Chinese migrant labor trades, sometimes with great fanfare, but the early vessels were not particularly fast or safe and were very costly to build and run. Only with the development of more efficient high-pressure boilers in the 1870s were steamships able to rival the fastest clippers in speed. A few steamers were used in the last years of the Chinese trade to Latin America but steamships remained rare in the Indian labor trade to the West Indies. Only two made the passage up to 1873, and the slightly cheaper costs of the sailing vessels enabled them to retain two-thirds of the trade to the British West Indies even at the end of the century.[5]

Steamships became important earlier on shorter runs within the Indian Ocean where their ability to operate year round without regard to the monsoon winds gave them a distinct advantage. The British India Steam Navigation Company had started steamer service from India to Southeast Asia after the 1857 Rebellion and all emigrants to Burma and Malaya traveled by steamer in the final quarter of the century. The majority of migrants from India to Mauritius and Natal went in steamers from 1889, but this was not the case for those going to more distant Fiji until 1905 and to the West Indies until 1908.[6]

The second major innovation in maritime passenger travel in the nineteenth century was in government regulation. In the late eighteenth century Great Britain had pioneered measures to improve conditions and cut losses during the middle passage of the African slave trade. Legislation in 1788 and 1799 effectively reduced the number of slaves carried per 100 tons burthen from over 250 to fewer than 100.[7] Britain's outlawing of the African slave trade in 1807 ended this experiment, but other sea travelers soon felt the effects of new regulations governing passenger density as well as the type and amounts of food, water, and medical equipment passenger ships had to carry. After 1828 British passenger acts became increasingly detailed in their specifications and increasingly effective in their enforcement. In 1840 ships from British possessions whose routes crossed the equator had to provide 15 square feet of space per passenger with decks no lower than 5.5 feet and containing no more than two tiers of berths. These rules applied to vessels carrying indentured Indians and Africans as well as Chinese shipped from Hong Kong. The Colonial Land and Emigration Commission was created in 1840 to keep track of passenger movement and mortality, issue more detailed regulations, and insure

---

[5]The use of the early British naval steamer *Growler* to transport migrants from Sierra Leone to the British West Indies in 1847–48 was not a success; Mary Elizabeth Thomas, *Jamaica and Voluntary Laborers from Africa, 1840–1865* (Gainesville,. University Presses of Florida, 1974), p. 127. The first steamship, the *SS Clarendon*, left Calcutta on 7 March 1857 with 421 passengers and arrived in British Guiana 91 days later. The only other steam vessel to carry indentured Indians to the British Caribbean before 1875, the *SS Far East* in 1869, reached British Guiana in 89 days. Hugh Tinker, *A New System of Slavery: The Export of Indian Labour Overseas, 1830–1920* (London: Oxford University Press, 1974), p. 146; U.K., Statement Exhibiting the Moral and Material Progress and Condition of India . . . , 1898–99, 1899–1900, 1900–1; Meagher, "Introduction of Chinese Laborers," table 46.

[6]Tinker, *New System of Slavery*, pp. 146–47; John McDonald and Ralph Shlomowitz, "Contract Prices for the Bulk Shipping of Passengers in Sailing Vessels, 1816–1904: An Overview," *International Journal of Maritime History* 5.1 (1993): 90.

[7]Herbert S. Klein and Stanley Engerman, "Slave Mortality on British Ships, 1791–1797," in *Liverpool, the African Slave Trade, and Abolition*, ed. Roger Anstey and P. E. H. Hair (Liverpool: Historic Society of Lancashire and Cheshire, 1976), pp. 113–25.

their enforcement. Spurred on by high passenger mortality associated with Irish famine victims and cholera epidemics in the British Isles, new passenger acts by 1855 required more head room and reduced passenger densities to no more than 100 adults per 200 tons burthen. The British example led other national carriers to adopt similar codes, though few approached the rigor of British enforcement.[8]

Because of these regulations, passenger accommodations on most labor ships became fairly uniform. At the beginning of the trade there were few ships specifically designed for passengers, so cargo holds were partitioned horizontally by adding long shelves along both sides (and down the middle if space permitted). Each shelf was divided into "berths" six feet long and 21 to 24 inches wide.[9] Emigrants were segregated by sex, except for married couples. By the mid-1850s regulations on British ships specified that migrant laborers receive a space allotment of 72 cubic feet per adult ($2 \times 6 \times 6$ feet), somewhat greater than the 66 cubic feet then allowed per British soldier on troop ships. Tinker notes with regard to Indian migrants, "From the 1870s, the rules aboard coolie ships were more comprehensive, and more effectively enforced, than on most other passenger ships."[10]

As Figure 4.2 shows, the average passenger density on indentured labor ships was far smaller than on those of the African slave trade, just over 40 migrants per 100 tons on ships from India and China to the British West Indies in the third quarter of the century and 55 migrants per 100 tons on ships from China to Cuba and Peru. Less cramped were indentured laborers on ships from Africa to the West Indies, which averaged a bit under 30 per 100 tons, similar to the 20 to 30 passengers per 100 tons on European immigrant ships to North America in the 1840s and 1850s. In contrast, densities in the peak decades of the nineteenth-century slave trade averaged 257 persons per 100 tons, well above the maximum of 167 adults that would have been permitted by the British regulations adopted for slave ships in the late eighteenth century. Indeed, one response to the risk of capture by British patrols was for captains to pack their vessels with as many as 300 to 350 slaves per 100 tons.[11] Nineteenth-century indentured

---

[8]Fred H. Hitchins, *The Colonial Land and Emigration Commission* (Philadelphia: University of Pennsylvania Press, 1931), pp. 119–53; Robert L. Irick, *Ch'ing Policy toward the Coolie Trade, 1847–1878* (Taipei: Chinese Materials Center, 1982), pp. 87, 209. The application of these rules to British ships from China was regularly evaded in the early 1850s. Spain and Macao adopted limits of 100 passenger per 200 tons in 1860 as did Peru in 1868; Meagher, "Introduction of Chinese Laborers," pp. 167–68.

[9]Meagher, "Introduction of Chinese Laborers," p. 166, with reference to a voyage from Macao to Havana in the 1860s.

[10]Tinker, *New System of Slavery*, p. 145.

[11]Emigrant ships from Europe tended to sail only partially full, at least in the first half of the century, since more capacity was needed for the cargoes of cotton and timber on the return trip; David Eltis, "Free and Coerced Transatlantic Migrations: Some Comparisons," *American Historical Review* 88.2 (April 1983): 271–72. Eltis, *Economic Growth*, pp. 135–36.

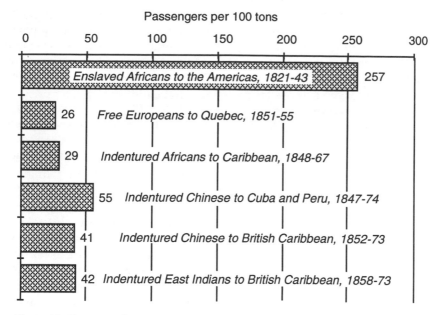

Figure 4.2. Passenger densities on selected nineteenth-century routes.
Source: Table A.4.

migrants were also much less crowded than indentured European migrants in the previous century, who commonly endured densities of 100 to
150 persons per 100 tons.[12]

Routes and experiences

It took some time for the changes in ship design and passenger regulation
to become uniform. As a result, accommodations on different migrant
routes in the early decades of the indentured labor trade varied considerably. Ships in the early Chinese labor trade were commonly fitted
out in the manner of African slave ships so as to control victims of
kidnapping or deceit, with "iron gratings over hatchways, walls between
crew and coolie quarters, armed guards, [and] cannons trained on hatch-

---

[12]Sharon V. Salinger, *"To Serve Well and Faithfully": Labor and Indentured Servants in Pennsylvania, 1682–1800* (Cambridge: Cambridge University Press, 1987), pp. 91–94, suggests that
indentured servant mortality may have been worse than slave mortality on transatlantic
voyages, citing instances of losses in excess of 50% in the German and Irish indentured
trade to Pennsylvania in 1729 and 1738, falling to about 20% for the Germans and rather
more for the Irish at midcentury. The records are fragmentary and those she cites may be
worst cases.

ways." Under these appalling circumstances some Chinese migrants sought to escape through suicide, while others participated in attempts to take over the ship and force its return to China. These "mutinies" were put down with great brutality and loss of life. Meagher has catalogued 68 "mutinies" out of 736 voyages from China, including some believed to have been instigated by pirates pretending to be migrants. Such uprisings gradually tapered off as the recruitment abuses that caused them were checked, "mutinies" being half as common in the 1860s as they had been a decade earlier.[13]

Indentured Chinese migration was also characterized by a wider variety of destinations and national carriers than was true of other migrant groups. The opening of the trade in 1842 had brought ships of every size, condition, and nationality to the Chinese ports. According to Meagher, "'The bigger and better equipped ships, mostly belonging to British and United States companies, were snatched up for the trade to California which was at its height in 1853, while the agents for Cuba, Peru and British Guiana had to be content with anything that could stay afloat." When the Californian and Australian gold rushes subsided, fast American clipper ships entered the emigrant trade from China, until an 1862 law, prompted by revelations of kidnapping and fears of mutinies, prohibited American ships from engaging in the "coolie trade." By 1865 Italian ships dominated the Chinese labor trade.[14]

The voyages of indentured Africans were much shorter than those endured by the Chinese, but also displayed a wide variety of circumstances. After the failed experiment with a royal navy steamer, the firm Hyde, Hodge and Company held the exclusive contract to convey liberated Africans from Sierra Leone and St. Helena to the West Indies from 1849 to 1861. The twenty thousand Africans recruited from western Africa between 1854 and 1862 for the French Caribbean colonies were mostly transported by Maison Maës and Victor Régis.[15] In the final years of the Atlantic slave trade about 5 percent of the liberated Africans on St. Helena were picked up by ships carrying migrants from India to the West Indies.

The transport of Indian laborers was more uniform because it was dominated by a single carrier, Britain, whose regulations governed the departure, passage, and landing of the indentured laborers. Except for

[13]Irick, Ch'ing Policy, pp. 209–10 (for quotation); Meagher, "Introduction of Chinese Laborers," pp. 201–2.

[14]Meagher, "Introduction of Chinese Laborers," pp. 153 (for quotation), 156–60; Irick, Ch'ing Policy, pp. 153–54, 209.

[15]Johnson U. J. Asiegbu, Slavery and the Politics of Liberation, 1787–1861: A Study of Liberated African Emigration and British Anti-Slavery Policy (London: Longmans, 1969), pp. 139, 149; Monica Schuler, "The Recruitment of African Indentured Labourers for European Colonies in the Nineteenth Century," in Colonialism and Migration; Indentured Labour before and after Slavery, ed. P. C. Emmer (The Hague: Martinus Nijhoff, 1986), pp. 143–44.

regulations isolating the single women from the males, passengers were relatively free to move about in the holds and on the decks, weather conditions permitting. The size of the Indian trade and its longer duration also enable one to see more clearly the improvements in recruitment and transportation over time. Perhaps because they were more likely to be voluntary and better informed than Chinese migrants, indentured Indians were generally resigned to their conditions and their protests were "isolated," "insignificant," and "not very ominous."[16]

Overall, the ships carrying indentured migrants had a good safety record. Few sank and the small number that were unable to complete the voyage because of damage due to storms or running aground were generally able to transfer passengers to other vessels. Only seven ships were lost in the twenty-eight years of the China emigration, a fact that is probably attributable to the skill of those who braved the China trade. Several of these disasters were the result of uprisings on board ship. For example, three days after the *Flora Temple*, a U.S. ship under British charter, sailed from Macao in October 1858 some 850 Chinese migrants staged a "mutiny." When the ship struck a reef during the melee, all of the Chinese, who had been locked below decks to quell the uprising, were lost. In 1855 the *Bald Eagle*, a large American clipper with 744 Chinese from Swatow, sank with a loss of all passengers after catching fire during a "mutiny."[17] Of over 350 sailings from India to the British West Indies between 1851 and 1873, just four failed to reach their destinations, of which only one went down with all passengers.[18] Stranded passengers were taken to their destinations on other ships.

Despite the changes in design and law, ocean travel in the mid-nineteenth century was no pleasure cruise. Even under the new regulations, passengers had minimal elbow room and little privacy. Sanitary facilities were rudimentary and the quality of food and water could deteriorate considerably during the long voyages from Asia to the Americas. Bad weather and mechanical failures prolonged the length of the trip and increased its discomforts.

Such conditions were not unique to the indentured migrants. Even on well regulated European migrant ships in the latter part of the nineteenth century, comfort was at a premium. The words used by Joseph Chamberlain, the president of the British Board of Trade, in commenting on com-

---

[16]Tinker, *New System of Slavery*, p. 168.

[17]Irick, *Ch'ing Policy*, p. 61n; Basil Lubbock, *The China Clippers* (Taipei: Ch'eng-Wen Publishing, 1966), pp. 44–49; Meagher, "Introduction of Chinese Laborers," pp. 165–66, 403.

[18]The *Hanover* ran aground at St. Helena in 1859, suffering a loss of 15. The *Fusilier* was wrecked in 1865 at Port Natal, with a loss of 86 passenger lives. The *Eagle Speed* was totally wrecked on the Roy Mutlah Sands in 1865 with a loss of all 497 passengers. The *Jason*, wrecked at Cape Town in 1868, suffered no losses. The 598 passenger deaths on these wrecks represent a loss of 4.4 per thousand passengers embarked during this period.

plaints about conditions of Irish migrants en route to North America in 1881 could as well apply to most indentured laborers:

The condition of steerage passengers in an emigrant ship must always be a subject of painful interest. The limited space, the rude accommodation, the poor and often dirty bedding and clothing, the awkwardness and novelty of the cooking and sleeping arrangements, the strangeness of the poor passengers to each other, the rough and unclean habits of some, and the helplessness of others, and, added to all, the discomforts of sea-sickness, necessarily create a scene even in the best managed ships which is too well calculated to rouse feelings both of pity and disgust. . . . It must, however, be remembered that the conditions . . . are to a great extent inseparable from the carriage at moderate fares of a large number of poor persons on a long sea voyage, and that they cannot be much changed for the better without increasing expenses and demanding fares which would put an end to emigration.[19]

The future colonial secretary also reminded his readers that "the conditions which appear so intolerable to persons accustomed to comfort and luxury, appear very different to the emigrants themselves." Late twentieth-century readers, like contemporary upper-class critics, judging by very different circumstances of travel to which they are accustomed, may rightly find such voyages unimaginably horrible and disgusting. The perspectives of most migrants would have been quite different. This is not because the poor felt pain less acutely, though it is likely their lives had inured them to conditions that those in other strata and times might find intolerable. Rather their frame of reference and their frame of mind are likely to have been different.

Most would have been uncertain and confused about what lay before them, having been ill-informed by recruiters or lacking a knowledge of geography sufficient to grasp the implications of what they had agreed to. The magnitude and strangeness of the undertaking caused some to desert on the eve of departure and even those who persisted would have suffered from the sadness of leaving home and kin. All but a few would have found the life on a large passenger vessel strange and disorienting. If the food served up was also unfamiliar or at variance with their dietary preferences, the ship's mess would have been more regular and wholesome than what many had been able to obtain prior to their departure. More significantly, the truly voluntary migrants would have accepted these discomforts as the means to bettering their circumstances. For all the uncertainty, sadness, and strangeness of the voyage, it was the way to a better life and to fulfill a dream of returning home with riches. This hopeful frame of mind was

[19]Joseph Chamberlain, Minute by the President of the Board of Trade . . . , 5 July 1881, no. 1, in "Emigrant Accommodation on Board Atlantic Steam Ships," *PP* 1881 lxxxii [c. 2995].

thus the greatest difference between indentured migrants and slaves, for whom the mental depression known to contemporaries as "fixed melancholy" was one of the greatest horrors of the middle passage.

Mortality and its causes

Their hopes and dreams may have buoyed most indentured migrants' spirits, but the fact remains that large numbers died of physical ailments during the long voyages. Mortality among indentured migrants stands apart from among other nineteenth-century passengers, both free and enslaved. Deaths on voyages of indentured Chinese to Latin America were nearly 120 per thousand. Indian migrants en route to the British West Indies from 1851 to 1870 perished at the rate of 65 per thousand and those from Africa at 35. At first glance these losses seem comparable to those in the Atlantic slave trade, which from 1811 to 1863 averaged about 70 per thousand. Death rates on indentured ships would seem to have little in common with those on nineteenth-century European migrant ships to North America and Australia, which averaged less than 10 per thousand.[20]

However, such comparisons are misleading since they disregard the very different durations of these voyages. It is more meaningful to measure deaths over a standard time period, a month being most suitable since most voyages lasted between one and three months.[21] Figure 4.3 shows that passenger mortality rates through the last quarter of the nineteenth century fell into three fairly distinct groups. The Atlantic slave trade stands alone at the high end of the spectrum with deaths of nearly 60 per thousand per month. European migrants, with average losses of 10 per thousand or less are at low end. The death rates among Chinese, Indian, and African indentured migrants stand between these two, at around 20 to 30 per thousand per month.

Why did the mortality of indentured laborers occupy this middle position, distinct from both the middle passage of the slave trade and from voyages of European migrants? Variations due to differences in the routes can be discounted, since the voyages of indentured Africans were quite

---

[20]See Table A.5.

[21]This follows the lead taken in studies of the Atlantic slave trade by Joseph C. Miller, "Mortality in the Atlantic Slave Trade: Statistical Evidence on Causality," *Journal of Interdisciplinary History* 11.3 (1981): 385–423; David Eltis, "Mortality and Voyage Length in the Middle Passage: New Evidence from the Nineteenth Century," *Journal of Economic History* 44.2 (1984): 301–8; and R. L. Cohn, "Maritime Mortality in the Eighteenth and Nineteenth Centuries: A Survey," *International Journal of Maritime History* 1.1 (June 1989): 159–91. It should be noted that the death rates are measured against the estimated "population at risk" (average of the number leaving and the number arriving). The formula used for calculating mortality rate is: [(total deaths ÷ total passengers at risk) ÷ average length of voyage in months] × 1000.

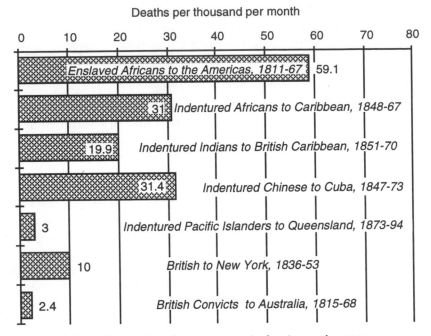

Figure 4.3. Mortality on selected ocean voyages in the nineteenth century.
Source: Table A.5.

similar to those of enslaved Africans, while indentured Indians and Chinese going to the West Indies passed through the same waters and endured voyages of similar durations to those of European migrants to Australia. The key factors to be considered are the circumstances of the voyages themselves and the conditions of the passengers at the time of their embarkation.

Were indentured passengers treated so much worse than free migrants that they died in larger numbers? Given the cultural and linguistic differences between passengers and crew during a period of growing racism, more callous care or mistreatment would not be unexpected. Indeed, Irick has suggested that the early Chinese suffered from severe neglect and abuse because ship captains were paid $70 to $100 for each migrant boarded – not landed, although Meagher cites considerable evidence to show that this often repeated assertion is based on extremely slender evidence and argues that weightier evidence and common sense support the view that captains and physicians had financial incentives to land passengers alive and were penalized for losses. Even such incentives did not prevent the occurrence of many abuses. After reviewing the frequent and often grisly abuses in the Chinese coolie trade, Meagher still concludes, "it would seem that most captains were genuinely concerned with the well being of their passengers, if only to have them reach their destination alive."[22]

The fact that indentured passengers from India and Africa were covered by British regulations similar to those of transatlantic free migrants, or even stricter after 1855, cannot be taken to mean they escaped ill-treatment, since regulations were not always effectively enforced. Indeed, contemporaries regularly blamed the high mortality on ships from India on shortcomings in care and treatment. For example, British investigators attributed the loss of 45 out of 380 Indians on the *Bucephalus* while en route to British Guiana in 1856–57 to the "total absence of all hospital accommodation," to problems with food and cooking, and to "the excessive and mistaken kindness which induced the surgeon and captain to allow the people to remain below [deck] the greater part of the voyage."[23] Another investigation of exceptional mortality on two ships from Bombay to Mauritius in 1864 (a year when mortality from Bombay to Mauritius averaged 74 per thousand per month) blamed the "misconduct and inefficiency of the surgeons, who are said to have been constantly intoxicated" and the insufficiency of food and fresh water, as well as an outbreak of smallpox and fever.[24] An inquest concerning the French vessel *Auguste*, carrying indentured migrants to Réunion from the French enclave of Pondicherry "revealed that some of the sick had been thrown into the sea while they were still alive and that the passengers had been deprived of water and food and had been whipped by the officers. Some of the women had been raped and several had died as a result."[25] These examples demonstrate ill-treatment of indentured migrants occurred, but such anecdotal evidence does not provide a basis for deciding whether these incidents were sufficiently widespread and severe to produce a measurable increase in the aggregate number of deaths.

A broader comparative approach suggests that regulations may have

[22]Irick, *Ch'ing Policy*, p. 209; Meagher, "Introduction of Chinese Laborers," pp. 179–80.

[23]*PP* 1859 xvi [c.2452], Papers relative to Emigration to the West Indian Colonies, J. G. Austin, Immigration Agent-General, and H. G. Butts, M.D., Acting Health Officer, to Hon. W. B. Wolesley, Georgetown, 17 February 1857, pp. 225–27. It is likely that the investigators underestimated the role of cholera (dysentery), which so debilitated the already emaciated emigrants that many were so weak and/or depressed that they relieved themselves in their clothing. Further evidence that it was not factors peculiar to the *Bucephalus* that were primarily to blame is that eight other ships (out of thirteen) arriving in the British West Indies from India in 1857 had worse death rates. Moreover, death rates on ships from India to British Guiana from 1856 to 1860 were nearly three times higher than those from 1851 to 1855.

[24]*PP* 1865 xviii [3526], 25th Report of CLEC 1865, p. 19. Despite the investigation, mortality was even higher from Bombay the next year: 82.6‰ per month; *PP* 1866 xvii [3679], 26th Report of CLEC 1866, from appendix no. 17.

[25]Hubert Gerbeau, "Engagées and Coolies on Réunion Island: Slavery's Masks and Freedom's Constraints," in Emmer, *Colonialism and Migration*, p. 224. Gerbeau does not give the date of the voyage.

been quite effective in reducing onboard mortality. Thus the fact that losses in the trade from China to Cuba were nearly double those on British vessels carrying Chinese to British West Indies in the same period might reasonably be expected to be due in some substantial measure to more effective British regulation. The trade from China to Peru suggests a similar inference. Losses in the early years of the trade to Peru (1851–54) were particularly appalling, averaging over 80 per thousand, but mortality on Peruvian ships (often old passenger vessels or converted cargo ships that were described as "floating hells") was ten times that on British ships. After the adoption of new regulations in 1864 mortality on Peruvian ships from China dropped by nearly three-quarters.[26]

However, it is more difficult to determine which aspects of the regulations were responsible for the variations in passenger losses. Is it significant, for example, that the Peruvian ships of 1851–54 carried many more indentured Chinese per ton than their British counterparts or that the Peruvian ships averaged 400 tons in size while the British vessels averaged almost 660 tons? As already noted, contemporaries firmly believed that overcrowding was closely linked to high mortality rates. One can also not fail to notice that the differences in mortality rates in Figure 4.3 generally correspond to the passenger densities in Figure 4.2: slaves were far more crowded than indentured migrants; indentured Asians were somewhat more crowded than contemporary European migrants.

Yet it is difficult to demonstrate a positive correlation between the degree of crowding and rate of mortality even during the period when losses were greatest. Table 4.1 shows that on the 119 known voyages from China to Cuba from 1847 to 1860 densities varied over a significantly broad range: 18 ships carried over 70 migrants per 100 tons and 13 had under 40 per 100 tons with the rest spread out in between. Yet there was virtually no difference in the mortality rates of the most crowded and least crowded groups of ships. On voyages from British India to the British West Indies the table does show a positive correlation between crowding and mortality, but because of British regulations there were only small variations in passenger density.[27] Highly significant in casting doubt on the connec-

---

[26]Watt Stewart, *Chinese Bondage in Peru: A History of the Chinese Coolie in Peru, 1848–1874* (Durham NC: Duke University Press, 1951), pp. 18, 56–57, 62. Records from Meagher, "Introduction of Chinese Laborers," tables 25–28. If one adds to the sample the one ship of each nation in 1850, the losses rise to 83‰ for Britain versus 157% for Peru, since a mutiny on the British ship resulted in the deaths of 199 Chinese.

[27]Indeed, the density is largely attributable to differences in the number of children and infants. British regulations permitted 50 "statute adults" per 100 tons, with children counted as half an adult and infants not counted at all. That infants and children died at a higher rate than adults has been demonstrated from records of voyages from Calcutta from 1858 to 1862, which separated deaths by age category and from regression analysis of other records; Ralph Shlomowitz and John McDonald, "Mortality of Indian Labour on Ocean Voyages, 1843–1917," *Studies in History* 6 (1990): 45–50. A smaller proportion of

Table 4.1. *Mortality among Chinese to Cuba, 1847-1860, and Indians to the British Caribbean, 1851-1870, by passengers per 100 tons*

Passengers per 100 tons	Chinese to Cuba		Indians to British Caribbean	
	Ships	Deaths/1,000	Ships	Deaths/1,000
20-39.9	13	135	90	48
40-49.9	22	159	157	57
50-59.9	33	151	28	66
60-69.9	33	164	--	--
70-96.9	18	134	--	--
	119		275	

tion between crowding and mortality is the fact that mortality on ships leaving French Indian ports for the French West Indies was no greater than on British ships from Madras, even though the former carried twice as many passengers per ton. British officials speculated that this was due to the French having higher selection standards and a superior understanding of the passengers' needs because they employed Indian doctors, while the British had switched to European doctors.[28]

Although contrary to commonsense expectations of both contemporary and modern observers, the conclusion that the discomforts imposed by shipboard crowding in the indentured labor trade bore little relation to mortality is in line with the general conclusions of studies of the African slave trade. Nor has a high correlation between mortality rates and shipboard densities been found on European migrant ships.[29] To be sure,

nonadults after 1892 was a factor in the decline in deaths at sea in the last years of the trade from India.

[28] *PP* 1859 xxxiv [2569-I] no. 115–16, 119, Consul Lawless to Earl of Malmesbury, Martinique, 12 May 1858, 13 October 1858, 17 January 1859, enclosing the records of twelve ships arriving from French India with 5,795 passengers that can be calculated to have suffered an average mortality of 9.7% per month. The ten ships from Madras to the British Caribbean in this period suffered a mortality of 9.9%. See comments of the Agent General of Immigrants in the Trinidad Annual Report, 1858, *PP* 1860 xliv [2711], pp. 36–37, and the CLEC, 17th General Report 1857, *PP* 1857 xvi [2249-II], pp. 47–48. Because they did not factor out the much larger number of ships that sailed from Calcutta, British officials believed that mortality on the French ships was actually significantly lower than on British, an inference that is unwarranted for reasons to be explained here.

[29] See summaries of evidence in Charles Garland and Herbert S. Klein, "The Allotment of Space for African Slavers aboard Eighteenth-Century British Slave Ships," *William and Mary Quarterly* 42 (1985): 238–48, and Eltis, *Economic Growth*, pp. 265–68. For a recent contrary view, based on ninety-two surgeons logs in the 1790s, see Richard H. Stechel and Richard A. Jensen, "New Evidence on the Cause of Slave Mortality in the Atlantic Slave Trade," *Journal of Economic History* 46.1 (1986): 72–73. For other migrants, see Eltis, "Free and Coerced Transatlantic Migrations," p. 273.

Table 4.2. *Chinese to Cuba, 1847-60, and Indians to the British Caribbean, 1851-70,*
by size of mortality (deaths per 1,000 embarked per month)

Mortality	Ships	Average tons	Deaths per 1,000	Days	% of passengers	% of deaths
Chinese						
80.1-132	13	896	390	124	11	28
60.1-80	10	762	321	138	8	17
40.1-60	18	791	221	145	15	23
20.1-40	31	921	123	130	27	22
0.1-20	48	779	39	119	39	10
Total	119				100	100
Indians						
80.1+	6	1,010	351	108	2	12
60.1-80	8	969	225	93	3	9
40.1-60	21	914	165	102	7	18
20.1-40	70	921	91	97	22	31
0.1-20	203	968	29	94	66	30
Total	308				100	100

confinement in the tight quarters of a ship certainly facilitated the spread of infectious diseases through the air and through contaminated water and food, but *by itself* the degree of crowding was not a significant variable.

Approaching the issue of mortality more directly, Table 4.2 looks for a correlation between mortality and other measurable factors. Despite a great spread in the mortality rates, this analysis fails to uncover any clear correlation between mortality and any other measurable factor. Both ship size and length of voyage vary independently of mortality rates. Indeed, the most striking fact to be drawn from Table 4.2 is how variable average mortality rates were. Two-fifths of Chinese migrants and two-thirds of Indian migrants traveled on ships with mortality of 20 per thousand or less, half of whom were on ships with a mortality of 10 per thousand or less. Put another way, for both groups over two-thirds of the deaths occurred on one-third of the voyages.

Although the overall conditions indentured migrants experienced on their voyages may still have affected their survival rate, it has proved impossible to establish a clear connection between mortality and any single carrier-defined circumstance. The best regulated voyages generally had lower mortality than those poorly supervised, but overcrowding was not the main issue. Ships that carried fewer passengers per ton were also likely to have better regulated food and water supplies, a factor whose significance cannot be measured. Nevertheless, it is notable that even on the best regulated migrant routes indentured passengers suffered higher mortality than free migrants, leading one to conclude that some other variable was responsible.

Thus, by process of elimination one is led to turn from the conditions of the voyages to the condition of the migrants who embarked upon them. Does the fact that mortality was higher among Asians than among Europeans, among Chinese than among Indians, and among Indians from Madras that those from Calcutta have to do with the place of origin? Three separable factors about the place of origin can be identified as affecting mortality on the voyages overseas: the general physical debility of the migrants before recruitment, their care between recruitment and boarding, and the likelihood of epidemic disease being introduced from the local environment.

As the previous chapter has argued, those who became indentured migrants were often victims of social and economic distress. They included Africans rescued from slavery, Indians and Chinese fleeing famine and political upheaval, victims of poverty and deprivation. The southern Chinese who became indentured, for example, were not just poorer than the larger number of migrants leaving China without becoming indentured in this period but were also more likely to be suffering from physical debilities brought on by their poverty. A recent comparative study of Chinese migrants points out:

Of the two streams of Cantonese who ventured overseas, those who traveled as free or semifree emigrants to the gold rushes in California, the Pacific Northwest, and Australia were probably upwardly mobile people who saw emigration as a way to obtain the funds that would enable them to benefit from the expansion of commercial agriculture, while those who left under the coercive conditions of the "coolie trade" to Cuba and Peru, as well as the ones who went to California *after* the placer mines there had given out, were more likely victims of imperialism, war, land dispossession, debt bondage, and natural disasters.[30]

Meagher has also drawn attention to the undesirable psychological and physical condition of indentured Chinese migrants in the 1850s. Some were prone to violence, either because they were the victims of kidnapping who wished to escape or because they were criminal types who accepted

[30]Sucheng Chan, "European and Asian Immigration into the United States in Comparative Perspective, 1820s to 1920s," in *Immigration Reconsidered: History, Sociology, and Politics*, ed. Virginia Yans-McLaughlin (New York: Oxford University Press, 1990), p. 44. A similar point was made by a contemporary British investigator: in contrast to the men who freely migrated to southeast Asia and the goldfields of California and Australia, indentured Chinese were and were likely to remain "the very poor and needy . . . and destitute"; James T. White, "Remarks on Emigration from China, and on the General Management of Chinese Emigrants in the British West Indies," Hong Kong, 8 February 1854; *PP* 1859 xvi [c.2452], Papers Relating to Emigration to the West Indian Colonies, pp. 35–36.

indenture in hopes of staging a successful mutiny and seizing control of the ship – in the words of a contemporary source, "the scum of the empire." For others, indenture was a last desperate act to save their lives, the overwhelming majority "feeble, sickly, emaciated wretches, whom hardship, disease and hunger had reduced to the lowest ebb of vitality," in the words of a ship's doctor who had examined them.[31]

Because those willing to emigrate were often in poor physical condition, an important part of recruitment was screening out those suffering from chronic health problems. The procedure in China left much to be desired. At midcentury recruits were collected in sheds, empty warehouses, or floating hulks known as baracoons (the term borrowed from the slave trade) by speculators and crimps who then sold them to the captains or shipping companies, whose responsibility it was to select out the weakest while still making their quotas. Conditions were better at the government-regulated depots later established in Canton and Macao, but on the whole the selection process was fraught with irregularities.[32]

In contrast, the government depots where Indian recruits normally spent one to three weeks awaiting the departure of their ships strove to maintain the hygienic standards of the day. Under the supervision of the emigration agent, recruits were bathed, issued clean clothing (including woolens for those passing through cool latitudes en route to Fiji and the West Indies), and well fed. Two medical inspections were conducted, an initial one by an Indian doctor (or nurse in the case of the females) and a final examination by the surgeon superintendent just prior to sailing. Tinker stresses that, under the pressure of numbers and the need to fill quotas, these examinations could be very superficial (especially in the case of the women): "any coolie who was not suffering from an obvious malformation, or displaying evidence of disease, would pass."[33] Although conditions in the Indian depots were far from ideal, such exclusions of the physically unfit could account for some of the difference in the mortality rate of Indian migrants compared with that of the Chinese, which in the case of Indians going from Madras to Mauritius and the West Indies was one-sixth that of Chinese to Latin America.

However, the difference between mortality rates among Indians from Madras and Calcutta is attributable to yet another factor, epidemic disease, which would appear to have been the most important single cause of death among all indentured migrants. The contrast between Madras and Calcutta is striking. In the typical year 1858 migrants en route from Calcutta to Mauritius perished at the rate of 19 per thousand while fewer than 5 per

---

[31]Meagher, "Introduction of Chinese Laborers," pp. 154, 181–82.
[32]Meagher, "Introduction of Chinese Laborers," pp. 97–139.
[33]Tinker, *New System of Slavery*, pp. 137–44 (quotation from p. 139).

thousand died on the voyage from Madras.[34] On the longer sea routes to the West Indies, migrants from Calcutta (327 vessels in 1851–73) perished at the rate of 20 per thousand, while losses from Madras (23 vessels 1856–62) were slightly over 4 per thousand. In some years there were even greater divergences. Despite efforts to improve conditions on ships from Calcutta, mortality among migrants from that port in 1856–57 was eighteen times higher than that from Madras. The reason was clear to both officials in India and to the British Emigration Commissioners: those departing from Calcutta came on board infected with disease, most commonly cholera.[35]

The case of the *Sir Robert Seppings* from Calcutta to British Guiana in 1856–57 may illustrate how the prevalence disease in the port, imperfections in the screening process, and the eagerness of Indians to be accepted as migrants could combine to produce high mortality during the voyage. Cholera had been raging in Calcutta at the time of departure. On the second day out of the port 40 of the ship's 291 passengers were suffering from diarrhea and dysentery, 61 eventually dying before reaching their destination and 57 others having to be hospitalized on their arrival. According to the captain, passengers reported "that most of them had been attacked [by illness] in depôt, but had been told that unless they suppressed the fact they would lose their opportunity of emigrating." Who told them to conceal their illness is not clear, but it is suggestive of their desire to be accepted that they did so, even though, as the captain also reported, most of them "had come to Calcutta with the wish to go to Mauritius" (to which immigration had been halted for six months after 24 October 1856 because of cholera among Indians arriving earlier in the year).[36]

---

[34]As elsewhere in this chapter mortality rates have been calculated on the basis of a 30-day period to offset the different sailing times from the two ports. Tables of emigrants arriving in Mauritius in 1865 and 1866 show that vessels from Calcutta (50 ships) averaged 41 days in passage, while those from Madras (19 vessels) averaged 32 days; CLEC Report 1866, appendix 17, and 1867, appendix 18. The CLEC reported death rates to Mauritius by port of origin in India (as percentages of those embarking) for the years 1858 to 1866; of that series the 1858 rates were the median and the number of migrants that year was the second highest in the series (after 1859, which showed similar mortality rates). A smaller number of ships sailing to Mauritius from Bombay experienced mortality rates similar to those from Madras, except in 1864 and 1865 when they jumped to 74 and 82.6‰ per month.

[35]PP 1857–58 xxiv [2395], CLEC, 18th General Report 1858, p. 53. F. J. Mouat, *The Report on the Mortality of Emigrant Coolies on the Voyages to the West Indies in 1856–57*, cited in Tinker, *New System of Slavery*, pp. 163–64.

[36]PP 1859 xvi [2452], Papers Relating to Emigration to the West Indian Colonies, T. W. C. Murdoch and Frederic Rogers, Emigration Officers to Herman Merivale, 4 May 1857, pp. 125–26. The *Roman Emperor*, which left Calcutta a few days later, lost 88 of its 313 passengers to cholera, dysentery, and bad weather and 63 others had to be hospitalized on arrival.

The great variation in mortality on Chinese migrant ships that was noted in Table 4.1 is consistent with the outbreak of epidemics of cholera or dysentery while at sea, as was the case on voyages from India. A correlation of high mortality on ships with preboarding conditions was also characteristic of indentured Africans. The Colonial Land and Emigration Commissioners' report for 1848 blamed the high death rate among the earliest shiploads of liberated Africans from Sierra Leone principally on "the state of debility to which the emigrants have been reduced by their previous hardships," which put them in need of better than ordinary feeding, as well on the high proportion of children and some deficiencies in sanitation. Of course, one should be skeptical of explanations that blame mortality on causes which the responsible officials could claim were beyond their control, but that does not make them untrue. Indeed, the correlation of unusually high shipboard mortality with the condition of the passengers who boarded is common to other migration studies. For example, losses of 163 per thousand among Irish sailing to Canada in 1847 (compared with an average of 6 per thousand in the previous five years) were attributed to "fever," likely the cholera that reached Britain that year. Studies of mortality in the African slave trade have also found that the condition of the slaves at the time of their boarding was unexpectedly significant in explaining large variations among different African ports.[37]

Does such a conclusion lead back to blaming the recruiters? Did the eagerness of recruiters to provide cheap labor to colonial plantations or the carelessness of medical personnel in the port and on ship lead them to overlook adverse medical conditions? One must keep in mind that up through the middle nineteenth century even the best Western medical practice was still very crude. Medical examinations of Europeans did not routinely include taking temperatures, measuring blood pressure, or performing laboratory blood tests. Inoculations existed only against smallpox (Indian migrants were customarily vaccinated before leaving the depots)[38] and the germ theory was not generally accepted. Cholera epidemics were still claiming thousands of lives in western Europe in the 1850s. Thus, while the medical staff that screened the migrants and accompanied them

[37]PP 1847–48 xxvi [961], CLEC, 8th General Report 1848, pp. 14–17, 22. Indeed, mortality among children was five times as high as among adults on the fourteen ships from Sierra Leone to the West Indies in 1848–49, before the reforms in feeding were put into effect. See PP 1849 xxii [1082], CLEC, 9th General Report 1849, p. 67. Cf. Asiegbu, *Slavery and the Politics of Liberation*, p. 115, citing C.O. 386/5. The high Irish mortality was a major impetus behind the new regulations governing shipboard densities and health measures. For a summary of the slave trade literature, see Eltis, *Economic Growth*, p. 137.

[38]Blue Book of Mauritius, 1865, p. 128.

on their voyages might well have done a better job, it can be doubted if it was within their abilities in the middle third of the century to identify or treat diseases in ways that would have reduced the mortality on shipboard by any large amount. Meagher's comment on the China trade is more broadly relevant: "it would seem that the enormous death rate can be attributed to no single cause but to a combination of factors such as, ill-equipped ships, lack of government supervision, overcrowding, the semi-involuntary nature of the migration, lack of proper food, water, and medical care, and above all the weakened state of the migrants themselves, which was aggravated by the conditions on board the vessels."[39]

Trends

Examining changes in mortality over the course of several decades highlights the major changes taking place in the indentured labor trade. As Figure 4.4 depicts, there was a very significant decline in passenger deaths on all major indentured migrant routes during the second quarter of the nineteenth century. Mortality from Africa to the British West Indies stabilized near 10 per thousand per month after midcentury, down from 44 per thousand in the 1840s. Deaths among migrants from India to the British West Indies fell from over 26 per thousand per month in 1851–60 to about 9 per thousand in the 1870s. Although it remained significantly higher, mortality among Chinese migrants to Cuba, Peru, and the British Caribbean colonies also declined from 40 per thousand per month in 1851–60 to 25 per thousand at the end of that trade in the early 1870s.

During the last half-century of trade indentured migrants had much less reason to fear dying during the voyage overseas than had their predecessors. Among the more than 100,000 Indians who took passage to British Guiana in the quarter century after 1875 mortality averaged 6.4 per thousand a month, rising somewhat to 7.3 per thousand for 1901–17 (about a third the rates of the 1860s). Mortality on Indian voyages to Mauritius fell from 10 per thousand in the 1870s to under 4 per thousand at its end in the 1890s. Rates for Indians on the new routes to Fiji and Natal were also in that range,[40] and other routes were even lower. Losses from death and desertion averaged 3.8 per thousand a month on the revived Chinese voyages to the Transvaal in 1904–7, a tenth of the level

[39]Meagher, "Introduction of Chinese Laborers," p. 184.
[40]British Guiana figures are calculated from Dwarka Nath, *A History of Indians in British Guiana* (London: Thomas Nelson, 1950), tables 2 and 3. Shlomowitz and McDonald, "Mortality of Indian Labour," table 6.

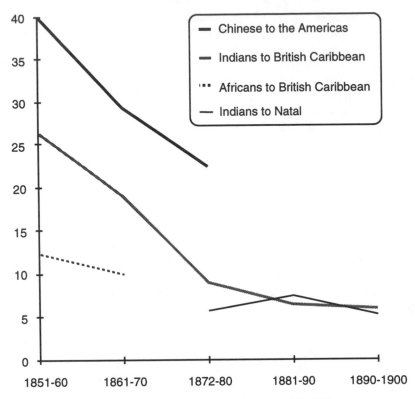

Figure 4.4. Indentured passenger deaths per thousand, 1850–1900.
Source: Table A.6 and Ralph Shlomowitz and John McDonald, "Mortality of Indian Labour on Ocean Voyages, 1843–1917," Studies in History 6.1 (1990): table 16.

of those to Latin America in 1847–74. Migrants from lands new to the trade also experienced very much lower mortality rates. Pacific islanders suffered losses of 3.0 per thousand per month en route to Queensland in 1873–94 and 3.6 per thousand en route to Fiji in 1882–84 and 1891–1911. There was only one death on the first voyage of Japanese indentured migrants to Hawaii in 1868, none during the first larger government-sponsored voyage in 1885, and there is no mention of deaths during frequent voyages thereafter.[41]

It is much easier to establish how sharply mortality diminished on

[41]Ralph Shlomowitz, "Epidemiology and the Pacific Labor Trade," Journal of Interdisciplinary History 19 (1989): table 3; Peter Richardson, Chinese Mine Labour in the Transvaal (London: Macmillan, 1982), pp. 157, 197; Hilary Conroy, The Japanese Frontier in Hawaii, 1868–1898 (New York: Arno Press, 1978), pp. 68–81.

indentured labor voyages than to explain precisely why the decline occurred. It is likely that improvements in shipboard accommodations, in the screening of embarking passengers, and in the application of practical sanitary measures all played a part. The trend toward larger and safer ships continued during the last half-century of the trade. The size of ships from India to British Guiana, for example, rose from an average of about 1,100 tons in 1872 to over 2,000 tons after 1908. By the early twentieth century most indentured passengers traveled aboard steamships, which greatly shortened the voyage. Passage times from India to British Guiana, for example, fell from an average of 96 days in 1851–73 to just 41 days in 1908–17. The steamships that carried Chinese laborers from Hong Kong to Durban in 1904–7 took only 30 days.[42] Steamships were also standard on Pacific migration routes in the late nineteenth century. In December 1891 a steamship executive and a Tokyo businessman organized the Nihon Yoshisa Emigration Company to carry Japanese contract laborers to Hawaii and other locations in the South Pacific. By the end of the century twelve separate companies were carrying Japanese contract laborers abroad and the 5,000-mile voyage from Japan to Hawaii took a mere 10 days.[43]

The greater size and faster speed of these vessels did not reduce mortality directly, but they provided a more salubrious environment and shorter time for contagious diseases to spread and fester. Infectious diseases were less likely to come onboard with the embarking passengers during this period. The Pacific islanders came from generally healthy rural communities, not squalid cities. The northern Chinese and Japanese migrants of this era came from healthier climates than had the more tropical southern Chinese, Africans, and Indians of the earlier period. Measures taken in the ports of departure also made Indian migrants less likely to be carrying disease when they embarked in these later decades, though infectious diseases such as dysentery and measles not detected in the screening process still led to deaths on some of the voyages. Brij V. Lal has demonstrated that in the 1890s over a sixth of those recruited in northern India were rejected as unfit at the subdepot or the Calcutta depot before departure. There were also improvements in Indian cities, such as the installation of a new piped water system in 1892 that reduced cholera contamination, although it certainly did not eliminate it, as the 1900 out-

---

[42]Tinker, *New System of Slavery*, pp. 146–47; Nath, *Indians in British Guiana*, tables 3–4; McDonald and Shlomowitz, "Contract Prices," p. 90.

[43]Yuji Ichioka, *The Issei: The World of the First Generation Japanese Immigrants, 1885–1924* (New York: Free Press, 1988), pp. 47–48. Wayne Patterson, *The Korean Frontier in America: Immigration to Hawaii, 1896–1910* (Honolulu: University of Hawaii Press, 1988), pp. 49–50.

break that claimed the lives of 2.3 percent of Calcutta migrants at sea amply demonstrated.[44]

Improvements in shipboard sanitation and medical care are also likely to have played a role in enhancing the safety of the migrants. Although scientific medicine was still in its infancy, the medical personnel on board seem to have become more effective in ensuring that the diet was nutritious and that food and water remained uncontaminated, and in limiting the spread of infection. Such improvements were part of a much larger trend that reduced mortality not only among indentured migrants but also among nonindentured overseas travelers and among Europeans generally both at home and in the tropics.[45]

Conclusions

This chapter has highlighted several aspects of the ocean voyages of indentured laborers. Although the rude shipboard accommodations, mistreatment, and appalling mortality experienced by many of these migrants certainly merit comparison with the experiences of the ongoing slave trade, an examination of these voyages across the full spectrum of their distribution and the full term of their operation suggests still more comparisons with the larger contemporary experiences of unindentured migrants from Europe and Asia.[46]

The great increase in ocean travel in this period was made possible by increased ship size and speed and increased government regulation that were shared by most indentured laborers. While still rudimentary, conditions were safer and less uncomfortable than in any earlier period. Even so, mortality among indentured migrants was distressingly high for young persons healthy enough to agree to several years of manual labor. The chapter argues that while conditions on shipboard were to some degree responsible for these losses, no one measurable factor – not even overcrowding – can be assigned a large share of the blame. Far easier to

---

[44]McDonald and Shlomowitz, "Mortality on Chinese and Indian Voyages"; Ralph Shlomowitz, "Mortality and the Pacific Labour Trade," *Journal of Pacific History* 22 (January 1987): 41–45; Brij V. Lal, *Girmitiyas: The Origins of the Fiji Indians* (Canberra: Journal of Pacific History, 1983), tables 4 and 5.

[45]See Cohn, "Maritime Mortality," pp. 159–91; Philip D. Curtin, *Death by Migration: Europe's Encounter with the Tropical World in the Nineteenth Century* (Cambridge: Cambridge University Press, 1989).

[46]Dudley Baines, *Emigration from Europe, 1815–1930* (London: Macmillan, 1991), is a brief overview for Europe but there is no comparable summary of Asian migration, which was also considerable. For example, in 1883 and 1884 unindentured Chinese laborers were arriving in Singapore at the rate of 112,000 annually; Straits Settlements Blue Book for the Year 1884 in *PP* 1884–85 lii [c.4583], p. 205.

document is that the migrants' physical health and their exposure to endemic and epidemic diseases were highly significant in accounting for the mortality rates in transit. Finally, the chapter demonstrates that mortality was not uniformly high during all periods but fell sharply and steadily after the early decades of indentured recruitment. Evidence does not permit the measurement of which factors were most significant in producing this reduction, but it is likely that larger and better equipped and regulated ships, faster voyages, improved experience in handling large seaborne populations and increased medical knowledge all played a role.

5

Indentures

A man's destination is not his destiny,
Each country is home to one man
And exile to another. Where a man dies bravely
At one with his destiny, that soil is his.

T. S. Eliot, "To the Indians Who Died in Africa"

After weeks or months at sea the migrants came in sight of the lands to which they had bound themselves in indentured service. The rigors of the voyage over, they now faced the challenges of adjustment to a new land and a new life. Some spent their first weeks in quarantine or in infirmaries recovering from illnesses (or succumbing to them). At most destinations the new arrivals were allocated to employers by local authorities; in Cuba and Peru migrants endured the frightening and humiliating experience of being auctioned off to the highest bidder.

At their work camps migrants were housed in rudimentary lodgings – crude shacks inherited from the days of slavery, barracks nearly as crowded as the ships that had brought them, or, in the last decades of the trade, modest bungalows. The food furnished by employers (at least for the first few months) was often unfamiliar and sometimes in short supply. Clean water could be at a premium, sanitary facilities minimal or entirely lacking. The new diet, contaminated water, and the local disease environment posed new threats of illness, in the treatment of which the medical facilities guaranteed by their contracts often left much to be desired. Only a minority of new arrivals were already hardened to the arduous physical labor they had contracted to perform. The tasks were unfamiliar, the workday long, and the pace enforced by overseers and managers a test of their strength and stamina. Psychological adjustment could be almost as difficult. The new surroundings, the sickness and physical toils, the problems of mastering new skills and the rudiments of a new language, and the entry into a new community all taxed the minds as well as the bodies of the migrants.

The initial experiences of most migrants roughly approximated the circumstances just outlined, but as the first few days and weeks grew into months and years the variations multiplied. Each importing territory had its own laws and customs; each work assignment, its own challenges and rewards. Mining gold had little in common with mining guano; cutting cane in the boiling sun was not the same as boiling cane syrup in the factory. However much they shared the culture and attitudes of their common class, employers differed in temperament and humaneness. Though change came slowly and unevenly, time did not stand still. The experience of the pioneers in 1838 differed from those arriving in 1875 or 1900.

At least as important as these circumstances into which fate and fortune had dropped them were the differences among the migrants themselves. Their state of health on arrival and the immunities acquired from prior exposure to disease affected who sickened and died and who survived the challenges of the first year. Small differences in stamina, determination, and frame of mind could result in great disparities over the term of the indenture. Some gained in body strength and savings year by year, others lost their earnings in gambling or squandered them on drugs. Women generally earned less than men, but fortunes of individual women varied markedly. There were still more differences in what individuals decided to do at the end of their contracts. Some returned home with whatever money they had accumulated; others stayed on temporarily for another term to earn still more; many settled permanently in their new land.

The challenge of this chapter is to describe some common and normative features of the migrant experience abroad without losing sight of these many variations. It examines that experience under four headings. The first two examine the larger parameters that governed employment conditions: the changing mix of destinations and conditions over time, the economic constraints on their employers. The second pair of topics follows the migrants' life cycle: the challenges they faced over the years of indenture, what they gained and what they decided about the future after completing an initial indenture. It is not a story of villains and heroes, but of men and women confronting their circumstances. While attention is paid to variations over time and space, of necessity the emphasis falls on the ordinary, not the unusual, the typical rather than the extreme.

Periods and destinations

As Chapter 2 outlined, the indentured labor trade began as a daring experiment that sought to abolish slavery while preserving the colonial plantation economies. It took time to change employers' entrenched attitudes and labor practices and to establish new administrative and legal structures governing recruitment and employment. Given the magnitude of this task and the changes taking place in the global economy, it is not surprising that the new labor system had many shortcomings, or that those shortcomings aroused periodic attempts at reform.

Although each territory followed its own timetable, the indentured labor system as a whole underwent notable changes in the destinations, origins, and treatment of migrants that roughly correspond to the four quarter-centuries of its existence (see Figure 5.1). Changes in the circumstances of a typical migrant resulted from the elimination of the worst territories and from improvements in average living and working conditions brought about by improved government supervision. In most places wages showed little or no real improvement.

During the period before about 1850 indentured laborers suffered from the growing pains inherent in setting up a new labor system as well as from employer attitudes and practices inherited from the days of slavery. In structure it was a fairly simple era: nearly all recruits came from India and Africa; nearly all went to British colonies. As Chapter 2 has detailed, British imperial and colonial officials responsible for Indian migration had extended the system with some deliberation and considerable oversight, rejecting some early regulations, such as an 1835 ordinance in Mauritius and an 1838 one in British Guiana, as being too close to slavery. They had also halted the shipment of Indian migrants to Mauritius from 1839 to 1843, as they would later to French colonies from 1856 to 1860, to force receiving colonies to remedy abuses.

Despite these governmental efforts to protect indentured laborers and distinguish them from slaves, the inescapable fact was that their lives were controlled by employers who had recently been slave owners and protected by local officials who were closely allied with this class. Slavery had been ended over the protests of sugar planters, who in many cases were neither inclined nor capable of changing their labor practices. Associations with slavery were reinforced by the fact that in many early locations indentured laborers took over not merely the jobs but also the dwellings of the emancipated slaves. The early, Indian migrants to Mauritius and Réunion moved into the *Camp des Noirs;* their counterparts in British Guiana occupied the barracks of the "Nigger Yard"; the early Chinese in Cuba were processed through the *Deposito de Cimarrones,* a place of confinement for runaway slaves. In 1848 the governor of Trinidad reflected the class and cultural biases of the planter class in arguing to the colonial secretary that newly arrived "fatalistic worshippers of Mahomet and Bramah" and the "savages who go by the name of liberated Africans . . . must be treated like children, . . . and Wayward ones too." As Hugh Tinker observes, "The

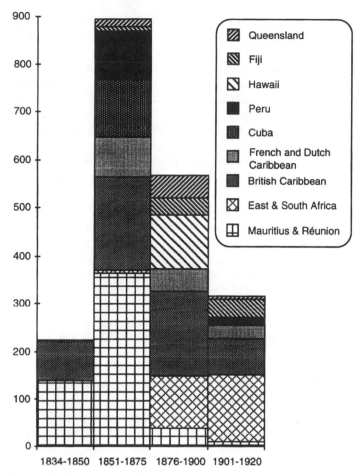

Figure 5.1. Destinations of indentured overseas migrants by period.
Source: Table A.2.

world of slavery still survived; the plantation was a world apart, on its own, subject to the laws – whims – of those in charge.[1]

Yet, in accounting for the treatment received by the early indentured laborers, the legacy of the past may have been less significant than the circumstances of the moment. What mattered more than the dead hand of

[1]Hugh Tinker, *A New System of Slavery: The Export of Indian Labour Overseas, 1830–1920* (London: Oxford University Press, 1974), p. 177; André Scherer, *La Réunion* (Paris: Presses Universitaires de France, 1980), p. 63; Duvon Clough Corbitt, *A Study of the Chinese in Cuba, 1847–1947* (Wilmore, Ky: Asbury College, 1971), p. 7. Lord Harris, governor of Trinidad to Earl Grey, February 1848, is quoted by William A. Green, *British Slave Emancipation: The Sugar Colonies and the Great Experiment,* (Oxford: Clarendon Press, 1976), p. 279.

slavery was the vital state of employers' purses. As a general proposition in this period, as later, it was better to be under contract to prospering employers than to ones near bankruptcy. The records of many investigations reveal that the latter were more likely to push workers beyond their limits and to fall behind in paying wages. Likewise, it was generally better to be employed in territories and in industries that were prospering than in ones that were faltering. Monica Schuler has painstakingly cataloged how it was the decline of the plantation economy in Jamaica in the late 1840s that led employers to reduce or suspend wages and increase the use of physical coercion. She concludes that it was not from the start but "after the first few years [that] the indentured labor system became the equivalent of slavery."[2]

Fortunately Jamaica was not the norm or an especially large importer of indentured labor. In Mauritius and British Guiana the prospering sugar industry's expanding demand for labor encouraged employers to treat their laborers in ways that would encourage them to extend their contracts, which were for as little as one year initially. These circumstances also permitted officials to withhold laborers from employers who abused them and allowed migrants to change employers or even leave the colony early at their own expense. Only a third of the migrants to Mauritius in the 1830s took advantage of the free passage home to which they were entitled at the end of their five years of service; fewer than 2 percent decided to leave early in the 1840s.[3]

During the quarter century after 1850 the indentured labor trade reached its peak volume and greatest diversity. Like their earlier counterparts in British colonies, indentured laborers newly introduced into Hawaii and Dutch, French, and Spanish colonies faced attitudes and conditions influenced by the slave system the planters had been forced to give up (or, in the case of Cuba, still continued). In the worst cases, planters and officials connived in the kidnapping of laborers and in their confinement in slave-like conditions. Pieter Emmer observes with regard to early indentured labor in Dutch Guiana, "Outside the plantation the words 'slavery' and

[2]Monica Schuler, *"Alas, Alas, Kongo": A Social History of Indentured African Immigration into Jamaica, 1841–1865* (Baltimore: Johns Hopkins University Press, 1980), pp. 9 (quotation), 45–64.
[3]*PP* 1846 xxviii (691-II), Papers Relative to Immigration of Labourers into the West Indies and the Mauritius, Rawson W. Rawson, Second Report of the Committee appointed for the purpose of inquiring into . . . the insufficiency of the Labouring Population, p. 160; Robert Neaves's, Notes on the Premature Return of the Immigrants to India and the Causes leading thereto, July 1845, p. 145, and Continuation of Mr. Neaves's Report upon Indian Immigration, 19 July 1845, pp. 147–48. Neaves learned that about 45% of the individuals leaving Mauritius early at their own expense disliked the work and an equal proportion felt they had earned enough or had family or personal reasons for leaving, while the remainder were actually labor recruiters.

'indentured labour' indicated a world of difference; for the workers on the plantation they meant continuity in recruitment, in work-load, daily life, health care, and, in resistance, crime and punishment."[4]

In British colonies stricter and longer contracts became the norm, a circumstance that permitted the abuses of indentured laborers to increase along with their numbers. An 1875 investigating commission reported that in Mauritius, the largest importer of indentured labor, beatings were a "common occurrence" and that on some estates "ill-usage has been systematic and long-continued." As Chapter 3 has detailed, the rapidly expanding Chinese recruitment and the early Pacific islander recruitment were the subject of many abuses. Chinese laborers in Cuba were compelled to work excessive hours, subject to beating that produced permanent injury and even death, inadequately fed, and forced to renew contracts of engagement.[5]

The Chinese indentured laborers on Peru's coastal plantations also experienced harsh treatment. Sold at auction in Callao, they customarily worked ten hours a day, six or seven days a week during the five to eight years of their indenture, with only three days off a year for celebrating each Chinese New Year. At its worst, their treatment by estate managers differed little from that accorded African slaves or native Peruvian peons, and small rebellions were not rare. After one of these, the liberal newspaper *El Commercio* charged in 1876: "Accustomed to the easy service of the slave laborer, our *hacendados* have constantly rejected every system that is not based on the absolute submission of the peon, or the complete denial of their natural right."[6]

As in Jamaica, some of the conditions on Peru's coastal plantations are attributable to economic constraints. In contrast, the Chinese at work building railroads into the Andes under the American entrepreneur Henry Meiggs were much better treated. However, an adequate capital base did not always ensure proper treatment. The most miserable of the Chinese in Peru were those mining the very profitable guano deposits on the waterless, treeless, offshore desert islands. They were compelled by the crack of a whip to dig a quota of five tons of acrid bird droppings per person per day. To foreign visitors, the barren landscapes, the strange objective of this

[4]Pieter Emmer, "The Importation of British Indians into Surinam (Dutch Guiana), 1873–1916," in *International Labour Migration: Historical Perspectives*, ed. S. Marks and Peter Richardson (Hounslow, Middlesex: M. Temple Smith, 1984), pp. 94–95.
[5]*PP* 1875 xxxiv [c.1115], Report of the Royal Commission appointed to inquire into the treatment of immigrants in Mauritius [hereafter Mauritius Commission Report], p. 583; Ch'ên Lanpin, A. Macpherson, and A. Huber, *Report of the Commission Sent by China to Ascertain the Condition of Chinese Coolies in Cuba* (Taipei: Ch'eng Wen Publishing, 1970), pp. 3–4.
[6]Watt Stewart, *Chinese Bondage in Peru: A History of the Chinese Coolie in Peru, 1849–1874* (Durham, N.C.: Duke University Press, 1951), pp. 82, 221 (quotation).

bustle of activity, and the enveloping clouds of yellowish ammonia-smelling dust that rose from their efforts appeared to be a scene from hell. And hell it was for the laborers, some of whom chose to escape from their inferno by leaping to their deaths from the guano cliffs. In the wake of the guano island scandals the government of Peru acted to suspend the importation of new laborers from 1856 to 1861. In the 1860s Chinese labor contracts normally contained clauses prohibiting their employment in guano mining, although these were not always observed.[7]

While chronic abuses were characteristic of this period, so too were efforts at correcting them. Governments wrote new labor codes and hired more officials to enforce them. Migrants to the older British plantation colonies, for example, were entrusted to the supervision of protectors of immigrants, who were charged with guarding their welfare. As the numbers of indentured laborers grew, there were added agents-general of immigration and various subagents, who personally conducted inspections of the migrants' welfare. Some countries that supplied laborers also took actions to correct abuses. Japanese officials suspended the shipment of laborers to Hawaii after problems with the first experiment in 1868, while the Chinese government terminated all shipments to Cuba and Peru in 1873 and 1874.

Of course, well-meaning regulations could be blunted by local government officials, who were generally more sympathetic to the interests of employers than of workers. The autonomy of the Peruvian planter on his estate was legendary, though reputations for kindness and cruelty varied by individual. A dispute between the governor of British Guiana and the colony's agent general for emigration in 1865–68 impaired the latter's effectiveness. The situation in Cuba was much worse; as Meagher points out:

Havana was far removed from Spain, and the colonial government traditionally made no effort to enforce decrees . . . which were not to its liking. In these circumstances it is not surprising that the provisions of the law which sought to protect the Chinese laborer from personal abuse and injustices were ignored or violated with impunity[8]

Nevertheless, the momentum for reform led to a series of investigating commissions in the early 1870s that, by exposing the sometimes scandalous shortcomings of the system's operation, were usually the occasion of

[7] Arnold J. Meagher, "The Introduction of Chinese Laborers to Latin America: The 'Coolie Trade'" (Ph.D. dissertation, History, University of California, Davis, 1975), pp. 247–48, 256; Jonathon V. Levin, *The Export Economies: Their Pattern of Development in Historical Perspective* (Cambridge, Mass.: Harvard University Press, 1960), pp. 31–33, 88–89.

[8] Meagher, "Introduction of Chinese Laborers," pp. 225–26 (quotation), 252; PP 1871 xx [c.393], Report of the Commissioners Appointed to Enquire into the Treatment of Immigrants in British Guiana [hereafter British Guiana Commission Report], June 1871, pp. 49–55.

important reforms. Although each territory followed its own cycle of re-cruitment and reform, actions taken as a result of the investigations of the 1870s marked a watershed in the system as a whole. The British Guiana Commission in 1871 led to legislation and increased vigilance that, in the later judgment of George William Des Voeux, the ex-magistrate whose accusations had led to its creation, "added at least something to the comfort and happiness . . . of indentured immigrants." An 1872 British commission of inquiry in Natal led to the adoption of reforms and the appointment of a new protector of Indian immigrants, while one to Mauritius in 1875 focused attention on the many shortcomings in that colony.[9]

As a result of these measures, the mistreatment of indentured laborers in the last quarter of the century was greatly reduced. Official supervision was everywhere the norm. In Queensland there were inspectors of Pacific islanders, while Indian migrants to Surinam were under the supervision of both government inspectors and the British consul. In Hawaii the resumption of Japanese migration in 1885 led to the creation of commissioners to oversee the welfare of all migrant laborers and, in time, an inspector general.[10] In addition, by the 1870s most indentured laborers were going to places such as Natal, Hawaii, and Queensland, which had never known plantation slavery or were under the control of a new generation with no personal experience of slavery.

Although discriminatory practices based on differences in class, cul-

[9]Des Voeux is quoted in Walton Look Lai, *Indentured Labor, Caribbean Sugar: Chinese and Indian Migrants to the British West Indies, 1838–1918* (Baltimore: Johns Hopkins University Press, 1993), pp. 138–40; for a largely negative assessment of the execution of the commission's recommendations, see Alan H. Adamson, *Sugar without Slaves: The Political Economy of British Guiana, 1838–1904* (New Haven: Yale University Press, 1972), pp. 14–45. Jo Beall, "Women under Indentured Labour in Colonial Natal, 1860–1911," in *Women and Gender in Southern Africa to 1945*, ed. Cheryl Walker (Cape Town: David Philip, 1990), p. 147. Mauritius Commission Report concluded (p. 583): "We find that assaults upon labourers are of common occurrence, and that there are estates upon which ill-usage has been systematic and long-continued. We have not been able to discover the great physical, moral, and intellectual advance accruing to Indians that is asserted to be the consequence of their immigration to Mauritius." There were also parliamentary investigations of indentured labor in Queensland in 1869 and 1876.

[10]British Guiana Commission Report, pp. 45–46; Judith Ann Weller, *The East Indian Indenture in Trinidad* (Rio Piedras, Puerto Rico: Institute of Caribbean Studies, 1968), pp. 30–32; Edward D. Beechert, *Working in Hawaii: A Labor History* (Honolulu: University of Hawaii Press, 1985), pp. 95–96; Pieter Emmer, "Importation of British Indians," p. 94; J. Ankum-Houwink, "Chinese Contract Migrants in Surinam between 1853 and 1870," *Boletín de Estudios Latinoamericanos y del Caribe* 17 (1974): 66. Notable exceptions to improving conditions were found at the fringes of the overseas trade, such as in German New Guinea and the French South Pacific; see Stewart Firth, "The Transformation of the Labour Trade in German New Guinea, 1899–1914," *Journal of Pacific History* 11.1–2 (1976): 51–65; D. Shineberg, " 'Noumea No Good. Noumea No Pay,' " *Journal of Pacific History* 26.2 (1991): 187–205; M. Panoff, "The French Way in Plantation Systems," *Journal of Pacific History* 26.2 (1991): 206–12; and Ralph Shlomowitz, "Marx and the Queensland Labour Trade," *Journal de la Société des Océanistes*, 96.1 (1993): 12.

tural, gender, and race persisted, it is fair to say that after 1875 (and much earlier in many places) the principal labor shortcomings were more the product of the economic and political conditions in which most indentured laborers (and their employers) operated rather than a holdover from slavery or a failure of administration. The clearest examples of how structural rather than personal issues governed conditions come in the 1880s and 1890s when a sharp decline in sugar prices led many employers to try to squeeze more labor out of their employees and, where possible, to reduce their wages. In Hawaii, at the bottom of the crisis in the mid-1890s, wages for Japanese contract workers were reduced from $15 to $12.50 a month (though the workers' contribution to their repatriation expenses was also cut from $65 to $13); wages for beginning contract workers fell from $14 (1889–92) to $11 (1895–99) a month. When lower wages led to a great increase in runaways in the 1890s, criminal penalties of three month's hard labor and imprisonment were added. Similar reactions occurred in some other colonies. Laborers in Trinidad, for example, experienced a fall in real wages and a sharp rise in prosecutions for contract infringements. However, wages in Queensland were unaffected because labor from the Pacific islands was in short supply, despite wider-ranging recruitment efforts that also raised recruitment costs.[11]

In the early twentieth century the destinations of the indentured labor trade shifted again. Low sugar prices cut production and thus ended labor imports in the Mascarenes and other less efficient producers. Hawaii's annexation by the United States in 1900 ended indentured labor there, as did Australia's adoption of a white labor preference a few years later. But as some labor trades closed down, others were opened, expanded, or revived. China's repeal of the long-standing ban on emigration in 1893 led to a new migration from northern China to the mines of southern Africa. A quarter century after the end of Chinese labor imports, Peruvian plantations began to import Japanese laborers. The early Japanese suffered high losses from disease and complained of mistreatment, but by a large margin they preferred to stay on in Peru at the end of their contracts rather than return home or emigrate elsewhere.[12] The labor trades from Java to Dutch

[11]Katharine Coman, *The History of Contract Labor in the Hawaiian Islands* (New York: Arno Press, 1978), table D; Gary Y. Okihiro, *Cane Fires: The Anti-Japanese Movement in Hawaii, 1865–1945* (Philadelphia: Temple University Press, 1991), pp. 27, 35; Tin-Yuke Char, comp. and trans., *The Sandalwood Mountains: Readings and Stories of Early Chinese in Hawaii* (Honolulu: University of Hawaii, 1975), pp. 280–83; Dorothy Ochai Hazama and Jane Okamoto Komeiji, *Okage Sama De: The Japanese in Hawai'i, 1885–1985* (Honolulu: Bess Press, 1986), p. 25. K. O. Laurence, *Immigration into the West Indies in the Nineteenth Century* (Kingston, Jamaica: Caribbean Universities Press, 1971), pp. 56–57; Bridget Brereton, "The Experience of Indentureship: 1845–1917," in *Calcutta to Caroni: The East Indians of Trinidad*, ed. John Gaffar LaGuerre (Trinidad: Longman Caribbean, 1974), p. 30.

[12]Stewart, *Chinese Bondage in Peru*, pp. 82, 102, 105, 137 (quotation from p. 221); see also his references to charges of slavery or near slavery on pp. 21, 55, 117–20. Toraje Irie, "History

Guiana and from India to Fiji were both growing in this period. Though not free of faults, these migrations were still more carefully supervised than those in earlier decades. In 1910 the last and broadest of the British inquiries into Indian indentured labor, the Sanderson Committee, found "that the arrangements for housing, medical treatment, and general well-being of the indentured immigrants leave little to be desired, and that the wages earned are such as to enable them to save a substantial sum during the period of the indenture." Emphatic in its insistence that indentured labor was a system of free labor and in no way a disguised continuation of slavery, the committee pronounced its "unhesitating opinion, after examining the best, most authoritative evidence that we could obtain on the subject, . . . that whatever abuses may have existed in the more remote past, no such charge can be substantiated against the system as it at present exists and has been in practice during the last 20 or 30 years." In its view, the only major fault remaining was the excessive use of criminal prosecution to enforce contracts. The committee also recommended that future migration be restricted to colonies in good economic health and able to provide land for settlement to those time-expired migrants who wished to stay on.[13]

While the numerous investigations reveal that keeping indentured labor from reverting to slavery was an uphill fight in which not all battles were won, it seems fair to say that over time the reform-minded governments succeeded in keeping indentured labor within limits acceptable to the standards of the time. They pruned the worst abuses and shut off the access of some individuals and territories to new labor. Such actions did not alter the underlying economic realities of indentured labor. The next section explores the relationship of labor conditions to three factors: the costs of labor recruitment, the productivity of the labor obtained, and the profitability of the plantation economies.

Costs, productivity, and profits

Importing labor was not cheap. During the third quarter of the nineteenth century the cost of recruiting and transporting an individual indentured laborer averaged $50 to $60 on the shorter routes and $100 to $200 on longer ones, not counting the cost of eventual repatriation, to which most migrants were entitled (Table 5.1). The actual cost to the employer varied. Where shipping was done by private entrepreneurs who could sell the

of Japanese Migration to Peru," trans. William Himel, *Hispanic American Historical Review* 31 (1951): 437–52, 648–64.
[13]*PP* 1910 xxvii [c.5192], Report of the Committee on Emigration from India to the Crown Colonies and Protectorates, 26 April 1910 [hereafter Sanderson Committee Report], pp. 12–24; quotation from pp. 13 and 23.

Table 5.1. *Costs of indentured labor on various routes, 1847-1913*

Route	Date	Recruiting	Transport	Return	Total	Term	Wage
1847-1880							
India to BWI[a]	1847-73	*ca.* $25	$60-65	$40	$125-130	3-5	
India to Mauritius[b]	1865		25	NA		5	$2.50+
India to Br. Guiana[c]	1874		64		102	5	4.00+
China to Br. Guiana[c]	1874			NA	>200	5	4.00+
China to Cuba[d]	1847-71	42-102	50-75	NA	92-177	8	4.00+
China to Peru[d]	1852	70	80	NA	150	6-8	4.00+
China to Hawaii[e]	1852			NA	50	5	3.00+
Japan to Hawaii[f]	1868			NA	70	3	4.00+
Pacific to Queensland[g]	1875-80			25	85	3	2.50+
Pacific to Fiji[h]	1866-80			12.50	58	3	1.25+
1881-1913							
Pacific to Queensland[g]	1886-90			25	160	3	2.50+
China to Hawaii[i]	1881-89			NA	54	3	15.50
Japan to Hawaii[i]	1885-93			NA	60-70	3	15.-17.
China to Transvaal[j]	1904-6	18	35	35	88	3	6.50+
India to Fiji[h]	1884-1913	42	40	NA	82	5	6.00
India to Br. Guiana[k]	1907-8				115	5	5.30
India to Trinidad[k]	1909				101	5	5.44

Notes: Wages are monthly for an initial basic contract by adult males. BWI = British West Indies; NA = not applicable; "+" indicates that rations were provided in addition to the wages.

Sources: (a) Records of the Colonial Land and Emigration Commission; Judith Weller, *The East Indian Indenture in Trinidad* (Rio Piedras, Puerto Rico: Institute of Caribbean Studies, 1968), p. 140. (b) Blue Book of Mauritius, 1865, p. 115; Larry W. Bowman, *Mauritius: Democracy and Development in the Indian Ocean* (Boulder, Colo.: Westview Press, 1991), p. 22. (c) Alan H. Adamson, *Sugar without Slaves: The Political Economy of British Guiana, 1838-1904* (New Haven: Yale University Press, 1972), p. 105. (d) Arnold J. Meagher, "The Introduction of Chinese Laborers to Latin America: The 'Coolie Trade,' 1847-1874," Ph.D. dissertation, History, University of California, Davis, 1975, tables 8-9. (e) Clarence E. Glick, *Sojourners and Settlers: Chinese Migrants in Hawaii* (Honolulu: University Press of Hawaii, 1980), pp. 7-8. (f) Hilary Conroy, *The Japanese Frontier in Hawaii, 1868-1898* (New York: Arno Press, 1978), p. 28. (g) Ralph Shlomowitz, "Markets for Indentured and Time-Expired Melanesian Labour in Queensland, 1863-1906: An Economic Analysis," *Journal of Pacific History* 16.2 (1981): table 3. (h) Ralph Shlomowitz, "The Fiji Labor Trade in Comparative Perspective, 1864-1914," *Pacific Studies* 9.3 (1986): tables 2-5, 12. (i) Katharine Coman, *The History of Contract Labor in the Hawaiian Islands* (New York: Arno Press, 1978), table D. (j) Peter Richardson, *Chinese Mine Labour in the Transvaal* (London: Macmillan, 1982), p. 191. (k) *Parliamentary Papers* 1910 xxvii [c. 5192], Report of the Committee on Emigration to the Crown Colonies and Protectorates, 1910, pp. 55-56, 65.

contracts of their recruits at auction to eager buyers, the price of a contract might run well above actual expenses. For example, Chinese laborers regularly sold for $400 each at Callao (Peru) and those landed in Cuba between 1847 and 1871 fetched an average of $340. To avoid bidding wars, in most other territories a private association or the government contracted for delivery of migrants at a predetermined price. In addition, governments often subsidized the expenses of recruitment from general revenues. After some disastrously expensive early shipment by a planters' Voluntary Subscription Immigration Society in British Guiana, for example, the colony's government took over the financing of the migrations, generally underwriting a third of the cost in the 1870s and 1880s, which taxes on planters only partially covered. From 1868 the government of Queensland closely supervised private recruitment at predetermined prices, charging employers a "capitation fee" for its services. Fiji had both government and private recruitment of Pacific islanders in the years after 1876, with its Immigration Department on occasion subsidizing recruiting and repatriation costs. The government of Surinam underwrote 40 percent of the cost of obtaining Chinese labor for its planters from 1863 to 1873. The first Chinese contract workers were brought to Hawaii for $50 each in 1852 by the Royal Hawaiian Agricultural Society, a planters' organization that coordinated recruitment from 1852 to 1865; thereafter recruitment was subsidized by the Hawaiian government's Bureau (or Board) of Immigration, which from 1888 onward recouped part of its expenses by deductions from the migrants' wages.[14]

Table 5.1 also shows a positive correlation between recruitment costs and contract lengths, reflecting employers' need to recoup their investments in recruiting expenses. Thus initial contracts of high-cost Chinese recruits in Cuba and Peru were typically for eight years, compared with five years in the British and Dutch Caribbean colonies where passage and recruiting costs were subsidized, and three years for the lower-cost routes from East Asia to Hawaii. This was not entirely a market calculation.

[14]Levin, *Export Economies*, pp. 82, 113; Meagher, "Introduction of Chinese Laborers," pp. 233–34; Ralph Shlomowitz, "Markets for Indentured and Time-Expired Melanesian Labour in Queensland, 1863–1906: An Economic Analysis," *Journal of Pacific History* 16 (1981): 70–91; Ralph Shlomowitz, "The Fiji Labor Trade in Comparative Perspective, 1864–1914," *Pacific Studies* 9 (1986): 116–17; William A. Green, "The West Indies and Indentured Labour Migration: The Jamaican Experience," in *Indentured Labour in the British Empire, 1840–1920,* ed. Kay Saunders (London: Croom Helm, 1984), p. 22; Emmer, "Importation of British Indians, p. 98; Adamson, *Sugar without Slaves,* pp. 43, 139–41; Alan H. Adamson, "The Reconstruction of Plantation Labor after Emancipation: The Case of British Guiana," in *Race and Slavery in the Western Hemisphere: Quantitative Studies,* ed. Stanley L. Engerman and Eugene D. Genovese (Princeton: Princeton University Press, 1975), p. 471; *PP* 1898 1 [c.8657], Report of the West Indian Royal Commission, appendix C, 2:119; Okihiro, *Cane Fires,* p. 27.

Governments also regularly imposed limits on contract length, although it is equally true that employers had success in raising legal limits that were uneconomic. For example, as employers in British Guiana were forced to implement reforms in other areas, they succeeded in raising the length of a standard contract from one year to five from 1854 and in gaining greater control over their new laborers. Since short-term labor contracts (generally no longer than a year) were the hallmark of progressive labor legislation in the nineteenth century, Alan Adamson can rightly argue that these changes constituted "a counterrevolution in Guyanese society [that] . . . reduced to zero what little social and economic freedom the immigrant had previously possessed." On the other hand, it is difficult to imagine how indentured labor trade to British Guiana would have continued without longer contract terms.[15]

Five-year contracts became the norm in other British colonies at this time with migrants in those closer to their homelands having the right to a free return passage after five years. Official opposition blocked any further lengthening of indenture contracts. Even though the rising demand for Pacific island labor required ever longer voyages that drove up the cost of recruiting an indentured Melanesian in Queensland from about $85 in 1875–80 to about $160 in 1886–90 (plus fees and local transportation costs), the standard contract there remained three years. The three-year contracts signed by Chinese in the Transvaal gold mines were the minimum length over which mine owners could recoup their recruitment costs and the maximum length to which authorities would agree.[16]

Despite the high costs of recruitment, indentured labor was in much demand in places where local supplies were limited or where local labor was even more expensive. In Cuba, for example, indentured Chinese migrants were cheaper than African slaves. In the older British plantation colonies indentured labor was initially much cheaper than local labor. By

[15]Adamson, *Sugar without Slaves*, pp. 54 (quotation), 55, 110, and "Reconstruction of Plantation Labor," pp. 467–70. See Donald Wood, *Trinidad in Transition* (London: Oxford University Press, 1968), pp. 133–35. The passage quoted from Adamson omits his charge that the 1854 laws represented "a movement back toward slavery"; rather than a reversion to an older labor system the longer contracts were a recognition that the costs of long-distance transport necessitated a longer payback period.

[16]Shlomowitz, "Markets . . . in Queensland," pp. 78–79; Peter Richardson, *Chinese Mine Labour in the Transvaal* (London: Macmillan, 1982), pp. 166–67. Government regulation could also impede shortening contracts: officials in British Malaya (Straits Settlements) in the later 1880s repeatedly argued that the three-year contract mandated by law was too long (when tied to the low wages also mandated) to attract Indian labor of sufficient quality; cf. *PP* lxxii 1888 [c.5249], Straits Settlements, Administrative Reports for 1887, p. 13. The term of indenture was finally reduced to two years in November 1899 and to 600 days in January 1905; Ralph Shlomowitz and Lance Brennan, "Mortality and Indian Labour in Malaya, 1877–1913," *Indian Economic and Social History Review* 29 (1992): 61.

one calculation indentured Indian labor cost one-eighth as much as free African labor in Mauritius in 1840, though two-thirds as much was probably closer to the truth. The first Indians brought to British Guiana in 1838 were paid wages of just 80¢ a month (plus benefits) at a time when newly emancipated field hands were receiving 32¢ a day.[17]

But over time, the gap between the wages of experienced indentured laborers and nonindentured laborers tended to close, partly because the growing number of indentured laborers had the desired effect of forcing down wages other laborers could command, partly due to legal requirements in Dutch and British Guiana that indentured laborers be paid at prevailing wage rates. In time the growing population of out-of-indenture laborers also created an alternative (and more experienced) labor supply, which commanded superior wages. For example, in Queensland in the late 1880s the annual wage during first indenture contracts was £6 ($28.80), during a subsequent reindenture £8.70 ($41.76), and for Melanesians no longer under indenture £16 to £18 ($76.80 to $86.40). Most time-expired Melanesians worked on small farms, not plantations. Some employers in the British West Indies also made a habit of hiring time-expired migrants, finding their experience made them worth a premium price.[18]

The other side of the initially competitive cost of indentured labor was its lower productivity, at least by novice recruits unaccustomed to the tasks they were required to perform and experiencing many other problems of adjustment. Dissatisfied with the low productivity of their first Japanese recruits, for example, Peruvian planters cut their wages and dismissed those who objected, but planters became more satisfied as both sides gained experience working with each other.[19] Other employers also complained of the low productivity of new arrivals, of women, and of people whom they termed malingerers.

After finding it impossible to import sufficient numbers of the African and European labor that they preferred and too expensive to import more Chinese, employers in the British West Indies came to depend on a labor supply they esteemed less, the East Indians. Because Indians were physically smaller and weaker than Africans, they were not as productive. In Trinidad in 1872 it was estimated that an indentured Indian man required five to six hours to do field work that a Creole male performed in four to

---

[17]PP 1841 xvi (45); the majority report put the cost of Indian labor at £8.90 a year compared to £68.90 for freed slaves, but the calculations in Mr. Dawson's minority report of £13.18 versus £19.20 seem better founded.

[18]Adamson, *Sugar without Slaves*, pp. 42, 119; Shlomowitz, "Markets . . . in Queensland," pp. 76–79; see pp. 89–91 for a discussion of the work preferences of out-of-indenture Melanesians.

[19]Irie, "Japanese Migration to Peru," p. 447.

five hours. With some exaggeration investigators in British Guiana at the same time reported that an Indian could do only half as much work as a Creole.[20]

To promote maximum effort (and reduce costs) employers in the British West Indies, Peru, and elsewhere took steps to tie wages to productivity. Instead of paying laborers for a certain number of hours of work, wages were linked to the completion of a "task," a system that had been commonly used during apprenticeship to define a day's work. In practice, the best Creole men could complete two tasks a day, though few were willing to work more than three or four days a week. Some experienced Indians could also do more than 1 task a day, such as the man in the fifth year of indenture in British Guiana who completed 42 tasks a month, but indentured Indians typically accomplished much less. One study of thirty-nine estates in British Guiana showed that of the theoretical 260 tasks that the law set as a year's work, Indian laborers actually averaged only 122 in 1854 and 140 in 1855. Another study in 1870 found that the average daily earnings of an ordinary Indian migrant laborer was 28¢ (14d.) versus the statutory wage of 40¢ (20d.), which would represent the completion of 182 tasks a year. While the trend was up, most likely because the proportion of first-year migrants in the work force was falling, productivity was still well below planters' expectations.[21]

This disappointing output was due not only to Indian migrants' typically accomplishing less in a day, but also to their working fewer days a year than anticipated. In the mid 1870s Indian migrants worked an average of 153 days a year in French Guiana; in Trinidad the average was 200 days. Because of high absenteeism an Indian in British Guiana typically worked 4 (rarely 5) days a week, not the 6 days the contract specified. On one well-run plantation on Trinidad in the mid-1890s a typical Indian was absent from work a third of the time. In 1909 at least 20 percent of indentured Indians failed to turn out for work in British Guiana in any given week, while in Fiji absenteeism for indentured Indian males averaged 11.4

[20]PP 1871 xviii [c.768], Report of CLEC, appendix 26. Creole women took 5 to 6 hours per task, indentured Indian women 6 to 6.5 hours. In 1872 the agent-general of immigration in Trinidad reported that indentured Indian men generally took 5.5 to 7 hours to complete a task; Indian women took 6 to 7 hours; PP 1873 xviii [c.768], Report of CLEC, appendix 26, table 2. See Barry W. Higman, "The Chinese in Trinidad," Caribbean Studies 12 (1972): 21ff.

[21]Adamson, Sugar without Slaves, p. 111; British Guiana Commission Report, appendix, part 1, p. 97. In 1854 38% of the total number of indentured Indian migrants arriving in the previous five years were in their first year of service. In 1855 that figure was down to 19%. Although the corresponding figure for 1870 would be 30%, by then many indentured laborers had been in the colony more than five years. Thus, a more meaningful calculation, supporting the correlation of the absentee rate with the proportion of neophyte migrants, can be made for 1872, when first-year migrants were 9% of the total indentured labor force. These calculations are based on Dwarka Nath, A History of Indians in British Guiana (London: Thomas Nelson & Sons, 1950), table 1, and Adamson, Sugar without Slaves, table 9.

percent and for females 23.7 percent.[22] Illness accounted for a significant part of the lost time, but many employers believed that much illness was exaggerated or imaginary and that Indians were chronic malingerers.

Because absenteeism undermined the principal rationale for importing indentured labor in the older plantation areas (the need for a tractable labor force) and added to its cost, employers responded with a variety of coercive measures that added greatly to the harshness of plantation life. One method was to force migrants to make up missed days. In Mauritius, a migrant incurred a two-day penalty (a "double cut") for every day of labor missed, even for illness. As a consequence of such penalties, it was officially estimated in the late 1850s that a five-year contract in Mauritius took seven years to complete, while a five-year contract in Trinidad (where only one day had to be made up for each day missed) took six years.[23]

Legal action against migrants for unauthorized absences and other violations of contract were also very common. In the first decade of the twentieth century 24 percent of indentured Chinese in the Transvaal gold mines were prosecuted in a year and in British Guiana the proportion was 38 percent; convictions in Trinidad were 16 percent, in Fiji 20 percent. Most convicted for vagrancy in Trinidad were first offenders, suggesting that the fines may have had the desired effect.[24]

This overview of costs and productivity supports the conclusion that for employers indentured labor was a success, but a limited one. It enabled older plantation areas to obtain labor for less than newly freed persons were willing to accept and with new legal basis for long-term control and discipline. In addition, by increasing the available labor supply, it drove general wage rates down from the high levels of the postemancipation years. In newer colonies indentured migrations furnished a labor supply that was otherwise unavailable in sufficient numbers or at an affordable price. Yet when the high costs of recruitment and the low productivity and absenteeism are calculated in, indentured labor was not cheap, especially not to the sugar planters struggling with falling commodity prices. To sustain productivity, employers relied more on the stick of enforcement than the carrot of wages. No doubt, the actions of some employers and supervisors reflected ingrained prejudices and personality defects, but the

---

[22]Eric Williams, *From Columbus to Castro: The History of the Caribbean, 1492–1969* (New York: Vintage Books, 1984), pp. 354–55; Laurence, *Immigration into the West Indies*, p. 56; British Guiana Commission Report, p. 90; Sanderson Committee Report, 1910, p. 56.

[23]On Trinidad in 1858 a typical Indian worked over two days a month more than a typical Creole or other migrant laborer; *PP* 1860 xliv [2711], Report of the Agent General of Immigrants, Annual Report Trinidad, 1858, pp. 36–37; Tinker, *New System of Slavery*, pp. 186–89.

[24]Richardson, *Chinese Mine Labour*, p. 174; Tinker, *New System of Slavery*, p. 194; Weller, *East Indian Indenture*, p. 56.

larger political and economic realities of the times sufficiently explain the overall pattern of wage rates and labor conditions.

The migrants' experience

Employers, governments, and markets constructed the political economy within which indentured labor operated, but the migrants themselves also shaped its operations by their actions and reactions. Although information on the perceptions of individual migrants is limited, it is possible to outline the differences in physical, mental, and social adjustment of migrant groups, in their earnings, and in the decisions they made at the end of their initial indenture. Which historical period (outlined in the previous section of this chapter) a migration took place in significantly affected the individual experience, but the stress here will be on the changes over the cycle of an individual life: the differences in the first year and the last of indenture, the choices and benefits of a migrant in a second contract (or out of contract) compared with those of a first termer.

One might expect to find a sharp difference between the experiences of those migrants who were true volunteers and those who were recruited by deception or even kidnapping, but this does not appear to have been the case. First of all, the line between these categories was not clear-cut, since few first-time recruits had a realistic image of what they were getting into, partly because of misinformation but mostly due to their own inability to imagine the geography and conditions they would encounter at their destinations. In addition, once overseas, most migrants seem to have adopted a fatalistic attitude toward what they had to endure, which further blurred the differences between their forms of recruitment. Instead, recruits' reactions were more likely to be formed by the actual conditions at their destinations and by their individual abilities to cope with unfamiliar circumstances. Like other migrants crossing ecological frontiers, they were stricken by unfamiliar illnesses, which sometimes proved fatal. Like other cross-cultural travelers, they suffered greatly from homesickness and other psychological problems of adjustment. In time most learned to cope with the conditions they found at their work sites and some succeeded in changing them. While circumstances varied by territory and by employer, so too did the individual's response.

No aspect of the migrant experience is more shocking than the high mortality they suffered. In January 1847, George R. Bonyun, a British doctor who had recently examined the survivors of the 36,000 migrants introduced to British Guiana during the previous decade, discovered that mortality varied widely among the different migrant groups. Least healthy were the Portuguese from Madeira, who had experienced an average annual mortality of at least 70 per thousand. While migrants from India were somewhat better off as a whole, their survival differed sharply by origin: South Indians departing from Madras had suffered mortality rates of 80-90 per thousand, whereas North Indians from Calcutta had experienced losses of about 27 per thousand (the reverse of the situation of these two groups during the voyages out from India). The healthiest of Guiana's migrants were those from Africa, whose mortality of 14 per thousand was virtually the same as that of the Creole African population in the colony.

Dr. Bonyun attributed these differences to three factors: the physical condition of the immigrants on arrival (Madeirans being debilitated by famine), their different susceptibility to diseases in Guiana, and the differences in medical care to which they had access in the colony, laying particular emphasis on the disease factor. The American consul in Mauritius concurred, attributing high death rates among Indian migrants there in the 1850s to cholera introduced from Calcutta in 1854 and to malaria in the 1860s. Modern research, particularly by Ralph Shlomowitz, has confirmed the primary role played by epidemiological factors among all indentured migrant groups. As Table 5.2 shows, Pacific island laborers in Fiji died at about twice the rate of Indian migrants there, since the latter had come from a more similar disease environment. Indeed, those from the isolated Pacific islands suffered high mortality almost everywhere they went (or even, as in Hawaii and Fiji, when they stayed at home). So did those moving from the temperate environment of Europe to tropical plantations. Mortality among other migrants varied with their exposure to unfamiliar diseases and unhealthy conditions.[25]

For this reason mortality also varied widely among the same migrant group at different locations. As Shlomowitz and Brennan demonstrate, Indians suffered far greater losses in Assam, Malaya, and Mauritius, where the intensity and virulence of malaria was greater, than in Natal and the West Indies. Among most migrant groups the worst losses occurred during the first year of their residence abroad and declined as the survivors acquired greater immunity or resistance to the new diseases. Shlomowitz of-

---

[25]George R. Bonyun, M.D., to Henry Light, governor of British Guiana, Demerary [sic], 6 January 1848, pp. 63–64; PP 1854–55 xvii [1953], 15th General Report of CLEC 1855, appendix 62, p. 207, cites mortalities for Guiana in 1853 of 113‰ for Chinese, 79‰ for Portuguese, 36‰ for Indians, and 14‰ for Africans. Of the first 4,312 Madeirans to arrive in British Guiana in 1841, 282 died within nine months; Brian L. Moore, "The Social Impact of Portuguese Immigration into British Guiana after Emancipation," Boletín de Estudios Latinoamericanos y del Caribe 19 (1975): 5. Of the first 200 Madeirans entering Trinidad in May 1846, 91 died by the end of the year; Wood, Trinidad in Transition, p. 103. Nicolas Pike, Sub-tropical Rambles in the Land of Aphanapteryx: Personal Experiences, Adventures, and Wanderings in and around the Island of Mauritius (New York: Harper & Brothers, 1873), pp. 91–110, 471. Philip D. Curtin, Death by Migration: Europe's Encounter with the Tropical World in the Nineteenth Century (Cambridge: Cambridge University Press, 1989).

Indentured labor in the age of imperialism

Table 5.2. *Mortality of adult indentured laborers (deaths per 1,000 per year)*

Indians	1868-70	1871-80	1881-90	1891-1900	1901-10	1911-20
Old Colonies						
Surinam		53.6	20.9	16.8	14.1	13.9
British Guiana	44.8	23.0	24.1	22.5	18.1	
Trinidad	45.3	30.9	22.7	18.2	19.9	13.5
Jamaica	29.8	32.3	20.3	20.8	23.7	24.3
New Colonies						
Natal				13.5	19.7	16.1
Assam		76.7	59.4	50.3	40.9	54.6
Province Wellesley (Malaya)		57.3	39.7	49.6	56.9	
Fiji			31.3	20.9	15.4	11.2

Pacific islanders	1879-87	1888-92	1893-1906	1907-13
Fiji	82	66	33	38
Queensland	82	53	35	

Sources: The first entry for British Guiana (actually for the period 1855-72 and not confined to adults) is from Alan Adamson, *Sugar without Slaves: The Political Economy of British Guiana, 1838-1904* (New Haven: Yale University Press, 1972), p. 145, and the last entry for Trinidad (actually 1911-15) is from Judith Ann Weller, *The East Indian Indenture in Trinidad* (Rio Piedras, Puerto Rico: Institute of Caribbean Studies, 1968), table 11. All the rest are from Ralph Shlomowitz and Lance Brennan, "Epidemiology and Indian Labor Migration at Home and Abroad," *Journal of World History* 5.1 (1994) table 1, and Ralph Shlomowitz, "Epidemiology and the Pacific Labor Trade,". *Journal of Interdisciplinary History*, 19.4 (1989): 597.

fers graphic evidence of this in the case of Pacific islanders in Fiji: among the 2,444 migrants arriving in 1880 the death rate was 1445 per thousand in their first year, 42 in their second year, and 27 in their third. Similarly mortality among the Japanese contract laborers to Peru was 157 per thousand in the first year (1899) but averaged only 8 per thousand during the next nine years despite the arrival of 5,500 new Japanese migrants. The mortality in Peru was made worse by an epidemic in 1899 and, although its decline was hastened by some reforms, it also reflected the growing proportion of older migrants in a colony. In cases where the migrant population was rapidly expanding or where there was a heavy turnover in migrants (both true of Assam and Malaya) mortality did not decline.[26]

[26]Ralph Shlomowitz and Lance Brennan, "Epidemiology and Indian Labor Migration at Home and Abroad," *Journal of World History* 5. (1994): 58–64; Ralph Shlomowitz, "Epide-

Mortality records do not exist for all migrant groups. Indeed, some of the most notorious destinations are the least documented. Even there, however, disease is likely to have been the major factor governing death rates. No annual population records were kept for Chinese migrants in Cuba, for example, but a Chinese investigating committee estimated that there remained 68,825 Chinese alive there in 1874 (of the approximately 125,000 brought there since 1847).[27] Those figures would be consistent with either of the worst mortality patterns in Table 5.2 – sustained losses at a 50 per thousand rate (the Malaya pattern) or very high initial losses (the Pacific islander pattern). The latter, reflecting the gradual adjustment to a new disease environment, is more likely and was the pattern among Chinese in British Guiana, where mortality declined from 113 per thousand in 1853 to 50 in 1867 to 30 in 1869.[28] Researchers have not bothered to calculate mortality rates among Asian and European indentured laborers in Hawaii because few premature deaths occurred in the islands' malaria-free and generally healthy environment, though diseases introduced by outside contacts decimated the indigenous Hawaiian population and Pacific island migrants.[29]

Table 5.2 also shows that colonies making the transition from slavery to indentured labor did not generally suffer higher mortality than those that had never known slavery, suggesting that whatever differences in treatment existed, they were not significant enough to affect overall survival rates. The paramount role played by epidemiology does not mean that poor sanitation, overwork, and the quality of medical care had no impact on the mortality curve. As Dr. Bonyun noted at midcentury, ailing migrants who were treated in hospitals (where they received doses of quinine) recovered at a significantly higher rate than those given more cursory treatment in infirmaries on the estates. However, the care accorded to migrants did not keep pace with the rapid improvements in medical

miology and the Pacific Labor Trade," *Journal of Interdisciplinary History* 19.4 (1989): 596; cf. Ralph Shlomowitz, "Differential Mortality of Asians and Pacific Islanders in the Pacific Labour Trade," *Journal of the Australian Population Association* 7.2 (1990): 116–27. Irie, "Japanese Migration to Peru," pp. 449–52. Grant McCall, "European Impact on Easter Island: Response, Recruitment and the Polynesian Experience in Peru," *Journal of Pacific History*, 11.1–2 (1976): 97–98.

[27]Meagher, "Introduction of Chinese Laborers," p. 236. Four years later their number was estimated to be about 50,000; *PP* 1878 lxvii [c.2051], Report on the Labour Question in Cuba, 1878, by H. Augustus Cowper.

[28]*PP* 1854–55 xvii [1953], 15th General Report CLEC 1855, p. 207; British Guiana Commission Report, p. 125. The latter rates may understate losses since the base population on which they are calculated includes deserters, some of whom were likely dead. Far worse rates are known: of 1,040 Chinese imported into Panama for railroad construction, half died in the first six months; 15th General Report CLEC 1855, p. 50.

[29]Judith A. Bennett, "Immigration, 'Blackbirding,' Labour Recruiting? The Hawaiian Experience," *Journal of Pacific History* 11.1–2 (1976): 21.

knowledge and procedures around the turn of the century. Aside from vaccinations against smallpox, no other inoculations were routinely provided by employers or local public health officials. Indeed, investigations revealed that elementary sanitary measures, regarding such things as water supply, drainage, and waste removal, were often poorly enforced before 1900.[30]

Problems of physical well-being went hand in hand with problems of mental health. As with disease, threats to mental health were usually worst during the first few months of residence abroad. Like migrants everywhere, newly arrived indentured laborers found difficulty in adjusting to new circumstances. Unfamiliar surroundings, strange food, the absence of reassuring religious sites and festivals, and separation from family and friends added to their alienation. A poignant example of the lengths to which homesickness drove some migrants (and of their limited grasp of geography) was recounted by an immigration agent in British Guiana in 1884:

On several occasions small parties of new coolies deserted from plantation Aurora[;] . . . all told the same story, viz. that they had been informed that after a few days' journey through the forest they would arrive at a mountain on the farther side of which a road was to be found leading to Calcutta.[31]

Adding to their psychological problems were the unaccustomed rigors of long hours of manual labor, coping with unexpected illness, and disappointments about wages and working conditions. Although each individual reacted differently, psychological adjustment was a major problem for most new migrants.

Many of these strains eased as migrants became more accustomed to their new circumstances, but the years brought little change in the shortage of women. This imbalance between the sexes inhibited the growth of stable family relations, promoted gambling and alcohol or drug abuse by male migrants to fight off loneliness, increased the demands on the existing women to perform traditional "female tasks" such as cooking, and sometimes produced more pathological effects. As was shown in Chapter 3, virtually all Pacific island migrants and Chinese migrants (except to British Guiana) were males. As few of the former became permanent residents abroad, their family lives had to be delayed (or interrupted) until their

---

[30]Weller, East Indian Indenture, chap. 7; Brereton, "Experience of Indentureship," p. 30. See the plantation-by-plantation record of health care shortcomings in 1870 in the British Guiana Commission Report, appendix C, pp. 3–149.

[31]Nath, Indians in British Guiana, p. 90. Pike, Sub-tropical Rambles, p. 475, suggests that it was "home-sickness" that drove large numbers of indentured Indians to besiege Mauritian authorities with pleas to be repatriated as invalids.

return from indenture. The unfortunate Chinese in Cuba and Peru were indentured for longer terms and had meager chances of returning home, although once out of indenture some, as in Hawaii, married women from other ethnic groups. Among indentured Indians overseas there were generally two to three men for every woman; among Japanese migrants to Hawaii men outnumbered women by over four to one. Because this imbalance forced most men into involuntary celibacy, homosexuality, or irregular relations with prostitutes, it was a major source of dissatisfaction among long-term migrants. Indeed, Tinker argues, "The disproportion between men and women was the main factor in shaping the life of the coolie lines."[32]

Like other factors in their lives, this disproportion affected individuals differently. About a quarter of Indians migrated as married couples, though many such arrangements had been made in the recruiting stations or during the outward voyages and not all such pairings lasted as long as the term of the contract. Other couples were able to form agreeable temporary or permanent relationships overseas. However, in the competition for women, richer and stronger men, especially foremen and overseers, had distinct advantages, a fact that drove other men to despair. Some researchers argue that this male competition offered women distinct advantages, whether they chose to change partners, to raise their status through relationships with more affluent and powerful individuals, or to enhance their independence from the sale of their favors. Because of their enhanced freedom, as well as because migration offered to widows, wives, and single women an escape from unhappy situations at home, Pieter Emmer suggests that "emigration can also be regarded as a vehicle for female emancipation." However, such apparent advantages could be overshadowed by risks. Women migrants were commonly under a double bondage: to the indenture holder and to accompanying husbands or kinsmen. Those who sought to loosen the latter bond suffered moral condemnation or worse, as unfaithful wives were sometimes murdered by jealous spouses or kinsmen. For these reasons other pioneering research on Indian women under indenture emphasize their negative experiences. Brij. V. Lal stresses that Indian women in Fiji "suffered greater hardships than men," a view to which Shaista Shameem agrees, and Jo Beall places indentured Indian women in Natal "at the very bottom of the class-race-gender hierarchy." These different perspectives are not incompatible. As with indentured

[32]Tinker, *New System of Slavery*, p. 201. According to the British Guiana Commission Report, p. 86, "Nearly all the serious crime committed by Coolies is directly traceable to [the] disproportion of the sexes among immigrants." Brereton, "Experience of Indentureship," p. 32, views the disparity between the sexes as "One of the most monstrous features of the immigration system," the cause of tension, personal suffering, and even violence.

men, the fact that women migrants were still exploited under indenture does not preclude their using it as a means of improving their lives. More research on indentured women is needed to untangle these issues.[33]

It is also important to keep in mind the changing circumstances of indentured women over time. The small number of women accompanying migrating husbands in the early decades of the trade were not always considered part of the labor force nor bound by contracts. As their numbers rose as the result of legal requirements, contracts became the rule along with the need to perform field work, usually of the least skilled type. In the Caribbean and Fiji indentured women became important to the sugar estates; in Natal they became essential to both sugar and tea estates. Yet, women earned less than men, whether because it took them longer to complete a task, because they worked fewer days a year, or because they were paid at lower rates for their labor, reducing some to destitution. At the end of their indenture contract, like the African women before them at the end of slavery and apprenticeship, few Indian women remained in plantation labor. In Mauritius in 1898 less than 3 percent of out-of-indenture women engaged in agricultural labor; the proportion in Fiji in 1921 was only 1.8 percent. Researchers have differed as to where to place this clear trend on the spectrum running from women's successful reintegration of themselves into traditional family roles to their victimization by a reestablished patriarchal domination.[34]

Individuals dealt with their frustrations, alienation, and feelings of depression in a variety of ways. The most extreme reaction to conditions was suicide, which in places became quite high, particularly by men. In the 1850s suicide attempts among Chinese mining guano in Peru were a regular occurrence and the principal overseer reported over 60 succeeded in one year. Suicide among indentured Chinese in Cuba averaged almost 800 per million in 1855–56. Tinker argues that suicides among Indian migrants were several times the rate (50 per million) in the areas of India from which most migrants came, citing incidences of 728 per million in

[33]P. C. Emmer, "The Great Escape: The Migration of Female Indentured Servants from British India to Surinam, 1873–1916," in Abolition and Its Aftermath: The Historical Context, 1790–1916, ed. David Richardson (London: Frank Cass, 1985), p. 248; Brij V. Lal, "Kunti's Cry: Indentured Women on Fiji Plantations," Indian Economic and Social History Review 22.1 (1985): 71; Shaista Shameem, "Gender, Class and Race Dynamics: Indian Women in Sugar Production in Fiji," Journal of Pacific Studies 13 (1987): 10–35; Beall, "Women under Indentured Labour," p. 166. Okihiro, Cane Fires, p. 33, presents a moderately positive view of indentured Japanese women's experience in Hawaii; see also Tinker's pioneering treatment in New System of Slavery, pp. 201–5, and Look Lai, Indentured Labor, pp. 142–44.

[34]M. D. North-Coombes, "From Slavery to Indenture: Forced Labour in the Political Economy of Mauritius, 1834–1867," in Saunders, Indentured Labour, p. 98; Beall, "Women under Indentured Labour," pp. 151–53; Shameem, "Gender, Class and Race Dynamics," p. 31.

Mauritius in 1869–72 and 640 in Natal and 780 in Fiji in the early twentieth century. Although still indicative of serious personal alienation, lower averages are recorded for other periods; for example, suicides among Indians in Mauritius (1875–79) and in British Guiana (1865–70) were in the range of 250 to 350 per million and suicides were also less common in Fiji before 1900, perhaps because of a lower incidence of first-year migrants. Researchers agree that suicide was hardly ever directly linked to ill-treatment by employers and varied greatly by cultural community. Thus suicides were much more common among South Indian than North Indian migrants and three times as common among Chinese than among indentured Indians in British Guiana.[35] Moreover, although suicide attests to underlying tensions in many indentured communities, such a small proportion of migrants resorted to it even in the worst cases that this extreme action provides little insight into normative behavior.

Desertion was a much more common way of getting out of a bad situation and one that was more directly linked to the work experience. In the early years of migration, when long contracts were not the rule, some Indians in British Guiana abandoned plantation labor to become squatters on vacant land or itinerant beggars, an honorable profession in India. Among the Chinese brought to the mines of the Transvaal there were 1,700 desertions in 1905–6 "due to ill treatment and exploitation." In some territories migrants escaped indenture by fleeing to another state. From the 1870s growing numbers of indentured Indians deserted Trinidad for Venezuela, where they could easily obtain land. High wages in California and other parts of the Pacific Coast drew large numbers of migrants from Hawaii, many truncating contracts of indenture whether legally or illegally. An experiment with indentured Japanese for mines, railroads, and sugarcane plantations in Mexico from 1901 to 1907 came to an abrupt halt, after a series of strikes and other protests, when most of the migrants fled north of the border. Yet outright desertion was far less common generally

[35]Meagher, "Introduction of Chinese Laborers," pp. 241–47; Corbitt, *Chinese in Cuba,* pp. 79–80; Tinker, *New System of Slavery,* p. 201. Colonial Blue Book of Mauritius 1874, 1875, 1876, 1877, 1879, in *PP* 1875 li [c.1336], 1877 lix [c.1825], 1878–79 1 [c.2273], 1881 lxiv [c.2829]; records for 1875–77 attribute 28% of known suicides to ill-health, 19% to alcohol or drug abuse, 18% to temporary insanity, 16% to domestic troubles, while 7% occurred after a murder or attempted murder. British Guiana Commission Report, pp. 125–26, 136–37, gives data that yield a suicide rate of 250 per million for Indians and 830 per million for Chinese in British Guiana. Brij V. Lal, "Veil of Dishonour: Sexual Jealousy on Fiji Plantations," *Journal of Pacific History* 20 (1985): 135–55, shows that the highest incidence of suicide occurred during the first six months of indenture, that most who committed suicide were men, and that suicide was more common among Hindus than among Muslims. Suicides per million in England and Wales in 1861–70 were 99 (males) and 34 (females) and in 1901–10 were 158 (males) and 49 (females); Olive Anderson, *Suicide in Victorian and Edwardian England* (Oxford: Clarendon Press, 1987), table 2, pp. 80–81.

than the short-term absenteeism that has already been noted as a frequent occurrence, notably in the West Indies.[36]

More common than outright desertion were escapist activities that marked the end of the workday or -week. Drinking and gambling were common among Indians, as was the use of cannabis, said (improbably) by one source to have been introduced to Jamaica by the Indian migrants. Many Japanese in Hawaii celebrated payday with "all night drinking and gambling sessions," which left some of them perpetually broke or indebted (though, of course, enriched others). Gambling also added to the indebtedness or enrichment of many Chinese migrants. Many Chinese also turned to opium as an escape. Its use in Peru, for example, took a significant proportion of many Chinese migrants' incomes and some, who after years of addiction could no longer put in a full workweek, were forced to extend their bondage to pay their debts.[37]

As their numbers grew and the system became more rigidly institutionalized and impersonal, more and more migrants turned from escapist strategies to directly confrontational ones. Protests and strikes were commonly led by individuals with greater education or longer experience in the colonies and took place under adverse economic conditions. Chinese staged protests against conditions in Peru and were found among the rebels in the Ten Years' War (1868–78) in Cuba. There were a number of small strikes in British Guiana and Trinidad beginning in the 1880s, which were usually put down with severity. Labor militancy was also notable among Japanese in Hawaii, who staged twenty-three strikes during the first half of 1900 on the eve of formal U.S. annexation and who deserted in such numbers that planters turned to labor from Korea, China, and Puerto Rico. A major strike by Japanese on Oahu in 1909, after the end of indenture, cost planters over $2 million and won significant improvements in wages and living conditions.[38]

---

[36]Adamson, *Sugar without Slaves*, pp. 47–48; Weller, *East Indian Indenture*, p. 51; Richardson, *Chinese Mine Labour*, p. 174; Yuji Ichioka, *The Issei: The World of the First Generation Japanese Immigrants, 1885–1924* (New York: Free Press, 1988), pp. 69–70.

[37]Tinker, *New System of Slavery*, pp. 212–14, citing testimony of Dr. James Edwards to Sanderson Committee, "that *ganja*, the 'leaf of friendship,' had been introduced by Indians to the Blacks of Jamaica." Hazama and Komeiji, *Okage Sama De*, pp. 39–40. Michael J. Gonzales, *Plantation Agriculture and Social Control in Northern Peru, 1875–1933* (Austin: University of Texas Press, 1985), pp. 101–2, claims that a per-capita consumption of opium in Peru of 2.9 pounds a year in 1876–82 represented 95 percent of an average Chinese migrant's annual wage. Consumption rose to 3.6 pounds per capita in 1885–90, but a rise in wages made it 25–39% of average wage. The earlier figure seems improbably high.

[38]*PP* 1878 lxvii [c.2051], Report on the Labour Question in Cuba, 1878, by H. Augustus Cowper. Strikes in British Guiana averaged about 20 a year in 1886–90 (42 in 1888) and 12 a year in 1899–1903; Adamson, *Sugar without Slaves*, pp. 154–55; for Trinidad, see Weller, *East Indian Indenture*, pp. 49–50. Wayne Patterson, *The Korean Frontier in America: Immigration to Hawaii, 1896–1910* (Honolulu: University of Hawaii Press, 1988), pp. 12–13; Hazama and Komeiji, *Okage Sama De*, pp. 42–44.

Although indentured laborers engaged in both passive and active resistance, it is really the absence of large-scale protest that is more striking and may give greater insight into the mentality of indentured workers. To be sure, protest was impeded by penal codes, which created a climate intimidating to expressions of discontent, though such a climate was not so oppressive as that endured by slaves in the Caribbean and Brazil where violent uprisings were feared and frequent.[39] In addition, as for other transplanted populations, newly arrived migrants would have found organized resistance difficult. Disappointment and discontent there were, even despair, but there is also evidence to suggest that most migrants found in their indenture experience a sufficient measure of satisfaction of the dreams that had driven them into indenture. Most migrants made the best of the difficult conditions they encountered, worked hard, lived frugally, and survived to the end of their indentures.

Remuneration and repatriation

Contentment is impossible to quantify, but one can measure the financial returns migrants received. Here, too, there was a wide range of individual experiences. Earnings and savings varied considerably between novices and experienced workers, the vigorous and the ill, the ambitious and the less motivated, and between men and women. Fairly typical is the distribution shown in Figure 5.2 of annual earnings of Indian migrants on one Demerara (British Guiana) plantation in 1869. The average migrant earned $53.43, but one-sixth earned over $80 during the year, one-sixth under $30. For the women included in this work force the average annual income was $46. Such wages were modest but frugal migrants could save most of their salaries since most employers also furnished lodging, board, medical care, and some clothing.

Moreover, such wages were certainly higher than agricultural labor might earn in Asia and not far off the rates then being earned in Europe. The entire Demerara sample just cited received an average monthly wage of $4.45 and the top two-fifths averaged $6.68. Most other indentured laborers received wages within that range. In comparison rural monthly wages in the Madras Presidency of India were generally between $1 and $2. As Table 5.1 shows, starting wages in the West Indies about 1870 were $4 a month; a migrant who completed twenty-six tasks a month in Trinidad would earn $6.50. The Hawaiian government calculated that its average agricultural wage in 1870 was $7.50, which it suggested was higher than the corresponding wages of farm workers in Scandinavia and Ger-

---

[39]See the account of intimidation by an exceptionally articulate Indian migrant named Bechu to the West Indian Royal Commission of 1897, appendix C, 1:75–76, 131.

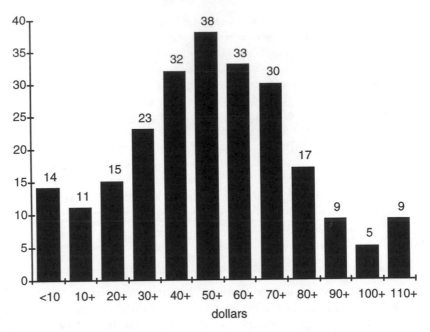

Figure 5.2. Distribution of annual earnings, British Guiana, 1869.
Source: Parliamentary Papers 1871 xx [c.393-II], Report of the Commissioners Appointed
to Enquire into the Treatment of Immigrants in British Guiana, June 1871, appendix,
1: 9. Based on records of 236 indentured Calcutta laborers on the Criming's Lodge
sugar estate, Demerara.

many ($3.30), Ireland ($4.25), and England ($6.50) and not far inferior to
those in Wales ($8.50) and the United States ($10.50).[40] To be sure, wages
do not measure satisfaction, but they do imply that most migrants need not
have been disappointed by their earnings.

Somewhat greater insight into the attitudes of migrants can be gathered
from the choices individuals made at the end of their term of indenture: to
return home, to sign a new contract, or to move into the labor market in
the land of their indenture. Of course, these decisions were not just the
product of individual preferences. In some cases making the return voyage
was a practical and financial impossibility. For example, early Indian and
African migrants in Jamaica found it difficult to return home because of the
absence of regular shipping, while most Chinese lacked the funds to pay
the passage back from Cuba and Peru (which was not provided by em-

[40]Beechert, *Working in Hawaii,* table 6, p. 107; M. Atchi Reddy, "Official Data on Agricultural
Wages in the Madras Presidency from 1873," *Indian Economic and Social History Review* 15.4
(1978): 453.

ployers).[41] In other cases there were equally great impediments to staying on. Virtually all of the Chinese who went to southern Africa faced compulsory repatriation, because of policies seeking to restrict the permanent residence of non-European settlers. White-preference legislation also forced the repatriation of most Pacific islanders and Chinese migants from Australia from the turn of the century.

Remarkably, the length of the return voyage does not seem to have had much effect on the rate of repatriation, perhaps suggesting that migrants harbored no great fear of the longer sea voyages. To be sure, over two-thirds of migrants returned to India and China on very short voyages from Southeast Asia and to Melanesia from Australia (enforced by repatriation policies in the latter case), but the proportion of Indian migrants who remained in Mauritius and Natal was about the same as those who remained in far more distant locations in the Caribbean (Table 5.3).[42] The lower rate of return from distant overseas locations may reflect many migrants' longer term of residence there and thus their greater assimilation.

Territories also adopted quite different policies about the rights of end-of-term migrants. Some tried to persuade or coerce migrants to sign new indenture contracts. Cuba's was the most draconian: from 1861 Chinese at the end of their first indenture had to leave the island (virtually impossible financially) or reindenture themselves. Only 140 are known to have managed to save enough to pay the long passage home; many who sought to evade the law were caught and ended up doing forced labor.[43] Some colonies chose the carrot rather than the stick. After 1854 in British Guiana, for example, those agreeing to a second five years of indenture received an immediate bonus of about $50 and the right to a free return passage after completing the new contract. Noting that over a third of the indentured labor force was under a second (or subsequent) term of indenture in 1870 and were investing some of their savings in livestock, the investigating commissioners reasoned that the migrants must perceive their situation to be "at least the equal of what it was in India."[44] Planter enthusiasm for reindenture collapsed after 1873 when the very high rate of labor imports

[41]Tinker, *New System of Slavery*, p. 87; Schuler *"Alas, Alas, Kongo,"* pp. 88–93.
[42]Figures for Malaya (Straits Settlements) include both indentured and unindentured migrants; 15.2% of arrivals were indentured. In 1900–21 59% of Indian migrants returned to India; Usha Mahajani, *The Role of Indian Minorities in Burma and Malaya* (Westport, Conn.: Greenwood Press, 1973), p. 106. Indenture had been abolished in 1910.
[43]Meagher, "Introduction of Chinese Laborers," pp. 223–25. As a way of encouraging end-of-term migrants to reindenture themselves, Mauritius and Natal levied a high tax on those staying on out of indenture; Tinker, *New System of Slavery*, pp. 232, 313.
[44]British Guiana Commission Report, pp. 33, 182. The commissioners calculated the value of livestock owned by Indians resident more than five years in the colony was worth $674,790 or about $33.44 per person.

Table 5.3. *Rates of repatriation of overseas migrants*

Region	Place of Indenture	Nationality	Period	Percentage
Indian Ocean	Burma	Indian	1892-1935	c.90[a]
	Malaya	Indian	1881-93	71[b]
	Thailand	Chinese	1882-1917	69[c]
	Mauritius	Indian	1836-1910	35[d]
	Natal	Indian	1860-1911	28[e]
Pacific Ocean	Queensland	Melanesian	1880-1904	75[f]
	Hawaii	Japanese	1885-94	37[g]
	Hawaii	Korean	1896-1910	17[h]
Caribbean	Surinam	Indian	1890-1931	34[i]
	Jamaica	Indian	1845-1916	33[j]
	British Guiana	Indian	1838-1918	28[j]
	Surinam	Javanese	1897-1938	c.25[k]
	Trinidad	Indian	1845-1918	20[j]
	Martinique/Guadeloupe	Indian	1853-85	21[i]

Note: These crude measures of arrivals against departures make no allowance for deaths or births (except in the case of Mauritius where departures exclude persons born in the colony). This results in an underestimation of the proportion of returns in cases where virtually all migrants were men (and thus births were far below deaths). Nor are repeat migrants factored out; where they were numerous (Southeast Asia, Queensland), their inclusion in the numerator may offset omission of deaths in the denominator.

Sources: (a) Usha Mahajani, *The Role of Indian Minorities in Burma and Malaya* (Westport, Conn.: Greenwood Press, 1973), p. 6. (b) Annual Report, Straits Settlements, 1890, 1893; (c) George William Skinner, *Chinese Society in Thailand: An Analytical History* (Ithaca: Cornell University Press, 1957), p. 61; (d) Larry W. Bowman, *Mauritius: Democracy and Development in the Indian Ocean* (Boulder, Colo.: Westview Press, 1991), table 2.2; (e) Jo Beall, "Women and Indentured Labour in Colonial Natal, 1860-1911," in *Women and Gender in Southern Africa to 1945*, ed. Cheryl Walker (Cape Town: David Philip, 1990), p. 147; (f) Peter Corris, *Passage, Port and Plantation: A History of Solomon Islands Labour Migration, 1870-1914* (Carlton: Melbourne University Press, 1973), p. 150; (g) Hilary Conroy, *The Japanese Frontier in Hawaii, 1868-1898* (New York: Arno Press, 1978), appendix E; (h) Wayne Patterson, *The Korean Frontier in America: Immigration to Hawaii, 1896-1910* (Honolulu: University of Hawaii Press, 1988), p. 106; (i) K. O. Laurence, *Immigration into the West Indies in the Nineteenth Century* (Kingston: Caribbean University Press, 1971), pp. 45, 57; (j) G. W. Roberts and J. Byrne, "Summary Statistics on Indentured and Associated Migration Affecting the West Indies, 1843-1918," *Population Studies* 20.1 (1966): 125-34; (k) Craig A. Lockard, "Repatriation Movements among the Javanese in Surinam: A Comparative Analysis," *Caribbean Studies* 18.1-2 (1978): 88.

finally resulted in a labor surplus, which was kept available to the planters by laws making it very difficult for end-of-indenture migrants to secure land for their own settlement.

Those colonies where end-of-term migrants could hope to advance themselves beyond the level of plantation laborer had the highest retention rates. Hawaii was attractive for its higher than average wages (partly offset by high costs of living) and was relatively free of coercive pressures to reindenture, but its greatest appeal was the many possibilities for employment outside the plantations. For example, of the 103 earliest Japanese migrants to Hawaii who completed their contract (1868–71), 90 chose to stay rather than to return to the poverty of their homeland, as did 57 percent of the 20,000 completing their contracts between 1888 and 1892. Most Chinese completing a contract in Hawaii also stayed on to take advantage of other employment opportunities. After the economic downturn in the 1890s, Hawaii's rate of retention of East Asian migrants dropped, mostly because of a drain to the more prosperous North American mainland.[45]

In other territories migrants showed similar interest in using their savings and rights of residence to enhance their economic positions. For example, despite efforts by authorities to discourage them by setting fees at prohibitive levels, many end-of-contract Indians in Mauritius bought licenses for trading and small manufacturing, or purchased land, animals, and equipment necessary for farming. As noted in Chapter 2, such Indian small producers sustained the island's sugar industry after the older plantations became unprofitable.[46]

After Mauritius went into decline, Natal became the most attractive Indian Ocean destination for Indian migrants because of southern Africa's expanding employment opportunities. Indeed, the rapid growth in the colony's Indian population in the late nineteenth century convinced white settlers that they would soon be outnumbered by Indians (as they were already by Africans) and led to the imposition of a £3 annual tax in 1895 on new Indian residents not under contracts of indenture. Despite this substantial penalty, only 11 percent returned to India at the end of their indenture in 1902, while 20 percent signed a new contract of indenture, 51 percent paid the £3 tax and joined the local free-labor market, and 18 percent disappeared (presumably to stay on while avoiding the tax). However, further restrictions on Indians (and protests led by the young Mohandas K. Gandhi), along with a recession after the South African War, made the decisions of those to end their indenture in 1908 very different:

---

[45]Beechert, *Working in Hawaii*, pp. 68, 131–33; Clarence E. Glick, *Sojourners and Settlers: Chinese Migrants in Hawaii* (Honolulu: University Press of Hawaii, 1980), p. 44.
[46]North-Coombes, "From Slavery to Indenture," pp. 111–12.

52 percent returned to India, only 6 percent paid the tax, while 43 percent reindentured themselves to avoid the tax and assure themselves of employment.[47]

Trinidad put a more positive twist on its labor retention policies, paying $50 from 1851 to over a thousand Indians to give up their right to a return passage. This inducement to stay on became even more attractive when free land was substituted for the cash from 1869, especially when in 1873 the offer included both land and cash. Between 1869 and 1880 2,643 Indian men settled on over 19,000 acres with their families. From 1885 to 1912 the rapidly growing Indian population on Trinidad was granted or purchased nearly 90,000 more acres, on which the Indians established villages and pioneered wet rice cultivation as well as sugar and cocoa farming. These land policies made Trinidad the most popular West Indian destination of Indian emigrants who stayed on at a higher rate than elsewhere.[48]

For those who chose to return home the decision was not irrevocable and many subsequently signed up for another indenture overseas. Naturally this was more common on routes where the voyage was of moderate duration, especially as ocean travel became faster and less harrowing. Thus repeaters accounted for 28 to 29 percent of Pacific island migrants to Australia in 1892–1903 and to Fiji in 1885–1911. Ten percent of the Indians entering Mauritius were veteran migrants in 1874–77, as were 14 percent of those a decade later in 1883–86. Even in distant Trinidad 7.4 percent of entering Indian migrants in 1885–94 were repeaters, over two-thirds of whom had served a previous indenture elsewhere, mostly in other West Indian colonies but one in five at Indian Ocean locations.[49]

In considering the motives of such repeat migrants, it is important to keep in mind both the continuing lack of employment opportunities at home as well as the cultural alienation that prolonged residence abroad may have produced. Emmer argues that such individuals "were the real victims of the system," since they failed to put down roots overseas yet

[47]Tinker, *New System of Slavery*, pp. 293, 313; Maureen Swan, "Ideology in Organized Indian Politics, 1891–1948," *The Politics of Race, Class and Nationalism in Twentieth-Century South Africa*, ed. Shula Marks and Stanley Trapido (London: Longman, 1987), pp. 186–87. According to Beall, "Women under Indentured Labour," p. 148, the peak came in 1912, when over 95% of end-of-contract Indians in Natal reindentured themselves.

[48]Bridget Brereton, *A History of Modern Trinidad, 1783–1962* (Kingston, Jamaica: Heinemann Educational Books, 1981), pp. 107–8; Brereton, "Experience of Indentureship," p. 34; Tinker, *New System of Slavery*, pp. 105–6, 120. After Chinese migrants refused to stay on or renew their contracts, Surinam also offered free land to Javanese migrants as an alternative to repatriation from 1895; Craig A. Lockard, "Repatriation Movements among the Javanese in Surinam: A Comparative Analysis," *Caribbean Studies* 18.1–2 (April–July 1978): 88.

[49]Shlomowitz, "Epidemiology and the Pacific," p. 589. Colonial Blue Book of Mauritius, 1874, 1875, 1876, 1877, 1886 (*PP* 1888 lxxii [c.5239]). Trinidad figures are calculated from appendixes vi and ix in Weller, *East Indian Indenture*, pp. 151–52, 165; sites of prior indentures in the Indian Ocean included Natal (8%), Mauritius (6%), and Fiji (4%).

could not readjust to their homelands. Michael Adas agrees that the "psychic costs" of migration were high, but argues that so too were the opportunities to improve one's social and material status.[50] The financial (as well as psychic) costs for Indians seeking to reenter the caste structure could also be high. Some returning migrants spent their entire savings to do so. Quantifying these different circumstances is impossible, but it is worth noting that oscillation between place of origin and overseas settlement area was also typical of migrating Europeans in this period.[51] Indeed, a high degree of alienation has long been an intrinsic part of every migrant's lot.

Had those choosing to return home fulfilled the migrant's dream of riches? In some cases, decidedly yes. Quite exceptional was the case of an Indian man returning from Trinidad with $10,000 in 1869, who had become a shopkeeper and moneylender after serving ten years of indenture. Less unusual but still not typical were the twenty Indian men who sailed from Trinidad in 1862 after five or six years under indenture who had an average of $450 each left over after paying their own return passage. Perhaps they were similar to the exceptionally strong and hard working Indian man encountered by investigators in British Guiana in 1871 who had earned over $200 during the fifth year of his indenture (more than double the average Indian man's earnings there) and was planning to return to India with accumulated savings of several hundred dollars.[52] At the other end of the spectrum, destitution and impoverishment were also common, perhaps particularly so for women. For example, fully one-eighth of the migrants returning to India from British Guiana between 1875 and 1910 were paupers repatriated at government expense.[53]

What was typical? A comparison of the existing evidence suggests that most returnees had accumulated modest savings. Interviews conducted with the ninety-three Indians returning from their first five-year contracts

[50]P. C. Emmer, "The Meek Hindu: The Recruitment of Indian Indentured Labourers for Service Overseas, 1870–1916," in Emmer, *Colonialism and Migration*, pp. 187, 197, calculates that second-indenture migrants amounted to 4.6% of all the migrants leaving Calcutta in 1878–1916. See Tinker, *New System of Slavery*, pp. 365–66, who argues that poor prospects of employment in India discouraged migrants from returning. Michael Adas, *The Burma Delta: Economic Development and Social Change on an Asian Rice Frontier, 1885–1941* (Madison: University of Wisconsin Press, 1974), pp. 90–102; Emmer, "The Great Escape," p. 247, make the same point regarding Indian women.
[51]Teodor Shanin, "The Peasants are Coming: Migants Who Labour, Peasants Who Travel and Marxists Who Write," *Race and Class* 19.3 (1978): 285, cites a total reemigration from the United States to Europe of 47% in 1897–1918. The reemigration rate from Argentina to Europe, 1859–1926, was also 47%; from New Zealand to Europe, 1853–1930, it was 78%; William Ashworth, *A Short History of the International Economy since 1850*, 2nd ed. (London: Longman, 1962), p. 186. Many of those returning home subsequently made a second attempt to settle abroad.
[52]Weller, *East Indian Indenture*, pp. 106–7; British Guiana Commission Report, p. 97.
[53]Nath, *Indians in British Guiana*, table 6.

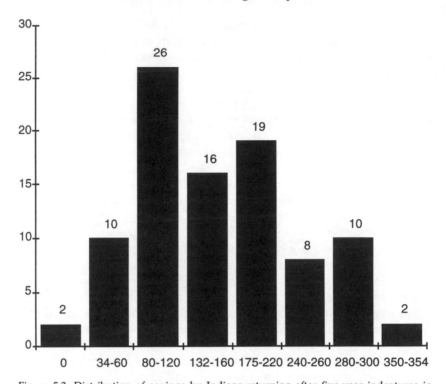

Figure 5.3. Distribution of savings by Indians returning after five-year indentures in Mauritius, 1840–41, in rupees.
Source: Parliamentary Papers 1841 xvi (427), Examination of Coolies Returned from Mauritius.

in Mauritius in 1840–41 show the considerable variation in individual savings (Figure 5.3; cf. Figure 5.2 for a similar distribution pattern in earnings). The median figure was 150 rupees (Rs.) ($81) and the average was a little higher, Rs.158 ($85.30). Twelve returned with virtually all of their five-years wages, Rs.300 ($162), or more. At the other end of the scale were twelve who had Rs.60 ($32.40) or less in savings, two of whom were identified as drunkards. Three-quarters had between Rs.100 and Rs.220. The first batch of Indians returning from five years in British Guiana in 1843 on average did even better, carrying savings of $117.70 per person.[54]

The average savings reported for Indian migrants returning in later years are somewhat smaller, in some cases reflecting the effects of economic downturns in the colonies, but also due to the different demographic composition of the immigrants, and to alternate means used to

[54]*PP* 1841 xvi (427); Nath, *Indians in British Guiana*, p. 20.

transmit money home. Indians returning from Mauritius in 1874–79 brought an average of $64.60 each, though 11.5 percent had no savings with them. Average savings held by Indians returning from other colonies are similar: $51 from British Guiana (1875–1910), $77 from Surinam (1870–1916), $48 from Natal (1902–7, down from double that in 1899 as a result of postwar conditions), and $67 from Trinidad (1899–1907, down from an average of $104.50 in 1851–91). Much of the decline in per capita savings among Mauritius migrants after 1843 can be accounted for by the fall in the value of the silver-based rupee against the gold-based pound. Per-capita totals were also reduced in the later decades of the trade by much higher proportions of lower-paid or nonworking women and children and somewhat higher proportions of paupers invalided home at government expense. The latter, forming about 13 percent of returnees from British Guiana during the four decades before 1914, included persons who were chronically ill, elderly, substance abusers, or destitute for other reasons. Their proportions, rose sharply during periods of economic distress, exceeding 20 percent between 1891 and 1900, perhaps reflecting efforts by colonial officials to reduce charity cases.

A final factor of importance in accounting for the fall in average savings per returnee is the omission from the totals of savings other than cash in hand. One significant omission is gold jewelry, which in the case of non-paupers from British Guiana between 1875 and 1910 averaged nearly $9 per person. Also uncounted is the considerable amount of money sent back to relatives in India by postal money order in the later decades. For example, nearly $570,000 was remitted to India from British Guiana and Trinidad between 1890 and 1912, mostly in small amounts. Post office remittances by Indians from Natal in 1903 averaged $6.25 per migrant, the highest of any colony. It is not possible to correlate post office remittances with specific batches of returnees, but it is likely that if accompanying noncash valuables and unaccompanying remittances could be taken into account, the apparent decline in savings by healthy Indian migrants in the latter part of the period of indenture would largely disappear. Even though savings were modest in most cases and far from evenly distributed, it seems fair to conclude that most Indians returning from a period of indenture had managed to better their financial status by laboring abroad.[55]

Less detailed records exist for other migrant groups. For East Asians the best available records concern remittances sent home by persons remaining

[55]Colonial Blue Books of Mauritius 1873–77, 1879; Nath, *Indians in British Guiana*, tables 6 and 8; Emmer, "Meek Hindu," pp. 199–200; *PP* Annual Reports India 1902–7; Sanderson Committee Report, 1910, pp. 69, 167; Williams, *From Columbus to Castro*, p. 356. The majority of witnesses told the Sanderson Committee (Report, pp. 12, 18) that Indians generally gained much more materially by serving several years in indentured labor overseas than they could have by staying home.

overseas. The Chinese in Latin America seem to have had the least chance to amass savings while under indenture. Although overseas Chinese remittances rose from an estimated 20 million taels in 1886 to 73 million in 1907, sums that provided substantial parts of all Chinese revenues and capital investments, little of this was likely to have come from indentured Chinese, except for those in Hawaii. Japanese migrants in Hawaii (whose numbers were about 20,000 at the end of that period) sent $2.6 million home between 1885 and 1894, not including what those who returned home carried on their persons. It was the custom for Melanesian migrants in Australia to bring back their savings in the form of trade goods, which became a vital part of the islanders' reciprocal gift giving. The value of such goods was not calculated, but Graves notes, "it was considered extremely shameful to return home without a box and commodities."[56]

It is hard to escape the conclusion that, in general migrants who had the good luck to survive the rigors of their migration and indenture were better off physically (as well as financially) than when they had started and healthier than they would have been had they stayed at home. Although no records of body weight were kept, the American consul in Mauritius believed that abundant food and hard labor produced a substantial transformation:

Look at the thin frail form of the Malabar when he arrives from India, and see him after some years' residence in the Island. His form assumes a roundness and his muscles a development, from exercise, wholesome and sufficient food and being well cared for, which speak volumes in praise of the civilizing influence he is unconsciously undergoing.[57]

Better health is also suggested by the much lower mortality rates on return passages than on outward voyages. Financial improvement was general, but there was wide variation. Some went home with significant savings, whereas others returned destitute or with little more than they had come with. Most fell somewhere in between. More research is needed, but it would appear that those who chose to remain abroad exhibited an equally broad range of financial conditions.[58]

[56]Ching-Hwang Yen, *Coolies and Mandarins: China's Protection of Overseas Chinese during the Late Ch'ing Period (1851–1911)* (Singapore: Singapore University Press, 1985), pp. 250–51; Marianne Bastid-Briguiere, "Currents of Social Change," in *The Cambridge History of China,* vol. 11: *Late Ch'ing, 1800–1911,* part 2, ed. John K. Fairbank and Kwang-Ching Liu (Cambridge: Cambridge University Press, 1980, p. 585). Adrian Graves "Colonialism and Indenture Labour Migration in the Western Pacific, 1840–1915," in Emmer, *Colonialism and Migration,* p. 242.
[57]Pike, *Sub-tropical Rambles,* p. 471.
[58]Weller, *East Indian Indenture,* pp. 104, 108. Mortality on ships from Mauritius carrying returning Indians averaged 2.5‰, compared with an average of 16.8‰ on ships from India to Mauritius in 1858–68; calculated from returns in CLEC reports.

This chapter has tried to understand the experiences of indentured migrants overseas by examining the forces that shaped their conditions and the ways in which migrants responded to them. In emphasizing that employers' actions were the product of economic and political forces, the chapter does not seek to deny the degree to which indentured labor was a form of exploitation or to minimize the suffering and abuse migrants endured. It does seek to distinguish impersonal economic and technological conditions from personal moral failings. Callous and cruel employers were not rare but at least during the second half of the period they were likely to suffer the loss of their best workers at contract renewal time and to be cut off from new indentured migrants by government officials. Ironically, this was both an age of growing capitalist domination and an age of heightened moral sensibilities and government regulation. Governments were also active (if not always entirely effective) in trying to set minimally acceptable standards and in mitigating the effects of too ruthless an application of supply and demand.

Given the power of employers, international capital, and government regulation, it is easy to reduce employees to mere passive victims. Despite the constraints imposed by the historical record, the chapter has argued that indentured migrants also shaped their indenture experiences in important ways. They brought cultural and personal norms with them, were affected by forces of nature (notably disease), worked according to their strength and ambition, saved and squandered their earnings, and experienced good or ill luck. It would be foolish to maintain that they had much effect on the larger political economy that created and defined the indentured labor system, but equally foolish to suggest that individuals did not succeed in extracting a measure of material benefit and personal improvement from it.

6

Conclusions

Every foreign land is a fatherland and every fatherland is a foreign land.
—Letter to Diognetes, second century C.E.

Ume Suenaga sailed from Japan to Hawaii in 1885 on the *City of Tokio* as an infant with her parents, Toranosuke and Saka. After completing their labor contracts on the Makee plantation on the island of Kauai, the elder Suenagas decided against returning to Japan and used money saved from their hard labors to open a grocery. Ume-san attended an English-language school on Kauai, but not wanting her to lose touch with the cultural traditions of their homeland, her parents arranged for her to live with a respected Japanese wholesaler in Honolulu in return for her performing household chores so that she could attend the new Japanese school founded there in 1896. A few years later at the age of sixteen she married Mankichi Yamada, who as a child of six had arrived on the same ship with his parents. A high school graduate, Mankichi (George) found work as an accountant, a court interpreter, and later as a successful contractor. He and Ume (Hazel) had six children before his death in 1926. The widowed Ume outlived her husband by fifty years, becoming a naturalized American citizen at the age of seventy-seven, a step that had been illegal for Asians until 1952.

Each set of lives is different. Even among the Japanese who came to Hawaii in 1885 on the *City of Tokio* the lives just described were not typical: Families constituted less than a majority of the total passengers (43 percent); nearly two-thirds of the migrants eventually returned to Japan; few of the girls received as much schooling as Ume; few were as successful in business as Mankichi. Yet these lives at least illustrate the personal poignancy of individuals striving to advance themselves and preserve their cultural heritage while settling in a new land. In that they represent the broader experience of postindenture migrants.[1]

This chapter draws the story of the new indentured labor to a conclusion. First, it describes how the indentured labor trade itself came to an end. But, as the Suenagas' lives show, endings are also beginnings. So there follows a brief sketch of some aspects of the new communities the indentured labor trade created around the world and of the labor systems that succeeded it. The interpretation of indentured labor also changed during the course of its existence as well as afterward. Viewed as a free-labor successor to slavery at its beginning, it was reviled as a new system of slavery at its end. In recent decades there has been an extensive reassessment of the indentured labor trade. Such debates will surely continue. By comparing the various streams of the trade and examining the historical forces that underpinned them, this study has sought to portray the broader context of this remarkable global phenomenon. But like the lives of those whom the trade affected, each segment also has its own story to tell.

The end of indenture

A long-standing debate about freedom and equality shaped the official decisions that ended indentured labor. The debate had begun with the abolitionists' prolonged campaign against slavery. They had argued that free labor would be superior in both morality and productivity. When the former slaves' own ideas of freedom led them to desert the plantation system in many key British colonies, the new indentured labor was organized, in part at least, as an alternative mechanism for demonstrating the abolitionists' second premise. In some ways the new system had never escaped from its origins as a marriage of high moral expectations with the grim practical realities of plantation labor. Commissioners investigating serious charges about the lack of freedom of indentured laborers in British Guiana in 1871 noted how the failures of slave emancipation weighed heavily on its successor: "The fact is, there is a prejudice against [indentured labor], partly sentimental, because it is the symbol of defeat to the too sanguine hopes for the future of the African race which were entertained at emancipation; partly practical, because the government experiment in this direction failed, which was made in the apprenticeship of slaves."[2]

---

[1]The story of the Suenagas is from Dorothy Ochai Hazama and Jane Okamoto Komeiji, *Okage Sama De: The Japanese in Hawai'i, 1885–1985* (Honolulu: Bess Press, 1086), pp. 20–21, supplemented with details from Franklin Odo and Kazuko Sinoto, *A Pictorial History of the Japanese in Hawai'i, 1885–1924* (Honolulu: Bishop Museum Press, 1985), pp. 39–42, 126, 206.
[2]*PP* 1871 xx (483), Report of the Commissioners Appointed to Enquire into the Treatment of Immigrants in British Guiana, p. 63.

These disappointments over emancipation were one aspect of the debate about freedom; more important was the changing context of that debate. The campaign to end slavery in the older British colonies had broadened during the nineteenth century, extending its geographical scope world-wide and including many other forced labor systems. In India debt- and caste-based peonage were outlawed as forms of slavery in 1843. Serfdom in Russia and slavery in the United States came to an end in the 1860s, followed by the remaining systems of slavery in the Americas in the late 1880s. The Brussels Act of 1890 bound its signatories to the suppression of slave trading elsewhere in the world, leading to pressures to end slavery in non-European states and in the Europeans' newly acquired African empire. The League of Nations Slavery Convention of 1926 expressed an even larger international consensus against slave and slavelike labor practices.[3]

The nineteenth-century campaigns against slave labor were paralleled by the struggles of the new industrial classes to improve their laboring conditions. As was discussed in Chapter 1, European workers' low pay, long hours, corporal punishment, and dangerous working conditions were sometimes said to constitute "white slavery." Here too prolonged reform movements led to changes in laws defining the rights of laborers and regulating their ages, hours, and lengths of contract. Here too champions from Marx and Engels to Pope Leo XIII drew close comparisons of the working classes with slavery. After World War I this aspect of free labor also produced international conventions from the International Labor Organization.

Judgments about the conditions of indentured labor could not help but be affected by the changing consensus about what legitimately constituted free labor in other contexts. Conditions conceived as "free labor" in one time and place were denounced as "slavery" at a later time or another place. The earliest and clearest shift in the perception of indentured labor came in the United States, some of whose territories had been major destinations for such labor in the seventeenth and eighteenth centuries. By the 1850s, as a result of the long struggle over slavery, the holding of adults in indentured servitude or peonage had come to be seen in nonslave states as equivalent to slavery and thus incompatible with free labor. After the Civil War the Anti-Peonage Act of 1867 extended the prohibition of "voluntary or involuntary servitude" to all states and territories of the United States.[4] When the United States annexed Hawaii in 1900, the prohibition of indentured contracts was extended to those islands.

[3]See Suzanne Miers and Richard Roberts, eds., *The End of Slavery in Africa* (Madison: University of Wisconsin Press, 1988), and Martin A. Klein, ed., *Breaking the Chains: Slavery, Bondage, and Emancipation in Modern Africa and Asia* (Madison: University of Wisconsin Press, 1993).
[4]Robert J. Steinfeld, *The Invention of Free Labor: The Employment Relation in English and American*

To be sure, changing perceptions were strongly influenced by the grim realities of some systems of indentured labor. The government of India refused to allow additional shipments of indentured Indians to French plantation colonies in the 1880s because local governments failed to safeguard their rights adequately and ensure their repatriation. The termination of indentured migrations between the Portuguese African colonies of Angola and São Tomé in 1909 was prompted by criticisms arising out of an investigation led by the Cadbury chocolate company and its subsequent boycott of cocoa from the island.[5] Elimination or reform of the worst cases fostered questions about the acceptability of indentured labor elsewhere even under the best of circumstances.

However, the final end of the indentured labor migrations was not simply the result of its perception as an unacceptable limitation of human freedom. It is a great irony that the age notable for its growing concern with universal human rights also saw strident new expressions of classism, racism, and nationalism. The clash between universal rights and particular interests often delayed the reform of laboring conditions. Yet the rise of strong expressions of nationalism in China and India also served to hasten the end of indentured labor.

In response to the humiliations of the Opium Wars and the scandals of the indentured labor trade, the Chinese central government adopted a more assertive foreign policy by the 1870s to restore its national honor abroad. No longer avoiding direct involvement with the migrations, China moved to regulate and then to abolish the trade. In 1874 an agreement between Chinese and Portuguese officials ended the export of Chinese contract labor from Macao (other ports having dropped out earlier). Subsequent official investigations of the condition of Chinese migrants in Cuba, Peru, and the United States were part of China's emergence from long-time isolation and resulted in the suspension of most indentured labor overseas.[6]

Law and Culture, 1350–1870 (Chapel Hill: University of North Carolina Press, 1991), pp. 122–84.

[5]William A. Cadbury, *Labour in Portuguese West Africa* (London: George Routledge & Sons, 1910); James Duffy, *A Question of Slavery* (Cambridge, Mass.: Harvard University Press, 1967); and William Gervase Clarence-Smith, "Cocoa Plantations and Coerced Labor in the Gulf of Guinea, 1870–1914," in Klein, *Breaking the Chains*, pp. 150–70.

[6]Arnold J. Meagher, "The Introduction of Chinese Laborers to Latin America: The 'Coolie Trade,' 1847–1874" (Ph.D. dissertation, History, University of California, Davis, 1975), pp. 307–36; Irich, *Ch'ing Policy*, pp. 237–392. This was less than a complete ban since Chinese continued to emigrate to Hawaii under debt bondage; by formal agreement between the respective governments Chinese contract laborers were brought to the Transvaal in 1904–7, and approximately 150,000 Chinese laborers were recruited by France and Britain for use in Europe during World War I. For the last, see Ta Chen, *Chinese Migrations, with Special Reference to Labor Conditions* (Washington, D.C.: Government Printing Office, 1923), pp. 142–48, 207–10.

As chapter 5 has shown, efforts to tar Indian indentured labor with the slavery brush were regularly rejected by British officials in the nineteenth century. The British Guinea commissioners in 1871 were emphatic in rejecting charges that the indentured laborers there were under a yoke like slavery, while not denying that, like other free persons, their civil rights were not always respected. After its broader investigation of Indian indentured labor in 1910, the Sanderson Committee was likewise unequivocal in concluding that indentured labor was free labor. To the long-standing criticism that it was a form of slavery, the committee rejoined: "Our unhesitating opinion, after examining the best and most authoritative evidence that we could obtain on the subject, is that whatever abuses may have existed in the more remote past, no such charge can be substantiated against the system as it at present exists and has been in practice during the past 20 or 30 years." It found that "the arrangements for housing, medical treatment, and general well-being of the individual immigrant leave little to be desired and that the wages earned are such as to enable them to save a substantial sum during the period of the indenture." The committee's endorsement of the benefits of such a free-labor system to both workers and employers was subject to only a few strictures: the excessive use of criminal prosecution to enforce contracts should be reduced; migration should be restricted to colonies in good economic health and able to provide land for the settlement of those time-expired migrants who wished to do so.[7]

Yet within less than a decade of this ringing endorsement, Indian indentured labor was banned for being incompatible with free labor. The change in official views was more a reaction to rising Indian nationalism rather than a reconsideration of the actual circumstances of indentured labor. When the young Mohandas K. Gandhi led protests in southern Africa over the general erosion of Indian rights there, nationalists back in India took up indentured labor as a convenient example of how Indians were treated unequally. To deflect criticism from the major issues of British rule in India, the government of India was willing to sacrifice a system of no particular importance to India as a whole, even if it remained important to the individual Indian migrants. Opposition by Indian members of the legislative council precluded the resumption of Indian indentured labor exports to Réunion and their extension to German Southwest Africa in 1911–12. It was in this context that the Indian viceroy, Lord Hardinge, in July 1915 urged the end of indenture "to remove a racial stigma that India deeply resents" by ending official support for "a system of forced labour

---

[7]*PP* 1910 xxvii [c.5192], Report of the Committee on Emigration from India to the Crown Colonies and Protectorates, 26 April 1910, pp. 12–24 (quotations from pp. 23 and 13 respectively).

entailing much misery and degradation and differing but little from a form of slavery." The government of India then made the decision to end the indentured labor trade from India as of March 1916, though most of the trade actually ceased a few months earlier because of the requisitioning of passenger ships for war use.[8]

Like the abolition of slavery in British colonies eight decades earlier, the cessation of indentured labor from British India was achieved through a combination high idealism and practical politics. This does not diminish the luster of either accomplishment. However achieved, the rescue of future generations from slavery and the servitude of long-term indenture and the erosion of the artificial line between the rights of European peoples and those of Asians and Africans are important milestones in the advancement of the human condition. But it would be equally wrong to ignore many other instances where high-minded rhetoric about the end of indentured labor masked a racist agenda.

This second path to the abolition of indentured labor resulted from a conflict between two forms of Western colonial expansion. During the century before 1920 there had been two quite distinct streams of overseas migration: one largely European and with rare exceptions unindentured, the other largely non-European and often indentured. To a remarkable degree they had gone to separate lands. As Chapter 1 related, this divergence was partly due to the economic resources of the migrants and partly to the different government subsidies applied to them. Where the two streams overlapped, as they did in the new overseas colonies of Australia, southern Africa, and Hawaii, European settlers were initially eager for ample supplies of indentured non-European laborers. However, this social and racial stratification lasted for a shorter time in the new colonies than had its settler-slave predecessor in the old colonial system, because indenture was not a permanent and hereditary condition. By the beginning of the twentieth century the growing numbers of non-Europeans out of indenture and their competition for jobs brought the governments of these hybrid societies to adopt overtly racialist labor and immigration policies.

One trend was to restrict the ability of end-of-term non-European migrants to compete politically and economically with European settlers by limiting their legal status and numbers. In the western parts of North America a large Chinese population, no longer needed in the 1880s now that unskilled European laborers were flooding in, was subjected to violent attacks and legal impediments. The United States Congress in 1882 passed the first of the exclusion acts that would deny Asian immigrants the rights accorded to white settlers. In short order, Canada passed less overtly discriminatory laws with similar results. As was explained in Chapter 1,

[8]Tinker, *New System of Slavery*, pp. 288–366 (quotation from pp. 339–40).

with rare exceptions the Chinese laborers in North America do not seem to have been under indentured contracts, but the issue of their status as free immigrants was the more edifying aspect of the debate over their rights.[9]

A similar instance occurred in Natal where by 1893 Indians were estimated to number 46,000 compared with 45,000 Europeans (and 470,000 Africans). To preserve whites' privileged position, the Natal government passed a series of laws in the 1890s aimed at confining Indian migrants to indentured roles as much as possible by imposing a £3 tax on those out of indenture, restricting the entry of unindentured ("free") Indians, and depriving unindentured Indians of the possibility of legal equality with whites. This was the context of Gandhi's protest movements, which stemmed the implementation of some laws and secured the repeal of the £3 tax, but it was also the context in which Natal planters chose to forgo future shipments of indentured Indians. Similarly in Britain's East Africa Protectorate (Kenya), although a trickle of indentured Indians continued to be imported until 1921–22, the laborers who had built the Uganda railroad from 1896 to 1902 were largely repatriated and policies were adopted that discouraged Indian entry and encouraged European settlement. For a time it was possible to maintain the illusion that both African territories could be "white man's countries" despite the overwhelming numerical preponderance of their indigenous populations. In both, Indians also continued to outnumber Europeans.[10]

In late nineteenth-century Queensland debate about the morality of indentured labor went hand in hand with the promotion of European labor at the expense of Pacific islanders. The public manifesto of a leading critic in 1892 clearly reveals the clumsy blend of idealism and racism:

I have been for many years one of the most determined opponents of the introduction of servile or coloured labour into Queensland. My objection has not been on account of the colour of men's skins, but I have maintained that the employment of such labour under conditions to which we had become accustomed, was injurious to the best interests of the Colony regarded as a home for the British race, and principally for the following reasons: 1. It tended to encourage the creation of large landed estates, . . . and so discouraged actual settlement by small farmers

---

[9]Shih-shan Henry Tsai, *China and the Overseas Chinese in the United States, 1868–1911* (Fayetteville: University of Arkansas Press, 1983), pp. 24–87; Persia Crawford Campbell, *Chinese Coolie Emigration to Countries within the British Empire* (London: P. S. King & Sons, 1923), pp. 41–56.

[10]B. Pachai, *The International Aspects of the South African Indian Question, 1860–1971* (Cape Town: C. Struik, 1971), pp. 6–19; Maureen Swan, *Gandhi: The South African Experience* (Johannesburg: Ravan Press, 1985); J. S. Mangat, *A History of the Asians in East Africa, c.1886 to 1945* (Oxford: Clarendon Press, 1969), pp. 39, 70–72; Robert G. Gregory, *India and East Africa: A History of Race Relations within the British Empire, 1890–1939* (Oxford: Clarendon Press, 1971), pp. 52–53.

working for themselves. 2. It led to field labour in tropical agriculture being looked down upon as degrading and unworthy of the white races. 3. The permanent existence of a large servile population amongst us, not admitted to the franchise, is not compatible with the continuance of our free political institutions.

Practical implementation of racial discrimination came piecemeal. In 1880 Pacific islanders were restricted to work in the sugarcane industry, in 1884 they were excluded from all skilled positions, and in 1892 excluded from all jobs in sugar mills. The movement toward exclusion took heart from Natal's anti-Indian measures. After Queensland's incorporation into the new commonwealth of Australia in 1901, all new indentures were banned and a subsidy of £2 per ton was granted to sugar grown exclusively with white labor, for the most part individuals cultivating small units around a central mill. Most Pacific islanders were repatriated in 1905–6 after the expiration of their contracts.[11]

Impressed with this small farmer approach in Australia, the Hawaiian Sugar Planters' Association also promoted several programs (of high cost and limited success) to Europeanize and Americanize their labor force after annexation, in order to reduce the East Asian presence on and off the plantations. On the American mainland, although indenture was not the issue, the laws excluding Chinese and Japanese laborers because they competed with poor European settlers were a closely analogous phenomenon.[12]

Consideration of the changing economic conditions also serves to diminish the luster of an explanation of the end of indentured labor that relies too much on reform as a motive. In the midst of the sugar crisis of the 1890s a major British commission, voicing concern that the continued importation of indentured Indian labor to British Guiana and Trinidad could impose a heavy burden on colonial treasuries for their repatriation if the economy eroded any further, recommended the phasing out of new imports, especially in light of the substantial populations the trade had built up there. The fact that Indian labor imports were already declining in several overseas locations (and had even ceased in Mauritius) made it much easier for the forces favoring the trade's abolition to succeed. A different economic circumstance favored the end of indenture in Malaya:

[11]"S. W. Griffith's Manifesto," *Brisbane Courier*, 13 February 1892, forwarded by governor to British secretary of state, Correspondence relating to Polynesian Labour and the Colony of Queensland, *PP* 1892 lvi [c.6686]. See other correspondence in *PP* 1892 lvi [c.6686], 1893 lvi [c.6808], 1893 lxi [c.7000], 1895 lxx [c.7912]. Ralph Shlomowitz, "Marx and the Queensland Labour Trade," *Journal de la Société des Océanistes* 96 (1993): 3, 12, points out that even after the expiration of the last indenture contract in 1904 only 27% of sugar qualified for the European-preference subsidy.

[12]Beechert, *Working in Hawaii* pp. 86, 121–33; Beechert errs in suggesting (p. 86) that this racist fear of former workers becoming "a threat to white power ... was unique to Hawaii" and absent from other sugar-growing areas. Queensland's success was not immediate.

prosperity had made wages sufficiently attractive to be able to draw enough unbonded labor.[13] If a century earlier "capitalism" had not in fact extinguished slavery quite so neatly as Eric Williams argued in his influential study, economic changes at least eased the way for its abolition. Similarly, the changing economic circumstances of the early twentieth century facilitated the ending of indentured labor, even though other factors dictated the timing.

The aftermath

The long-term cultural and demographic effects of indentured migration varied greatly. In some places the migrants' influence declined quickly after the trade ended. Having enjoyed the fruits of their labors, places such as Queensland and the Transvaal largely erased the migrants' presence by policies of repatriation and exclusion. Even in lands where most Chinese migrants did not or could not return home at the end of indenture, such as Cuba and Peru, the extreme imbalance in the sexes in time reduced their numbers. In some places, indentured migrants and their descendants blended into other population groups: for example, in the West Indies the descendants of indentured African migrants were absorbed into the much larger black population created under slavery and the descendants of European migrants, depending on marriage patterns, were similarly absorbed into other strata of the population. The arrival of substantial numbers of nonindentured migrants from the same homeland could also dilute communities dating from indentured migrations.[14]

If the vitality of migrant groups diminished in some lands, in many others their presence remained evident to even the most casual observer (see Table 6.1). East Indians replaced Africans as the largest part of the population in British Guiana, Mauritius, Réunion, and Dutch Guiana, in time becoming the majority in the first three, while Indians and Javanese together formed a majority in Dutch Guiana. By 1921 Indians were a third or more of the population of Trinidad and Fiji and continued to outnumber European settlers in Natal. Similarly Japanese and Chinese remained over half the population of Hawaii through the first quarter of the twentieth

[13]*PP* 1898 1 [c.8655], Report of the West India Royal Commission, 1897, pp. 26, 38–39. Tinker, *New System of Slavery*, pp. 314–15, 364. The clearest exception was Fiji, whose economy strongly favored continuing indentured labor and was in consequence the last major employer of Indian laborers to abrogate indentured contracts

[14]The Chinese population in Cuba declined until the turn of the century, then expanded as the result of large new migrations in the early twentieth century. The number of Chinese in British Guiana fell from 6,880 in 1871 to 2,622 in 1911, thereafter rising slowly due to new immigration; Look Lai, *Indentured Labour*, p. 301. Despite their amalgamation with the larger population, Schuler, "Alas, Alas, Kongo," p. 8, was still able to locate descendants of African migrants to Jamaica in 1971.

Table 6.1. *Share of total population in selected territories deriving from indentured migration, 1900-1960*

	1900-1	1920-21	1940-44	1957-60
Indians in Mauritius[a]	70%	71%	63%	67%
Indians in Trinidad[b]	32	33		36
Indians in British Guiana[b]	38 (1891)	42		48
Indians in Fiji[c]	15	40		49
Japanese in Hawaii[d]	40	43	37	32
Chinese in Hawaii[d]	17	9	7	6

Sources: (a) Auguste Toussaint, *Histoire des iles Mascareignes* (Paris: Berger-Levrault, 1972), pp. 335-36; (b) Walton Look Lai, *Indentured Labor, Caribbean Sugar: Chinese and West Indian Migrants to the British West Indies, 1838-1918* (Baltimore: Johns Hopkins University Press, 1993), tables 32-33; (c) Brij V. Lal, *Broken Waves: A History of the Fiji Islands in the Twentieth Century* (Honolulu: University of Hawaii Press, 1992), pp. 18, 33, 38, 63; (d) Franklin Odo and Kazuko Sinoto, *A Pictoral History of the Japanese in Hawai'i, 1885-1924* (Honolulu: Bishop Museum Press, 1985), pp. 18-19. All statistics for 1957-60 are from Chandra Jayawardena, "Migration and Social Change: A Survey of Indian Communities Overseas," *Geographical Journal* 58.3 (1968): table 1.

century until their proportions were diluted by the arrival of new Caucasian and Filipino migrants. Where the sexes were not too out of balance, natural reproduction equalized the proportion of females in the migrant population within a few decades. In the case of Japanese in Hawaii this process was accelerated by sending for "picture brides," a process that helped transform the male-to-female sex ratio from 4 to 1 under indenture in the 1890s to 3 to 2 by 1920. Less vulnerable to the diseases that had afflicted the first arrivals, generations born in the new lands flourished and sometimes (e.g., in Fiji and Hawaii) surpassed the growth rate of indigenous populations.[15]

The economic and social development of such substantial and self-sustaining expatriate communities was affected by the cultural heritage the migrants brought with them and by the opportunities open to them in their new homes. The Japanese in Hawaii benefited from both circumstances. As the result of the rapid growth in education in their homeland during the late nineteenth century, Japanese migrants arriving in Hawaii possessed a high degree of literacy and a devotion to formal education. In 1896 69 percent of male Japanese migrants in Hawaii were already literate, as were 25 percent of the females. After indenture they moved into a broad

[15]Odo and Sinoto, *Pictorial History of the Japanese,* p. 75.

Table 6.2. *Distribution of occupations after indenture, 1899-c.1938 (as percentage of total employed)*

	Chinese in Cuba 1899[a]	Chinese in Hawaii 1930[b]	Indians in British Guiana 1899[c]	Indians in Trinidad late 1930s[d]	Japanese in Hawaii 1926[e]
Agriculture				68	
laborers	53	27	77		39
owners, farmers		4	15		8
Servants	20	13	2	2	13
Day laborers (non-farm)				13	9
Commerce	20	35	3	6	11
Industry, construction	2	11	3	5	14
Learned professions	<1	5	<1	1	3
Other	5	6	<1	5	2

Sources: (a) Duvon Clough Corbitt, *A Study of the Chinese in Cuba, 1847-1947* (Wilmore, Ky.: Asbury College, 1971), pp. 92-94. (b) Clarence E. Glick, *Sojourners and Settlers: Chinese Migrants in Hawaii* (Honolulu: University Press of Hawaii, 1980), table 3. (c) Walton Look Lai, *Indentured Labor, Caribbean Sugar: Chinese and West Indian Migrants to the British West Indies, 1838-1918* (Baltimore: Johns Hopkins University Press, 1993), table 21. (d) Yogendra K. Malik, *East Indians in Trinidad: A Study in Minority Politics* (London: Oxford University Press, 1971), table 1.4. (e) Franklin Odo and Kazuko Sinoto, *A Pictoral History of the Japanese in Hawai'i, 1885-1924* (Honolulu: Bishop Museum Press, 1985), table 18.

spectrum of occupations in Hawaii's expanding economy and, as the example cited at the beginning of this chapter suggests, with the aid of successful Japanese residents who had not come as contract laborers, they educated their children in schools that transmitted both Japanese and Western cultural values. In 1920 16 percent of the entire Japanese population in Hawaii was attending school.[16] As Table 6.2 shows, a significant number of Japanese (in comparison to other migrant groups) also managed to enter the learned professions at an early date.

Chinese in Hawaii followed a pattern of occupational development similar to the Japanese, except for a higher proportion going into commerce. While this trajectory was partially due to the opportunities Hawaii offered, it does not appear to be explainable exclusively by that circumstance since the occupational profile of Chinese in Cuba a quarter century after the end of indenture is remarkably similar, with the notable absence of the learned professions. In part because of their smaller numbers Chinese in Cuba, Peru, and the British Caribbean were more likely than

[16]Odo and Sinoto, *Pictorial History of the Japanese,* pp. 127, 131.

Indians to lose their language, change religions, and marry outside their ethnic group.[17]

In contrast to the East Asians, Indian communities overseas generally underwent less rapid social change, even though they were larger and had emerged much earlier. In 1871 there were nearly 17,000 unindentured Indians resident in Trinidad (61 percent of the Indian community), 10,000 in British Guiana (23 percent), and 134,000 in Mauritius (61 percent). By 1910–11 the number of Indians not under indenture had grown to 96,000 in Trinidad (89 percent), almost 118,000 in British Guiana (93 percent), and 258,000 in Mauritius (100 percent).[18] In all three colonies, most Indians remained rural residents, working on their own or other persons' land.[19] This situation reflected the Indians' strong preference for becoming rural landowners as well as their more limited opportunities for advancement in these colonies compared with those in Hawaii. Moreover, Indian communities did not consider schools as means of social mobility until well into the twentieth century. As late as 1970 the proportion of Indo-Trinidadians, for example, with no formal education was ten times as high as for Afro-Trinidadians and as a consequence Indians were the most economically depressed ethnic group in Trinidad. The explanation partly reflects the absence of a literate tradition among most Indian migrants, who, as rural residents, also had limited access to schools. Cultural differences seem to have played an important role as well: long after the end of indenture most Indians remained aloof from both European and African cultures and tended to define career aspirations within the limits of caste status. Compared with East Asian migrants, both Hindu and Muslim Indians seem to have been more fearful of the cultural destructiveness of the Christian-dominated educational systems in their new homes. But in contrast to the Japanese in Hawaii, they lacked the financial resources (and strong motivation) to set up their own schools. As a result, in 1931 most Indians literate in English in Trinidad were Christians.[20]

[17]Look Lai, pp. 204–16, suggests that because of this greater acculturation and smaller numbers there was little friction between Chinese and persons of African descent, except in Jamaica.

[18]Look Lai, *Indentured Labour*, pp. 220–22, 283; *PP* 1873 xlviii [c.709-I], Report of the Protector of Immigrants, Mauritius, 1871.

[19]Even in the early 1960s, 87% of Indians in British Guiana were rural as were 80% of the Hindus and 57% of the Indo-Muslims of Mauritius, far higher than other segments of these populations; Peter Newman, *British Guiana* (London: Oxford University Press, 1964), table 5a; Burton Benedict, *Mauritius* (London: Praeger, 1965), p. 23.

[20]Dwarka Nath, *A History of Indians in British Guiana* (London: Thomas Nelson & Sons, 1950), pp. 166–68; Raymond T. Smith, *British Guiana* (London: Oxford University Press, 1962), pp. 108–12. Winston Dookerman, "East Indians and the Economy of Trinidad and Tobego," pp. 79–80; Kelvin Singh, "East Indians and the Larger Society," pp. 59–60, 67 n. 25; Bridget Brereton, "The Experience of Indentureship, 1845–1917," pp. 32–37; all three in John Gaffar LaGuerre, ed., *Calcutta to Caroni: The East Indians of Trinidad* (Trinidad: Longman Caribbean, 1974).

Contrasts within Indian communities were notable. The many fine distinctions of caste observed in India tended to be subsumed into the four broader orders or *varnas* of Hinduism, but these distinctions, as well as those between Hindus and Muslims and between North and South Indians, were usually maintained by marriage patterns. Language differences also reinforced distinctions. In the 1960s most Indians in Mauritius spoke an Indian language at home, with Hindi (Hindustani) predominating, but Marathi, Tamil, Telugu, Gujarati, and Urdu were also represented. In Natal hybridized versions of Hindi and Tamil evolved, with English serving as an important second language.[21] Contrasts among Indian communities were also notable. Those on Fiji and Natal became more highly urbanized and educated by the mid-twentieth century, in part because of restrictions against their ability to own land.[22] Even closely situated Indian communities in the Caribbean developed in quite different ways, often in complete ignorance of each other's existence.[23]

While the new Asian communities differed substantially in the direction and speed of their cultural evolution, they nevertheless shared some common features. All formed part of distinctly "plural societies," societies with sharply defined communities distinguished by "racial" and ethnic identities and, less rigidly, by cultural norms.[24] Naturally degrees of cleavage varied. Indian communities generally distanced themselves from the older African populations, though culturally they were drawn more toward the dominant European population. Both Indians and Africans in the West Indies showed hostility to the Portuguese migrants' rapid economic success. While often cited as one of the most harmonious multicultural societies in the world, Hawaii was also home to many forms of discrimination and antagonism, especially before the middle of the twentieth century. Another common feature of migrant communities overseas was their distancing from their home communities as well. In this they shared the common experience of other expatriate communities.

[21]Benedict, *Mauritius*, p. 40; Hilda Kuper, "'Strangers' in Plural Societies: Asians in South Africa and Uganda," in *Pluralism in Africa*, ed. Leo Kuper and M. G. Smith (Berkeley: University of California Press, 1971), p. 256.
[22]David Welch, "The Growth of Towns," in *Oxford History of South Africa*, ed. Monica Wilson and Leonard Thompson (Oxford: Oxford University Press, 1971), 2:179; Robert Norton, *Race and Politics in Fiji*, 2nd ed. (St. Lucia: University of Queensland Press, 1990), pp. 22–26; Brij V. Lal, *Broken Waves: A History of the Fiji Islands in the Twentieth Century* (Honolulu: University of Hawaii Press, 1992), pp. 85–86, 159, 229–31.
[23]V. S. Naipaul, himself descended from indentured Indian migrants to Trinidad, expressed great surprise at learning during a 1961 visit to Martinique that there had been a large indentured Indian migration there in the nineteenth century (of whose descendants only four or five thousand remained): *The Middle Passage* (New York: Vintage Press, 1981), pp. 204–5. This interesting volume records his impressions of Trinidad, British Guiana, Surinam, Martinique, and Jamaica.
[24]M. G. Smith, *The Plural Society in the British West Indies* (Berkeley: University of California Press, 1965); Kuper and Smith, *Pluralism in Africa*.

Another way to assess the legacy of indentured migration is to consider what replaced it as a labor system. As with the legacy of the migrants themselves, this is a vast subject. Like the end of slavery, the end of indentured labor was less a sharp break with the past than a redirecting of the forces that produced it under a new legal mandate in a partially altered economy. The demand for migrant labor was certainly not over, though in many of the largest importing colonies the indentured migration had created a sufficient demographic base. In South Africa there was growing mobilization of local African labor as well as that of migrants from neighboring colonies (especially Mozambique for the mines). The colonies of East Africa also adopted policies of taxation and labor recruitment that enabled them to rely upon their own growing populations for low-wage labor. To deal with the labor shortages resulting from the ending of both slavery and indentured labor, the Cuban sugar industry adopted the *colonato* system by which leaseholders produced sugarcane for a central factory. Unindentured migrants became increasingly important in the early twentieth century, including a half million poor Europeans from the Canary Islands and Spain during the two decades after 1898, 150,000 Chinese between 1902 and 1924, and migrants from neighboring Haiti and Jamaica beginning during World War I.[25] Hawaii and Australia also saw large new migrations of unindentured persons (including large numbers of Europeans) that enabled them to meet their labor needs. As was indicated in Chapter 2, the sugar industry also reduced its labor needs through the mechanization of many processes.

The second half of the twentieth century has witnessed even greater population movements than the half century before World War I, and with many similar features. Rapid population growth and deficiencies of local economic development in Asia, Africa, and Latin America have pushed many people to migrate regionally or to other continents. New advances in transportation have continued the pattern of falling costs and rising speed begun in the nineteenth century, which have facilitated such migrations. The demand for guest workers has been a feature of maturing industrial economies and of modern agrobusiness, sometimes with patterns of ill-treatment reminiscent of indentured labor.[26]

Such circumstances foster the flood of migrants from North Africa and the Middle East into Europe, from Islamic South and Southeast Asia into the oil-rich Middle East, from Mexico and Central America into the United States. In 1993 there was an almost perfect approximation of the motiva-

---

[25]Duvon Clough Corbitt, *A Study of the Chinese in Cuba, 1847–1947* (Wilmore, Ky: Asbury College, 1971), pp. 105, 117; Louis A. Pérez, Jr., *Cuba: Between Reform and Revolution* (New York: Oxford University Press, 1988), pp. 13–14, 202.

[26]See Alec Wiliamson, *Big Sugar: Seasons in the Cane Fields of Florida* (New York: Alfred A. Knopf, 1989).

tions and circumstances of indentured labor trade as young Chinese sold themselves into debt bondage and endured long voyages in crowded ships in a desperate effort to reach the employment Mecca of North America. While the motives and the means behind such migrations may be similar, what is different, of course, is that only in exceptional cases does modern labor migration duplicate the experiences common to indentured laborers in the nineteenth century, just as it was only in exceptional cases that indentured labor duplicated the experiences of slavery.

This study has sought to present the larger experience of indentured labor as a distinct historical phenomenon. It was not a continuation of slavery, though, like slavery, it was largely concerned with sugar production, largely confined to non-Europeans, and was abolished in a campaign that stressed its incompatibility with humane standards of free labor. Indentured labor was also distinct from the larger European migration of the nineteenth century in its composition, in its destinations, and in its legal circumstances. Yet indentured migrants' motives in emigrating, the voyages that carried them, and their struggles to establish a new life once their contract was over do resemble those of "free" migrants and deserve to be included in that larger story.

Appendix A: Tables A.1–A.6

Table A.1. *Decadal exports of indentured migrants by origins, showing intended destinations, 1831-1920.*

source↓		1831-40	1841-50	1851-60	1861-70	1871-80	1881-90	1891-1900	1901-10	1911-20	Total
Africans		**3,212**	**27,427**	**54,763**	**10,630**						**96,032**
British Caribbean	A	3,212	26,827	4,963	4,330						39,332
Réunion	B		600	36,600							37,200
French Caribbean	C			13,200	6,300						19,500
Chinese			**5,672**	**96,669**	**137,786**	**60,849**	**16,196**	**5,791**	**63,938**		**386,901**
British Caribbean	D			5,064	11,938	904	681				18,587
French Caribbean	B			2,250							2,250
Dutch Guiana	E			518	2,361	100					2,979
Cuba	E		612	58,460	65,013	14,071					138,156
Peru	E		2,260	24,355	55,966	34,851					117,432
Mauritius	E		600	250							850
Réunion	B		1,350								1,350
Tahiti	E				1,100						1,100
Transvaal	F								63,938		63,938
Queensland	E		850	5,100							5,950
Hawaii	G			672	1,408	10,923	15,515	5,791			34,309
Europeans		**3,451**	**25,140**	**13,830**	**205**	**931**	**11,534**	**936**			**56,027**
British Caribbean	A	3,451	23,960	13,555							40,966
French Caribbean	B		1,180								1,180
Dutch Guiana	H			275	205						480
Hawaii	G					931	11,534	936			13,401
Indians	I	**26,396**	**132,738**	**276,930**	**193,187**	**186,180**	**138,435**	**170,430**	**162,260**	**49,474**	**1,336,030**
British Guiana		396	12,075	22,713	39,674	52,212	38,867	39,827	23,918	9,179	238,861
Trinidad			5,512	16,516	19,903	25,147	24,085	23,603	24,548	10,309	149,623

	1	2	3	4	5	6	7	8	9	Total
Jamaica		4,615	2,412	8,142	8,569	2,676	4,020	5,265	2,896	38,595
Other BWI			2,714	4,307	2,278	1,693	160			11,152
Mauritius	26,000	93,360	188,372	69,669	37,923	19,299	8,706	11,858		455,187
Reunion		17,176	31,171	15,005	7,807	3,695				74,854
French Caribbean			12,250	28,855	27,238	10,746				79,089
Dutch Guiana					6,251	8,100	7,586	8,525	4,041	34,503
East Africa							*34,177*	*2,251*	*3,009*	*39,437*
Natal				7,632	18,257	20,004	39,943	63,695	3,401	152,932
Fiji					498	9,270	12,408	22,200	16,639	61,015
Japanese				**148**		**11,664**	**54,012**	**7,146**	**12,232**	**85,202**
Peru J							*790*	*7,146*	*12,232*	*20,168*
Hawaii G				*148*		*11,664*	*53,222*			*65,034*
Javanese			**8**	**21**	**94**	**94**	**3,470**	**6,558**	**9,085**	**19,330**
Dutch Guiana K			*8*	*21*	*94*	*94*	*3,470*	*6,558*	*9,085*	*19,330*
Pacific Islanders				**10,772**	**30,727**	**35,378**	**13,207**	**5,845**	**114**	**96,043**
Peru L				*3,470*						*3,470*
Queensland M				3,667	16,373	26,755	12,065	3,935		62,795
Fiji N				3,444	12,837	7,887	1,142	1,910	114	27,334
Hawaii G				*191*	*1,517*	*736*				*2,444*
North Americans	**1,367**	**297**		**178**						**1,842**
British Caribbean A	*1,367*	*297*		*178*						*1,842*
Totals	**34,426**	**191,274**	**441,418**	**352,927**	**278,781**	**213,301**	**247,846**	**245,747**	**70,905**	**2,076,625**

Note: Figures in italics are arrivals.

(continued)

Table A.1 continued

Sources: (A) G. W. Roberts and J. Byrne, "Summary Statistics on Indenture and Associated Migration Affecting the West Indies, 1843-1918," *Population Studies* 20.1 (1966): tables 2-8. (B) François Renault, *Libération d'esclaves et nouvelle servitude: Les rachats de captifs africains pour le compte des colonies françaises après l'abolition de l'esclavage* (Abidjan: Nouvelles Editions Africaines, 1976), pp. 16-17, 42, 72, 176-77, plus an allowance for estimated losses in transit. (C) David Eltis, *Economic Growth and the Ending of the Transatlantic Slave Trade* (New York: Oxford University Press, 1987), table A8, with an addition for estimated losses in transit and an estimate for 1831-50. (D) Walton Look Lai, *Indentured Labor, Caribbean Sugar: Chinese and Indian Migrants to the British West Indies, 1838-1918* (Baltimore: Johns Hopkins University Press, 1993), table 23. (E) Arnold J. Meagher, "The Introduction of Chinese Laborers to Latin America: The 'Coolie Trade,' 1847-1874," (Ph.D. dissertation, University of California, Davis, 1975), tables 4, 7, 13, 14, 24, 48, 49. Where departure figures are lacking (notably in the trade to Peru) an estimate has been added based on the average losses and passenger loads for the decade. (F) Peter Richardson, *Chinese Mine Labour in the Transvaal* (London: Macmillan, 1982), p. 197. (G) Katharine Coman, *The History of Contract Labor in the Hawaiian Islands* (New York: Arno Press, 1978), p. 63. (H) K. O. Laurence, *Immigration into the West Indies in the Nineteenth Century* (Kingston: Caribbean University Press, 1971), pp. 43-45. (I) Walter F. Willcox, ed., *International Migrations* (New York: National Bureau of Economic Research, 1929), 1:904-5, with these additions and modifications: the distribution to Trinidad, Jamaica, and other BWI in 1871-80 are based on the arrival series in Roberts and Byrne, "Summary Statistics on Indenture"; Great Britain, *Statistical Abstract Concerning British India* (London H. M. Stationery Office, 1840ff), has also been used for departures to other BWI in 1891-1900, to the French Caribbean, and to Natal; departures to Mauritius in 1834-39 are from *Parliamentary Papers* 1846 (691-II), Second Report of the Committee, p. 160, plus an estimate of mortality; arrival figures in Réunion for 1844-60 are from Hubert Gerbeau, "Engagées and coolies on Réunion Island: Slavery's Masks and Freedom's Constraints," in Emmer, ed., *Colonialism and Migration*, 216, 224. (J) Willcox, *International Migrations*, 1:938. (K) Willcox, *International Migrations*, 1: 537. (L) H. E. Maude, *Slavers in Paradise: The Peruvian Slave Trade in Polynesia, 1862-64* (Stanford: Stanford University Press, 1981), table 6. (M) Return of the Number of South Sea Islanders Introduced into Queensland, 11 August 1876, *Parliamentary Papers* 1877 lxi (29); Return Relating to Polynesian Labour during the Years 1886 to 1897; *Parliamentary Papers* 1899 lix (31); Ralph Shlomowitz, "Markets for Indentured and Time-Expired Melanesian Labour in Queensland, 1863-1906: An Economic Analysis," *Journal of Pacific History* 22.1 (1987): table 9. (N) Shlomowitz, "Mortality and the Pacific Labour Trade," table 7, with missing years completed from Ralph Shlomowitz, "The Fiji Labor Trade in Comparative Perspective, 1864-1914," *Pacific Studies* 9 (1986): table 6, and with an allowance appropriate for each decade for migrants who were rejected or who died before signing contracts.

Table A.2. Decadal imports of indentured migrants by destinations, showing origins, 1831-1920.

	source↓	1831-40	1841-50	1851-60	1861-70	1871-80	1881-90	1891-1900	1901-10	1911-20	Total
British Caribbean		**8,426**	**72,844**	**67,449**	**85,764**	**85,086**	**68,948**	**64,934**	**54,803**	**21,150**	**529,404**
Europeans	A	3,451	23,960	13,555							40,966
N. Americans	A	1,367	297		178						1,842
Africans	A	3,212	26,827	4,963	4,330						39,332
Indians	A	396	21,760	44,183	69,777	84,183	68,268	64,934	54,803	21,150	429,454
Chinese	B			4,748	11,479	903	680				17,810
Mauritius		**25,403**	**94,272**	**184,289**	**71,292**	**37,829**	**19,178**	**8,194**	**12,145**		**452,602**
Indians	C	25,403	93,690	184,055	71,292	37,829	19,178	8,194	12,145		451,786
Chinese	D		582	234							816
Réunion			**19,015**	**65,598**	**15,005**	**7,807**	**3,695**				**111,120**
Africans	E		574	33,645							34,219
Indians	F		17,176	31,953	15,005	7,807	3,695				75,636
Chinese	E		1,265								1,265
French Caribbean			**1,180**	**26,879**	**34,755**	**27,238**	**10,746**				**100,798**
Africans	G			12,500	5,900						18,400
Indians	H			12,250	28,855	27,238	10,746				79,089
Chinese	E			2,129							2,129
Europeans	E		1,180								1,180
French Pacific					**1,035**						**1,035**
Chinese	D				1,035						1,035
Dutch Guiana				**801**	**2,447**	**6,763**	**8,727**	**9,782**	**15,043**	**13,588**	**57,151**
Indians	I				2,221	6,569	8,633	6,312	8,485	4,503	34,502
Chinese	D			518		100	94				2,839
Javanese	I			8	21			3,470	6,558	9,085	19,330
Europeans	I			275	205	94					480

(continued)

Table A.2 continued

	source↓	1831-40	1841-50	1851-60	1861-70	1871-80	1881-90	1891-1900	1901-10	1911-20	Total
Cuba			**571**	**49,330**	**58,991**	**12,918**					**121,810**
Chinese	D		571	49,330	58,991	12,918					121,810
Peru			**1,500**	**20,000**	**47,116**	**32,000**		790	**5,311**	**11,663**	**118,380**
Chinese	H		1,500	20,000	45,000	32,000					98,500
Japanese	J							790	5,311	11,663	17,764
Pacific Islanders	K				2,116						2,116
Africa					**6,445**	**17,834**	**20,134**	**72,662**	**130,167**	**8,074**	**255,316**
Natal: Indians	L				6,445	17,834	20,134	38,485	64,221	5,065	152,184
Transvaal: Chinese	M								63,695		63,695
East Africa: Indians	H							34,177	2,251	3,009	39,437
Queensland			**780**	**4,350**	**3,667**	**16,265**	**26,621**	**12,054**	**3,935**		**67,672**
Chinese	D		780	4,350							5,130
Pacific Islanders	N				3,667	16,265	26,621	12,054	3,935		62,542
Fiji					**3,349**	**12,915**	**14,930**	**12,276**	**23,350**	**15,640**	**82,460**
Indians	O					410	7,395	11,161	21,504	15,530	56,000
Pacific Islanders	P				3,349	12,505	7,535	1,115	1,846	110	26,460
Hawaii	Q			**672**	**1,747**	**13,371**	**39,449**	**59,949**			**115,188**
Chinese				672	1,408	10,923	15,515	5,791			34,309
Japanese							11,664	53,222			65,034
Europeans					148	931	11,534	936			13,401
Pacific Islanders					191	1,517	736				2,444
Total		33,829	190,162	419,368	331,613	270,026	212,428	240,641	244,754	70,115	2,012,936

Note: Figures in italics are departures.

Table A.2 continued

Sources: (A) G. W. Roberts and J. Byrne, "Summary Statistics on Indenture and Associated Migration Affecting the West Indies, 1843-1918," *Population Studies* 20.1 (1966): tables 2-8. Indian arrivals in British Guiana are from Dwarka Nath, *A History of Indians in British Guiana* (London: Thomas Nelson & Sons, 1950), table 1. (B) Walton Look Lai, *Indentured Labor, Caribbean Sugar: Chinese and Indian Migrants to the British West Indies, 1838-1918* (Baltimore: Johns Hopkins University Press, 1993), table 23. (C) Larry W. Bowman, *Mauritius: Democracy and Development in the Indian Ocean* (Boulder, Colo.: Westview Press, 1991), table 2.2. (D) Arnold J. Meagher, "The Introduction of Chinese Laborers to Latin America: The 'Coolie Trade,' 1847-1874," (Ph.D. dissertation, University of California, Davis, 1975), tables, 4, 7, 13-14, 24, 48-49. (E) François Renault, *Libération d'esclaves et nouvelle servitude: Les rachats de captifs africains pour le compte des colonies françaises après l'abolition de l'esclavage* (Abidjan: Nouvelles Editions Africaines, 1976), pp. 16-17, 42, 72, 176-77. (F) Hubert Gerbeau, "Engagées and coolies on Réunion Island: Slavery's Masks and Freedom's Constraints," in Emmer, ed., *Colonialism and Migration,* pp. 216, 224; Table A.1 above. (G) David Eltis, *Economic Growth and the Ending of the Transatlantic Slave Trade* (New York: Oxford University Press, 1987), table 8A. (H) Table A.1 above (with allowances for mortality in the case of Chinese to Peru). (I) Walter F. Willcox, ed., *International Migrations,* vol. 1: *Statistics,* (New York: National Bureau of Economic Research, 1929), 1: 537. (J) Toraje Irie, "History of Japanese Migration to Peru," *Hispanic American Historical Review* 31.3-4 (1951): 444, 651-52, 659. (K) H. E. Maude, *Slavers in Paradise: The Peruvian Slave Trade in Polynesia, 1862-64* (Stanford: Stanford University Press, 1981), table 6. (L) Surendra Bhana, *Indentured Indian Emigrants to Natal 1860-1902* (New Delhi: Promilla, 1991), p. 2, with interpolations for decadal divisions. (M) Richardson, *Chinese Mine Labor,* p. 197. (N) Return of the Number of South Sea Islanders Introduced into Queensland, 11 August 1876, *Parliamentary Papers* 1877 lxi (29); Return Relating to Polynesian Labour during the Years 1886 to 1897; *Parliamentary Papers* 1899 lix (31); Ralph Shlomowitz, "Markets for Indentured and Time-Expired Melanesian Labour in Queensland, 1863-1906: An Economic Analysis," *Journal of Pacific History* 16.2 (1981): p. 74, and "Mortality and the Pacific Labour Trade," *Journal of Pacific History* 22.1 (1987): table 9. (O) Shlomowitz, "Mortality and the Pacific Labour Trade," table 1. (P) Ralph Shlomowitz, "The Fiji Labor Trade in Comparative Perspective, 1864-1914," *Pacific Studies* 9 (1986): table 6. (Q) Katharine Coman, *The History of Contract Labor in the Hawaiian Islands* (New York: Arno Press, 1978), p. 63.

Table A.3. *Indentured migration from British India, 1855-65, suggesting the impact of the 1857 Rebellion*

Season	From Calcutta	From Madras	From Bombay	Total
1855-56	9,942	6,673	700	17,315
1856-57	7,242	4,800	513	12,555
1857-58	12,531	6,244	1,983	20,758
1858-59	23,312	15,461	6,252	45,025
1859-60	25,590	12,461	3,471	41,777
1860-61	14,533	6,479	860	21,872
1861-62	22,600	6,804	0	29,404
1862-63	7,825	4,665	0	12,490
1863-64	6,189	4,371	706	11,266
1864-65	13,485	7,124	936	21,545

Source: Statistical Abstract for British India, 1867, 1870, 1874. Season runs from 1 May to 30 April.

Table A.4. *Ship size and passenger density in nineteenth-century transoceanic voyages (number of voyages in parentheses)*

Voyagers and sources	Period	Average tonnage	Average number of passengers per 100 tons
Enslaved			
Africans to the Americas[a]	1821-1843	172 (538)	257 (267)
Indentured			
Africans to West Indies[b]	1848-1867	632 (41)	29 (112)
Indians to British West Indies[b]	1858-1873	968 (277)	42 (275)
Chinese to Cuba[c]	1847-1873	728 (207)	55 (342)
Chinese to Peru[c]	1865-1874	839 (127)	55 (162)
Chinese to British West Indies[c]	1852-1873	870 (48)	41 (48)
Free			
Europe to Quebec[a]	1851-1855	450 (1580)	26 (1580)

Sources: (a) Calculated from David Eltis, "Free and Coerced Transatlantic Migrations: Some Comparisons," *American Historical Review* 88.2 (1983): 271; (b) Calculated from records of the Colonial Land and Emigration Commission; (c) Calculated from Arnold J. Meagher, "The Introduction of Chinese Laborers to Latin America: The 'Coolie Trade,' 1847-1874," (Ph.D. dissertation, University of California, Davis, 1975), tables 13-15.

Table A.5. *Mortality on ocean voyages in the nineteenth century (number of voyages in parentheses)*

Routes and sources	Period	Deaths per 1,000	Average days en route	Mortality per month per 1,000
Enslaved				
West Africa to the Americas[a]	1811-1863	69.0 (687)	37 (584)	59.1
Indentured				
Africa to British West Indies[b]	1848-1867	35.2 (112)	32 (110)	31.0
India to British West Indies[b]	1851-1873	63.8 (350)	96 (347)	19.9
India to Mauritius[b]	1858-1868	21.6 (463)	38 (72)	17.0
India to Martinique[c]	1853-1858	27.1 (12)	85 (12)	7.7
China to Cuba[d]	1847-1873	118.4 (342)	120 (207)	31.4
China to Peru[d]	1849-1874	123.5 (178)	110 (113)	33.6
China to British West Indies[d]	1852-1873	50.0 (47)	104 (46)	14.1
Pacific Islands to Queensland[e]	1873-1894	11.1 (558)	111 (558)	3.0
Free/Convict				
Europe to New York[e]	1836-1853		c.45 (1077)	c 10.0
Britain to Australia (Convicts)[e]	1815-1868	9.8 (693)	122 (693)	2.4
Britain to Australia (Free)[e]	1838-1853		109 (258)	7.4

Sources: (a) Calculated from David Eltis, *Economic Growth and the Ending of the Transatlantic Slave Trade* (New York: Oxford University Press, 1987), pp. 133, 137. (b) Calculated from records of the Colonial Land and Emigration Commission. (c) *Parliamentary Papers* 1859 xxxiv [2569-I], no, 115, 116, 119: Lawless to Malmesbury, 12 May 1858, 13 October 1858, 27 January 1859. (d) Calculated from Arnold J. Meagher, "The Introduction of Chinese Laborers to Latin America: the 'Coolie Trade,' 1847-1874," (Ph.D. dissertation, University of California, Davis, 1975), tables 13-15, 25-47. (e) John McDonald and Ralph Shlomowitz, "Mortality on Chinese and Indian Voyages to the West Indies and South America, 1847-1874," *Social and Economic Studies* 41.2 (1992), table 3.

Table A.6. *Changing mortality patterns in the nineteenth century (number of voyages in parentheses)*

	Chinese to Americas	Chinese to Peru	Chinese to Cuba	Chinese to BWI	Indians to BWI	Africans to BWI
1846-50	53.6 (5)	105.4 (3)	16.5 (2)	none	11.0 (NA)	44.4 (55)
1851-55	26.0 (47)	22.7 (13)	26.3 (25)	26.9 (9)	13.0 (48)	11.4 (13)
1856-60	43.6 (123)	93.9 (6)	43.5 (109)	9.3 (9)	33.0 (78)	8.9 (16)
1861-65	35.1 (114)	65.7 (40)	20.3 (46)	13.1 (28)	22.6 (91)	9.9 (27)
1866-70	24.9 (180)	21.6 (50)	27.4 (128)	5.2 (2)	15.6 (93)	
1871-75	22.2 (87)	22.6 (55)	24.4 (31)	1.0 (1)	10.3 (40)	

Note: Chinese to Americas = Peru + Cuba + BWI (British West Indies). Mortality = deaths per thousand per month, based on the average population at risk.
Sources: For Chinese mortality: Arnold J. Meagher, "The Introduction of Chinese Laborers to Latin America: The 'Coolie Trade,' 1847-1874," (Ph.D. dissertation, History, University of California, Davis, 1975), tables 13-15, 25-47; for Indian and African mortality: the Colonial Land and Emigration Commission records.

Appendix B: Source notes for maps

Map 2 (Latin America). All figures are from Table A.2. The distribution among the individual colonies is based on the sources listed in that table's notes with Portuguese migrants counted only up to 1860 and 20% of Africans to the French Caribbean colonies allotted to French Guiana.

Map 4 (Oceania). Table A.2, with some additional destinations and the distributions by source from Doug Munro, "The Origins of Labourers in the South Pacific: Commentary and Statistics," pages xxxix–li in *Labour in the South Pacific,* edited by C. Moore, J. Leckie, and D. Munro (Townsville: Department of History and Politics and Melanesian Studies Centre, James Cook University of North Queensland, 1990). Munro's figures produce totals at slight variance with those in Table A.2. The breakdown by European origin is from Katharine Coman, *The History of Contract Labor into the Hawaiian Islands* (New York: Arno Press, 1978), p. 63.

Map. 5 (Africa and Europe). Figures are from Table A.1 and the sources listed there, with these additions: coastal origins of liberated Africans are from David Eltis, *Economic Growth and the Ending of the Transatlantic Slave Trade,* (New York: Oxford University Press, 1987), tables 3, 4.

Map 6 (South Asia). Intercontinental migrations from Table A.1. Regional migrations from Walter F. Willcox, ed., *International Migrations* (New York: National Bureau of Economic Research, 1929–31), I: 913 (Malaya), 916 (Ceylon), and Usha Mahanjani, *The Role of Indian Minorities in Burma and Malaya* (Westport, Conn.: Greenwood Press, 1973), p. 106 (Burma).

Map 7 (East Asia). All intercontinental migration figures are from Table A.1. Other Chinese migrations are from Willcox, *International Migrations*, 1: 262–72 (United States), 525–27 (Cuba), 913 (Straits Settlements), 929–31 (other Southeast Asia). The sources of migrants within China are from

Arnold J. Meagher, "Introduction of Chinese Laborers into Latin America: The 'Coolie Trade,' 1847–1874," (Ph.D. dissertation, History, University of California, Davis, 1975), map 2. Nonindentured Japanese migrations are from Yamamoto Ichihashi, "International Migrations of the Japanese," in Willcox, *International Migrations*, 2: table 270.

Bibliography

PUBLIC DOCUMENTS

Great Britain, *Parliamentary Papers (PP)*

1810–11 ii (225). Report from the Select Committee appointed to consider the practicality and expediency of supplying the West India Colonies with Free Labourers from the East.

1812 x (370). Papers Relating to a Recruiting Depôt on the Coast of Africa for the West India Regiments.

1821 xxiii (61). Annual Returns by the Collectors of Customs of Negroes that have been apprenticed [1807–19].

1824 xxiv (442). Number of Slaves Condemned to His Majesty under the Abolition Acts, 16 June 1824.

1826–27 vii (312) (552). Report of the Commissioners of Inquiry into the State of the Colony of Sierra Leone, 9 May 1827.

1841 xvi (45). Report of the Committee appointed by the Supreme Government of India to inquire into the Abuses alleged to exist in exporting from Bengal Hill Coolies and Indian Labourers, of various Castes, to other Countries; together with an Appendix, containing the oral and written Evidence taken by the Committee, and official Documents laid before them, 14 October 1840.

1841 xvi (427). Mr. J. P. Grant's Minute on the Abuses alleged to exist in the Export of Coolies; etc.

1842 xi–xii (551). Report from the Select Committee on the West Coast of Africa.

1842 xiii (479). Report from the Select Committee on the West India Colonies.

1843 xxxiv (438). Emigration to the West Indies: Papers relative to Emigration from the West Coast of Africa to the West Indies.

1844 xxxv (530). Correspondence relative to Emigration of Labourers to the West Indies and the Mauritius, from the West Coast of Africa, the East Indies, and China.

1846 xxviii (691-II). Papers relative to Immigration of Labourers into the West Indies and the Mauritius.

1847 xxxix (191). Emigration to the West Indies: Further Papers relative to Emigration from the West Coast of Africa to the West Indies.

1847 xxxix (496). Free Emigration into Jamaica, British Guiana, Trinidad and the Mauritius, since the Abolition of Slavery in 1834.

1847–48 xliv (732). Copy of the Reports made in 1844 and 1845, by Mr. R. G. Butts and Mr. Robert Guppy, as Commissioners of Inquiry into the Subject of Emigration from Sierra Leone to the West Indies.

1847–48 xlvi (749). Distress in the Sugar Growing Colonies: Correspondence regarding Sierra Leone.

1850 xl (643). Papers relative to the Emigration of Labourers from Sierra Leone and St. Helena to the West Indies.

1851 xl (625); 1852 xxxi (231). Number of Immigrants and Liberated Africans admitted into the Mauritius, for each year, 1849 to 1851, 1852.

1857–58 xxxvii (209). Letter of Mr. John Spence relative to the Enlistment of Krewmen, 11 March 1858.

1859 xvi [c.2452]. Papers relative to Emigration to the West India Colonies, August 1857.

1859 xxxiv [2569-I]. Slave Trade, Correspondence, class B.

1866 xxx–xxxi [c.3682]. Report of the Jamaica Royal Commission.

1871 xx [c.393]. Report of the Commissioners Appointed to Enquire into the Treatment of Immigrants in British Guiana.

1873 xlviii [c.709-I]. Report of the Protector of Immigrants, Mauritius, 1871.

1875 xxxiv–xxxv [c.1115]. Sir William Frere and Victor A. Williams, Report of the Royal Commission appointed to inquire into the treatment of immigrants in Mauritius, 1875.

1875 lxxi [c.1215]. Correspondence respecting Slavery in Cuba and Puerto Rico and the State of the Slave Population and Chinese Coolies in those Islands.

1877 lxi (29). Return of the Number of South Sea Islanders Introduced into Queensland, 11 August 1876.

1878 lxvii [c.2051]. Report on the Labour Question in Cuba, 1878, by H. Augustus Cowper.

1889 lviii (281). Government of India. Dispatch, dated 22nd day of June 1889, with enclosures, including Reports by Mr. Tucker.

1892 lvi [c.6686]. Correspondence relating to Polynesian Labour in the Colony of Queensland.

1893 lxi [c.6808 and 7000]. Further Correspondence relating to Polynesian Labour in the Colony of Queensland.

1893 lxi (342). Return relating to Polynesian Labour during the Years 1886–92.

1895 lxx [c.7912]. Further Correspondence relating to Polynesian Labour in the Colony of Queensland.

1897 lix (31). Return relating to Polynesian Labour during the Years 1886–97.

1898 l–li [c.8655–57, 8669, 8799]. Report of the West India Royal Commission. Four Volumes.

1910 xxvii [c.5192–94]. Report of the Committee on Emigration from India to the Crown Colonies and Protectorates (Sanderson Committee Report).

Other official British reports (printed in Parliamentary Papers)

General Reports of the Colonial Land and Emigration Commission (CLEC), 1841–73. State of the Colonies, Annual Reports, Bluebooks, etc.

SECONDARY WORKS

Adamson, Alan, H. *Sugar without Slaves: The Political Economy of British Guiana, 1838–1904.* New Haven: Yale University Press, 1972.

"The Reconstruction of Plantation Labor after Emancipation: The Case of British Guiana." Pages 457–73 in *Race and Slavery in the Western Hemisphere: Quantitative Studies,* edited by Stanley Engerman and Eugene Genovese. Princeton: Princeton University Press, 1975.

"The Impact of Indentured Immigration on the Political Economy of British Guiana." Pages 42–56 in Saunders, *Indentured Labour (see below).*

Adas, Michael. *The Burma Delta: Economic Development and Social Change on an Asian Rice Frontier, 1852–1941.* Madison: University of Wisconsin Press, 1974.

Alapatt, George K. "The Sepoy Mutiny of 1857: Indian Indentured Labour and Plantation Politics in British Guiana." *Journal of Indian History,* 59 (1981): 295–314.

Ankum-Houwink, J. "Chinese Contract Migrants in Surinam between 1853 and 1870." *Boletín de Estudios Latinoamericanos y del Caribe* 17 (1974): 42–68.

Ashworth, William. *A Short History of the International Economy since 1850.* 2nd ed. London: Longmans, 1962.

Asiegbu, Johnson U. J. *Slavery and the Politics of Liberation 1787–1861: A Study of Liberated African Emigration and British Anti-Slavery Policy.* London: Longman, 1969.

Baines, Dudley. *Emigration from Europe, 1815–1930.* London: Macmillan, 1991.

Barr, Pat. *The Coming of the Barbarians: A Story of Western Settlement in Japan, 1853–1870.* New York: Viking Penguin, 1988.

Barth, Gunther P. *Bitter Melons: A History of the Chinese in the United States, 1850–1870.* Cambridge, Mass.: Harvard University Press, 1964.

Bastid-Bruguiere, Marianne. "Currents of Social Change." Chapter 10 in *The Cambridge History of China.* Volume 11, *Late Ch'ing, 1800–1911,* part 2, edited by John K. Fairbank and Kwang-Ching Liu. Cambridge: Cambridge University Press, 1980.

Beall, Jo. "Women under Indentured Labour in Colonial Natal, 1860–1911." Chapter 6 in *Women and Gender in Southern Africa to 1945,* edited by Cheryl Walker. Cape Town: David Philip/London: James Currey, 1990.

Beechert, Edward D. *Working in Hawaii: A Labor History.* Honolulu: University of Hawaii Press, 1985.

Benedict, Burton. *Mauritius.* New York: F. A. Praeger, 1965.

Bennett, Judith A. "Immigration, 'Blackbirding,' Labour Recruiting? The Hawaiian Experience, 1877–1887." *Journal of Pacific History* 11.1–2 (1976): 3–27.

Bhana, Surendra. *Indentured Indian Emigrants to Natal, 1860–1902: A Study Based on Ships' Lists.* New Delhi: Promilla, 1991.

Blouet, Brian, and Olwyn M. Blouet. Review of *A New System of Slavery,* by Hugh Tinker. In *Caribbean Studies* 16.2 (1976): 251–53.

Bowman, Larry W. *Mauritius: Democracy and Development in the Indian Ocean.* Boulder, Colo.: Westview Press, 1991.

Brereton, Bridget. "The Experience of Indentureship: 1845–1917." Pages 25–38 in LaGuerre, *Calcutta to Caroni (see below).*

A History of Modern Trinidad 1783–1962. Kingston, Jamaica: Heinemann Educational Books, 1981.

Brooks, George E., Jr. *The Kru Mariner in the Nineteenth Century: An Historical Compendium.* Liberian Studies Monograph Series, no. 1. Newark, Del.: Liberian Studies Association in America, 1972.

Buckley, Roger Norman. *Slaves in Red Coats: The British West Indies Regiments, 1795–1815.* New Haven: Yale University Press, 1979.

Cadbury, William A. *Labour in Portuguese West Africa.* London: George Routledge & Sons, 1910.

Campbell, Persia Crawford. *Chinese Coolie Emigration to Countries within the British Empire*. London: P. S. King & Sons, 1923. Reprinted Taipei: Ch'eng Wen Publishing, 1970.

Carter, Marina, and Hubert Gebeau. "Covert Slaves and Covert Coolies in the Early 19th Century Mascareignes." Pages 194–208 in *Economics of Indian Ocean Slave Trade in the Nineteenth Century*, edited by William Gervase Clarence-Smith. London: Frank Cass, 1989.

Chan, Sucheng. "European and Asian Immigration into the United States in Comparative Perspective, 1820s to 1920s." Chapter 2 in *Immigration Reconsidered: History, Sociology, and Politics*, edited by Virginia Yans-McLaughlin. New York: Oxford University Press, 1990.

Chang-Rodríguez, Eugenio. "Chinese Labor Migration into Latin America in the Nineteenth Century." *Revista de Historia de América* [Mexico], 46 (1958): 375–99.

Char, Tin-Yuke, comp. and ed. *The Sandalwood Mountains: Readings and Stories of the Early Chinese in Hawaii*. Honolulu: University of Hawaii Press, 1975.

Charlesworth, Neil. *British Rule and the Indian Economy, 1800–1914*. London: Macmillan, 1982.

Ch'ên Lapin, A. MacPherson, and A. Huber. *Report of the Commission Sent by China to Ascertain the Condition of Chinese Coolies in Cuba*. Shanghai: Imperial Maritime Customs Press, 1876. Reprinted Taipei: Ch'eng Wen Publishing 1970.

Clarence-Smith, William Gervase. "The Portuguese Contribution to the Cuban Slave and Coolie Trades in the Nineteenth Century." *Slavery and Abolition* 5.1 (1984): 24–33.

"Cocoa Planting and Coerced Labor in the Gulf of Guinea, 1870–1914." Chapter 6 in Klein, *Breaking the Chains (see below)*.

"Chinese Immigration and Contract Labor in the Late Nineteenth Century." *Explorations in Economic History* 24.1 (1987): 22–42.

"Chinese Immigration: Reply to Charles McClain." *Explorations in Economic History* 28.2 (1991): 239–47.

Cohn Raymond L. "Deaths of Slaves in the Middle Passage." *Journal of Economic History* 45.3, (1985): 685–92.

"Determinants of Individual Immigrant Mortality on Sailing Ships, 1836–1853." *Explorations in Economic History* 24.4 (1987): 371–91.

"Maritime Mortality in the Eighteenth and Nineteenth Centuries: A Survey." *International Journal of Maritime History* 1.1 (1989): 159–91.

Coman, Katharine. *The History of Contract Labor in the Hawaiian Islands*. Publications of the American Economic Association, 3rd series, 4.3 (1903). Reprinted New York: Arno Press, 1978.

Conroy, Hilary. *The Japanese Frontier in Hawaii, 1868–1898*. Berkeley: University of California Press, 1953. Reprinted New York: Arno Press, 1978.

Corbitt, Duvon Clough. *A Study of the Chinese in Cuba, 1847–1947*. Wilmore, Ky.: Asbury College, 1971.

Corris, Peter. *Passage, Port and Plantation: A History of Solomon Islands Labour Migration, 1870–1914*. Carlton: Melbourne University Press, 1973.

Cowan, Helen I. *British Emigration to British North America: The First Hundred Years*. Rev. ed. Toronto: University of Toronto Press, 1961.

Curtin, Philip D. *Death by Migration: Europe's Encounter with the Tropical World in the Nineteenth Century*. Cambridge: Cambridge University Press, 1989.

Davis, David Brion. *Slavery and Human Progress*. New York: Oxford University Press, 1984.

Davis, Kingsley. *Population of India and Pakistan*. Princeton: Princeton University Press, 1951.

Dharma, Kumar. *Land and Caste in South India: Agricultural Labour in the Madras Presidency during the Nineteenth Century*. Cambridge Studies in Economic History. Cambridge: At the University Press, 1965.

"Colonialism, Bondage, and Caste in British India." Pages 112–30 in Klein, *Breaking the Chains (see below)*.

Denoon, Donald. "The Political Economy of Labour Migration to Settler Societies: Australia, Southern Africa, and Southern South America between 1890 and 1914." Pages 186–205 in Marks and Richardson, *International Labour Migration (see below)*.

Dookerman, Winston. "East Indians and the Economy of Trinidad and Tobago." Pages 69–83 in LaGuerre, *Calcutta to Caroni (see below)*.

Duffy, James. *A Question of Slavery*. Cambridge, Mass.: Harvard University Press, 1967.

Elson, R. E. *Javanese Peasants and the Colonial Sugar Industry: Impact and Change in an East Java Residency, 1830–1940*. Singapore: Oxford University Press, 1984.

"Sugar Factory Workers and the Emergence of 'Free Labour' in Nineteenth-Century Java." *Modern Asian Studies* 20.1 (1986): 139–74.

Eltis, David. "Free and Coerced Transatlantic Migrations: Some Comparisons." *American Historical Review* 88.2 (1983): 251–80.

"Mortality and Voyage Length in the Middle Passage: New Evidence from the Nineteenth Century." *Journal of Economic History* 44.2 (1984): 301–8.

Economic Growth and the Ending of the Transatlantic Slave Trade. New York: Oxford University Press, 1987.

Emmer, P. C. "The Importation of British Indians into Surinam (Dutch Guiana), 1873–1916." Pages 90–111 in Marks and Richardson, *International Labour Migration (see below)*.

"The Great Escape: The Migration of Female Indentured Servants from British India to Surinam, 1873–1916." Pages 245–66 in *Abolition and Its Aftermath: The Historical Context, 1790–1916*, edited by David Richardson. London: Frank Cass, 1985.

" 'The Meek Hindu': The Recruitment of Indian Indentured Labourers for Service Overseas, 1870–1916." Pages 187–207 in Emmer, *Colonialism and Migration (see below)*.

ed., *Colonialism and Migration: Indentured Labour before and after Slavery*. Comparative Studies in Overseas History, volume 7. The Hague: Martinus Nijhoff, 1986.

Engerman, Stanley. "Economic Adjustments to Emancipation in the United States and British West Indies." *Journal of Interdisciplinary History* 13 (1982): 191–220.

"Contract Labor, Sugar, and Technology in the Nineteenth Century." *Journal of Economic History* 43 (1983): 635–59.

"Economic Change and Contract Labor in the British Caribbean: The End of Slavery and the Adjustments to Emancipation." *Explorations in Economic History* 21.2 (1984): 133–50. Also pages 225–44 in *Abolition and Its Aftermath: The Historical Context, 1790–1916*, edited by David Richardson. London: Frank Cass, 1985.

"Servants to Slaves to Servants: Contract Labour and European Expansion." Pages 263–94 in Emmer, *Colonialism and Migration (see above)*.

"Coerced and Free Labor: Property Rights and the Development of the Labor Force." *Explorations in Economic History* 29.1 (1992): 1–29.

Firth, Stewart. "The Transformation of the Labour Trade in German New Guinea, 1899–1914." *Journal of Pacific History* 11.1–2 (1976): 51–65.

Fyfe, Christopher. *A History of Sierra Leone*. London: Oxford University Press, 1962.

Galenson, David W. "The Rise and Fall of Indentured Servitude in the Americas: An Economic Analysis." *Journal of Economic History* 44.1 (1984): 1–26.

Galloway, J. H. *The Sugar Cane Industry: An Historical Geography from Its Origins to 1914*. Cambridge: Cambridge University Press, 1989.

Garland, Charles, and Herbert S. Klein. "The Allotment of Space for African Slaves aboard Eighteenth-Century British Slave Ships." *William and Mary Quarterly* 42 (1985): 238–48.

Gerbeau, Hubert. "Engagées and Coolies on Réunion Island: Slavery's Masks and Freedom's Constraints." Pages 209–36 in Emmer, *Colonialism and Migration (see above)*.

Gilchriese, Harry L. "Managing 200,000 Coolies in France." *Current History* 11 (1919): 522–26.

Gillion, K. L. "The Sources of Indian Emigration to Fiji." *Population Studies* 10 (November 1956): 139–57.

Glick, Clarence E. *Sojourners and Settlers: Chinese Migrants in Hawaii*. Honolulu: Hawaiian Chinese Center and the University Press of Hawaii, 1980.

Gonzales, Michael J. *Plantation Agriculture and Social Control in Northern Peru, 1875–1933*. Austin: University of Texas Press, 1985.

Gootenberg, Paul. *Between Silver and Guano: Commercial Policy and the State in Postindependence Peru*. Princeton: Princeton University Press, 1989.

Graham, Gerald. "The Ascendency of the Sailing Ship, 1850–85." *Economic History Review* 9 (1956): 74–88.

Graves, Adrian. "The Nature and Origins of Pacific Labour Migration to Queensland, 1863–1906." Pages 112–39 in Marks and Richardson, *International Labour Migration (see below)*.

"Colonialism and Indentured Labour Migrations in the Western Pacific, 1840–1915." Pages 237–59 in Emmer, *Colonialism and Migration (see above)*.

Graves, Adrian, and Peter Richardson. "Plantations in the Political Economy of Colonial Sugar Production: Natal and Queensland, 1860–1914." *Journal of South African Studies* 6.2 (1980): 214–29.

Green, William A. "The West Indies and British West African Policy in the Nineteenth Century: A Corrective Comment." *Journal of African History* 15.2 (1974): 247–59.

British Slave Emancipation: The Sugar Colonies and the Great Experiment. Oxford: Clarendon Press, 1976.

"The West Indies and Indentured Labour Migration: The Jamaican Experience." Pages 1–41 in Saunders, *Indentured Labour (see below)*.

"Plantation Society and Indentured Labour: The Jamaican Case, 1834–1865." Pages 163–86 in Emmer, *Colonialism and Migration (see above)*.

Gregory, Robert G. *India and East Africa: A History of Race Relations within the British Empire, 1890–1939*. Oxford: Clarendon Press, 1971.

Grubb, Farley. "The Incidence of Servitude in Trans-Atlantic Migration, 1771–1804." *Explorations in Economic History* 22.3 (1985): 316–39.

Hall, Douglas. *Free Jamaica, 1838–1865: An Economic History*. New Haven: Yale University Press, 1959.

"Bountied European Immigration to Jamaica with Special Reference to the German Settlement of Seaford Town up to 1850." *Jamaica Journal* 8.4 (1974): 48–54 and 9.1 (1975): 7–24.

Harkness, D. A. E. "Irish Emigration." Chapter 10 in *International Migrations*, volume 2, edited by Walter F. Willcox. New York: National Bureau of Economic Research, 1931.

Hazama, Dorothy Ochiai, and Jane Okomoto Komeiji. *Okage Sama De: The Japanese in Hawai'i, 1885–1985*. Honolulu: Bess Press, 1986.

Headrick, Daniel. *The Tentacles of Progress: Technology Transfer in the Age of Imperialism, 1850–1940*. New York: Oxford University Press, 1988.

Higman, Barry W. "The Chinese in Trinidad, 1806–1838." *Caribbean Studies* 12.3 (1972): 21–44.

Slave Populations of the British Caribbean, 1807–1834. Baltimore: John Hopkins University Press, 1984.

Hirata, Lucie Cheng. "Free, Indentured, Enslaved: Chinese Prostitutes in Nineteenth-Century America." *Signs* 5.1 (1979): 3–29.

Hitchins, Fred Harvey. *The Colonial Land and Emigration Commission*. Philadelphia: University of Pennsylvania Press/London: Oxford University Press, 1931.

Hobsbawm, E. J. *The Age of Capital, 1848–1875*. New York; New American Library, 1979.

Hobson, J. A. *Imperialism: A Study*. London: A. Constable, 1902.

Hopkins, A. G. *An Economic History of West Africa*. New York: Columbia University Press, 1973.

Ichioka, Yuji. The Issei: The World of the First Generation Japanese Immigrants, 1885–1924. New York: Free Press/London: Collier Macmillan, 1988.

Irick, Robert L. *Ch'ing Policy, toward the Coolie Trade, 1847–1878*. San Francisco and Taipei: Chinese Materials Center, 1982.

Irie, Toraje. "History of Japanese Migration to Peru." Translated by William Himel. *Hispanic American Historical Review* 31.3–4 (1951): 437–52, 648–64.

Iriye, Akira. "Japan's Drive to Great Power Status." Pages 759–62 in *Cambridge History of Japan*, volume 5: *The Nineteenth Century*, edited by Marcus B. Jansen. Cambridge: Cambridge University Press, 1989.

Jayawardena, Chandra. "Migration and Social Change: A Survey of Indian Communities Overseas." *Geographical Journal* 58.3 (July 1968): 426–49.

Kimura, Yukiko. *Issei: Japanese Immigrants in Hawaii*. Honolulu: University of Hawaii Press, 1988.

Klein, Herbert S., and Stanley Engerman. "Slave Mortality on British Ships, 1791–1797." Chapter 6 in *Liverpool, the African Slave Trade, and Abolition*, edited by Roger Anstey and P. E. H. Hair. Liverpool: Historic Society of Lancashire and Cheshire, 1976.

Klein, Martin A. "Introduction: Modern European Expansion and Traditional Servitude in Africa and Asia." Pages 3–36 in Klein, *Breaking the Chains (see below)*.

ed., *Breaking the Chains: Slavery, Bondage, and Emancipation in Modern Africa and Asia*. Madison: University of Wisconsin Press, 1993.

Kuczynski, Robert Rene. *Demographic Survey of the British Colonial Empire*. Volume 3: *West Indies and American Territories*. London: Oxford University Press, 1953.

Kuper, Hilda. "'Strangers' in Plural Societies: Asians in South Africa and Uganda." Chapter 8 in *Pluralism in Africa*, edited by Leo Kuper and M. G. Smith. Berkeley: University of California Press, 1971.

LaFargue, Thomas E. *China and the World War*. Stanford: Stanford University Press, 1937.

LaGuerre, John Gaffar, editor. *Calcutta to Caroni: The East Indians of Trinidad*. Trinidad: Longman Caribbean, 1974.

Lal, Brij V. *Girmitiyas: The Origins of the Fiji Indians.* Canberra: Journal of Pacific History, Australian National University, 1983.

"Kunti's Cry: Indentured Women on Fiji Plantations." *Indian Economic and Social History Review* 22.1 (1985): 55–71. Reprinted pages 163–79 in *Women in Colonial India,* edited by J. Krishnamurty. Delhi: Oxford University Press, 1989.

"Veil of Dishonour: Sexual Jealousy on Fiji Plantations." *Journal of Pacific History* 20.3–4 (1985): 135–55.

Broken Waves: A History of the Fiji Islands in the Twentieth Century. Honolulu: University of Hawaii Press, 1992.

Latham, A. J. H. "Southeast Asia: A Preliminary Survey, 1800–1914." Pages 11–29 in *Migration across Time and Nations: Population Mobility in Historical Contexts,* edited by Ira Glazier and Luigi de Rosa. New York: Holmes and Meier, 1986.

Laurence. K. O. *Immigration into the West Indies in the Nineteenth Century.* Chapters in Caribbean History 3. Kingston, Jamaica: Caribbean University Press, 1971.

Lenin, V. I. *Imperialism: The Highest Stage of Capitalism.* Moscow: Foreign Language Publishing House, n.d.

Levin, Jonathan V. *The Export Economies: Their Pattern of Development in Historical Perspective.* Cambridge, Mass.: Harvard University Press, 1960.

Lewis, W. Arthur. *The Evolution of the International Economic Order.* Princeton: Princeton University Press, 1978.

Lockard, Craig A. "Repatriation Movements among Javanese in Surinam: A Comparative Analysis." *Caribbean Studies* 18.1–2 (1978): 85–113.

Look Lai, Walton. *Indentured Labor, Caribbean Sugar: Chinese and Indian Migrants to the British West Indies, 1838–1918.* Baltimore: Johns Hopkins University Press, 1993.

Lovejoy, Paul. *Transformations in Slavery: A History of Slavery in Africa.* Cambridge: Cambridge University Press, 1983.

Lubbock, Basil. *The China Clippers.* Glasgow: James Brown and Sons, 1914. Reprinted Taipei: Ch'eng-wen Publishing, 1966.

Ly-Tio-Fane Pineo, Huguette. *Lured Away: The Life History of Cane Workers in Mauritius.* Moka, Mauritius: Mahatama Gandhi Institute, 1984.

McCall, Grant. "European Impact on Eastern Island: Responses, Recruitment and the Polynesian Experience in Peru." *Journal of Pacific History* 11.1–2 (1976): 90–105.

McClain, Charles. J., Jr. "Chinese Immigration: A Comment on Cloud and Galenson." *Explorations in Economic History* 27.3 (1990): 363–78.

McDonald, John, and Ralph Shlomowitz. "Mortality on Immigrant Voyages to Australia, 1838–1892." *Explorations in Economic History* 27.1 (1990): 84–113.

"Mortality on Chinese and Indian Voyages to the West Indies and South America, 1847–1874." *Social and Economic Studies* 41.2 (1992): 203–40.

"Contract Prices for the Bulk Shipping of Passengers in Sailing Vessels, 1816–1904: An Overview." *International Journal of Maritime History* 5.1 (1993): 65–93.

Mahajani, Usha. *The Role of Indian Minorities in Burma and Malaya.* Bombay: Vora and Company, 1960. Reprint Westport, Connecticut: Greenwood Press, 1973.

Malik, Yogendra K. *East Indians in Trinidad: A Study in Minority Politics.* London Oxford University Press, 1971.

Mangat, J. S. *A History of the Asians in East Africa, c. 1886 to 1945.* Oxford: Clarendon Press, 1969.

Manning, Patrick. *Slavery and African Life: Occidental, Oriental, and the African Slave Trades.* Cambridge: Cambridge University Press, 1990.

Marks, Shula, and Peter Richardson, eds. *International Labour Migration: Historical Perspectives.* Hounslow, Middlesex: M. Temple Smith, 1984.

Masaoka Kodama. "Japanese Emigration to U.S.A. in the Meiji Era." *Shakai Keizai Shigaka* 47.4 (1981): 6–7.

Mathieson, William Law. *British Slave Emancipation, 1838–1949.* New York: Octagon Books, 1967.

Maude, Henry Evans. *Slavers in Paradise: The Peruvian Slave Trade in Polynesia, 1862–64.* Stanford: Stanford University Press / Canberra: Australian National University Press, 1981.

Meagher, Arnold Joseph. "The Introduction of Chinese Laborers to Latin America: The 'Coolie Trade,' 1847–1874." Ph.D. dissertation, History, University of California, Davis, 1975.

Meleisea, Malama. "The Last Days of the Melanesian Labour Trade in Western Samoa." *Journal of Pacific History* 11.1–2 (1976): 126–32.

Miers, Suzanne, and Richard Roberts, ed. *The End of Slavery in Africa.* Madison: University of Wisconsin Press, 1988.

Miller, Joseph C. "Mortality in the Atlantic Slave Trade: Statistical Evidence on Causality." *Journal of Interdisciplinary History* 11.3 (1981): 385–423.

Mintz, Sindey W. *Sweetness and Power: The Place of Sugar in Modern History.* New York: Viking Penguin, 1985.

Mokyr, Joel. *The Lever of Riches: Technological Creativity and Economic Progress.* New York: Oxford University Press, 1990.

Mörner, Magnus. *Race Mixture in the History of Latin America.* Boston: Little, Brown, 1967.

Mookherji, S. B. *The Indentured System in Mauritius, 1837–1915.* Calcutta: Firma K. L. Mukhopadhyay, 1962.

Moore, Brian L. "The Social Impact of Portuguese Immigration into British Guiana after Emancipation." *Boletín de Estudios Latinoamericanos y del Caribe* 19 (1975): 3–15.

Moore, Clive. *Kanaka: A History of Melanesian Mackay.* Port Moresby: Institute of Papua New Guinea Studies and University of Papua New Guinea Press, 1985.

"Labour and Historiography in the Pacific." Chapter 9 in *Pacific Islands History: Journeys and Transformations,* edited by Brij V. Lal. Canberra: Journal of Pacific History, 1992.

"Revising the Revisionists: The Historiography of Immigrant Melanesians in Australia." *Pacific Studies* 15.2 (1992): 61–86.

Morris, Morris D. "Towards a Reinterpretation of Nineteenth-Century Indian Economic History." *Journal of Economic History* 23.4 (1963): 606–18.

The Emergence of an Industrial Labor Force in India: A Study of the Bombay Cotton Mills, 1854–1947. Berkeley: University of California Press, 1965.

Morris, Morris D., T. Matsui, B. Chandra, and T. Raychaudhuri. *The Indian Economy in the Nineteenth Century: A Symposium.* New Delhi: Indian Economic and Social History Association 1969.

Munro, Doug. "The Origins of Labourers in the South Pacific: Commentary and Statistics." Pages xxxix–li in *Labour in the South Pacific,* edited by Clive Moore, Jacqueline Leckie, and Doug Munro. Townsville, Queensland: Department of History and Politics, and Melanesian Studies Centre, James Cook University of North Queensland, 1990.

"The Pacific Islands Labour Trade: Approaches, Methodologies, Debates." *Slavery and Abolition* 14.3 (1993): 87–108.

Murayama, Yuzo. "Information and Emigrants: Interprefectural Differences of

Japanese Emigration to the Pacific Northwest, 1880–1915." *Journal of Economic History* 51.1 (1991): 125–47.

Naipaul, V. S. The Middle Passage: Impressions of Five Societies – British, French, and Dutch – in the West Indies and South America. New York: Vintage Books, 1981.

Nath, Dwarka. *A History of Indians in British Guiana*. London: Thomas Nelson & Sons, 1950.

Newbury, Colin W. "Historical Aspects of Manpower and Migration in Africa South of the Sahara." Pages 523–45 in *Colonialism in Africa*, edited by Peter Duignan and L. H. Gann, volume 4. Cambridge: Cambridge University Press, 1975.

"Labour Migration in the Imperial Phase: An Essay in Interpretation." *Journal of Imperial and Commonwealth History* 3.2 (1975): 234–45.

"The Melanesian Labor Reserve: Some Reflections on Pacific Labor Markets in the Nineteenth Century." *Pacific Studies* 4.1 (1980): 1–25.

Newman, Peter. *British Guiana*. London: Oxford University Press, 1964.

North-Coombes, M. D. "From Slavery to Indenture: Forced Labour in the Political Economy of Mauritius, 1834–1867." Pages 78–125 in Saunders, *Indentured Labour (see below)*.

Norton, Robert. *Race and Politics in Fiji*. 2nd ed. St. Lucia: University of Queensland Press, 1990.

Odo, Franklin, and Kazuko Sinoto. *A Pictorial History of the Japanese in Hawai'i, 1885–1924*. Honolulu: Bishop Museum Press, 1985.

Okihiro, Gary Y. *Cane Fires: The Anti-Japanese Movement in Hawaii, 1865–1945*. Philadelphia: Temple University Press, 1991.

Omvedt, Gail. "Migration in Colonial India: The Articulation of Feudalism and Capitalism by the Colonial State." *Journal of Peasant Studies* 7.2 (1980): 185–212.

Pachai, B. *The International Aspects of the South African Indian Question, 1860–1971*. Cape Town: C. Struik, 1971.

Panoff, M. "The French Way in Plantation Systems." *Journal of Pacific History* 26.2 (1991): 206–12.

Patterson, Wayne. *The Korean Frontier in America: Immigration to Hawaii, 1896–1910*. Honolulu: University of Hawaii Press, 1988.

Pérez, Louis A., Jr. *Cuba: Between Reform and Revolution*. New York: Oxford University Press, 1988.

Pike, Nicolas. *Sub-tropical Rambles in the Land of Aphanapteryx: Personal Experiences, Adventures, and Wanderings in and around the Island of Mauritius*. New York: Harper & Brothers, 1873.

Prakash, Gyan. *Bonded Histories: Genealogies of Labor Servitude in Colonial India*. Cambridge: Cambridge University Press, 1990.

"Terms of Servitude: The Colonial Discourse on Slavery and Bondage in India." Pages 131–49 in Klein, *Breaking the Chains (see above)*.

Price, Charles A., with Elizabeth Baker. "Origins of Pacific Island Labourers in Queensland, 1863–1904: A Research Note." *Journal of Pacific History* 11.2 (1976): 106–21.

Ramesar, Marianne. "Industrial Labour in Trinidad, 1880–1917." Pages 57–77 in Saunders, *Indentured Labour (see below)*.

Reddi, Sadasivam. "Aspects of Slavery during the British Administration [of Mauritius]." Pages 106–23 in *Slavery in South West Indian Ocean*, edited by U. Bissoondoyal and S. B. C. Servansing. Moka, Mauritius: Mahatma Gandhi Press, 1989.

Reddy, M. Atchi. "Official Data on Agricultural Wages in the Madras Presidency from 1873." *Indian Economic and Social History Review* 15.4 (1978): 451–66.

Renault, François. *Libération d'esclaves et nouvelle servitude: Les rachats de captifs africains pour le compte des colonies françaises après l'abolition de l'esclavage*. Abidjan: Nouvelles Editions Africaines, 1976.

Richardson, David, ed. *Abolition and its Aftermath: The Historical Context, 1790–1916.* London: Frank Cass, 1985.

Richardson, Peter. *Chinese Mine Labour in the Transvaal.* London: Macmillan, 1982.

"The Natal Sugar Industry, 1849–1905: An Interpretative Essay." *Journal of African History* 23.4 (1982): 515–27.

"Chinese Indentured Labour in the Transvaal Gold Mining Industry, 1904–10." Pages 260–90 in Saunders, *Indentured Labour (see below).*

"Coolies, Peasants, and Proletarians: The Origins of Chinese Indentured Labour in South Africa, 1904–1907." Pages 167–85 in Marks and Richardson, *International Labour Migration (see above).*

Roberts, G. W. "Immigration of Africans into the British Caribbean." *Population Studies* 7.3 (1954): 235–62.

Roberts, G. W., and J. Byrne. "Summary Statistics on Indenture and Associated Migration Affecting the West Indies, 1843–1918." *Population Studies* 20.1 (1966): 125–34.

Rodney, Walter. *A History of the Guyanese Working People, 1881–1905.* Baltimore: Johns Hopkins University Press, 1981.

Rozman, Gilbert. "Social Change." Pages 499–568 in *Cambridge History of Japan, volume 5: The Nineteenth Century*, edited by Marcus B. Jansen. Cambridge: Cambridge University Press, 1989.

Salinger, Sharon V. *"To Serve Well and Faithfully": Labor and Indentured Servants in Pennsylvania, 1682–1800.* Cambridge: Cambridge University Press, 1987.

Saunders, Kay. "The Pacific Islander Hospitals in Colonial Queensland: The Failure of Liberal Principles." *Journal of Pacific History* 11.1–2 (1976): 28–50.

ed. *Indentured Labour in the British Empire, 1840–1920.* London: Croom Helm, 1984.

Scarr, Deryck. "Recruits and Recruiters: A Portrait of the Pacific Island Labour Trade." *Journal of Pacific History* 2 (1967): 5–24.

Scherer, André. *La Réunion.* Que Sais-je? Paris: Presses Univérsitaires de France, 1980.

Schuler, Monica. "African Immigration to French Guiana: The *Cinq Frère* Group, 1854–1860." *Bulletin of the African Studies Association of the West Indies* 4 (1971): 62–78.

"Alas, Alas, Kongo": A Social History of Indentured African Immigration into Jamaica, 1841–1865. Baltimore: Johns Hopkins University Press, 1980.

"The Recruitment of African Indentured Labourers for European Colonies in the Nineteenth Century." Pages 125–61 in Emmer, *Colonialism and Migration (see above).*

"Kru Emigration to British and French Guiana, 1841–1857." Pages 155–201 in *Africans in Bondage: Studies in Slavery and the Slave Trade*, edited by Paul E. Lovejoy. Madison: African Studies Program, University of Wisconsin, 1986.

Liberated Africans in Nineteenth Century Guyana. The 1991 Elsa Goveia Memorial Lecture. Mona, Jamaica: Department of History, University of the West Indies, Mona, 1992.

Scott, Rebecca J. *Slave Emancipation in Cuba: The Transition to Free Labor, 1860–1899.* Princeton: Princeton University Press, 1985.

Shameem, Shaista. "Gender, Class and Race Dynamics: Indian Women in Sugar Production in Fiji." *Journal of Pacific Studies* 13 (1987): 10–35.

Shanin, Teodor. "The Peasants Are Coming: Migrants Who Labour, Peasants Who Travel and Marxists Who Write." *Race and Class* 19.3 (1978): 277–88.

Shineberg, D. " 'Noumea No Good. Noumea No Pay.' " *Journal of Pacific History* 26.2 (1991): 187–205.

Shlomowitz, Ralph. "Markets for Indentured and Time-Expired Melanesian Labour in Queensland, 1863–1906: An Economic Analysis." *Journal of Pacific History* 16.2 (1981): 70–91.

"Indentured Melanesians in Queensland: A Statistical Investigation of Recruiting Voyages, 1871–1903." *Journal of Pacific History* 16.3 (1981): 203–8.

"Fertility and Fiji's Indian Migrants 1879–1919." *Indian Social and Economic History Review* 23.2 (1987): 205–13.

"The Fiji Labor Trade in Comparative Perspective, 1864–1914." *Pacific Studies* 9.3 (1986): 107–52.

"Mortality and the Pacific Labour Trade." *Journal of Pacific History* 22.1 (1987): 34–55.

"Mortality and Indentured Labour in Papua (1885–1941) and New Guinea (1920–1941)." *Journal of Pacific History* 23.2 (1988): 70–79.

"Epidemiology and the Pacific Labor Trade." *Journal of Interdisciplinary History* 19.4 (1989): 585–610.

"The Pacific Labour Trade and Super-Exploitation?" *Journal of Pacific History* 24.2 (1989): 238–41.

"Differential Mortality of Asians and Pacific Islanders in the Pacific Labour Trade." *Journal of the Australian Population Association* 7.2 (1990): 116–27.

Review of *Indentured Indian Emigrants to Natal, 1860–1902*, by Surendra Bhana. In *Journal of Natal and Zulu History* 14 (1992): 113–21.

"Coerced and Free Migration from the United Kingdom to Australia, and Indentured Labour Migration from India and the Pacific Islands to Various Destinations: Issues, Debates, and New Evidence." Paper prepared for International Institute of Social History Conference, Amsterdam, September 1993.

"Marx and the Queensland Labour Trade." *Journal de la Société des Océanistes* 96.1(1993): 11–17.

Shlomowitz, Ralph, and Lance Brennan. "Mortality and Indian Labour in Malaya, 1877–1913." *Indian Economic and Social History Review* 29.1 (1992): 57–75.

"Epidemiology and Indian Labor Migration at Home and Abroad." *Journal of World History* 5.1 (1994): 47–67.

Shlomowitz, Ralph, and John McDonald. "Mortality of Indian Labour on Ocean Voyages, 1843–1917." *Studies in History* 6.1 (1990): 35–65.

Singh, Kelvin. "East Indians and the Larger Society." Pages 39–68 in LaGuerre, *Calcutta to Caroni (see above)*.

Skinner, George William. *Chinese Society in Thailand: An Analytical History*. Ithaca: Cornell University Press, 1957.

Slater, Henry. "The Changing Pattern of Economic Relationships in Rural Natal, 1838–1914." Chapter 6 in *Economy and Society in Pre-Industrial South Africa*, edited by Shula Marks and Anthony Atmore. London: Longman, 1980.

Smith, M. G. *The Plural Society in the British West Indies*. Berkeley: University of California Press, 1965.

Smith, Raymond T. *British Guiana*. London: Oxford University Press, 1962.

Spence, Jonathan D. *The Search for Modern China*. New York: W. W. Norton, 1990.

Steckel, Richard H., and Richard A. Jensen. "New Evidence on the Cause of Slave

Mortality in the Atlantic Slave Trade." *Journal of Economic History* 46.1 (1986): 57–77.

Steinfeld, Robert J. *Invention of Free Labor: The Employment Relation in English and American Law and Culture, 1350–1870.* Chapel Hill: University of North Carolina Press, 1991.

Stewart, Watt. *Chinese Bondage in Peru: A History of the Chinese Coolie in Peru, 1849–1874.* Durham, N.C.: Duke University Press, 1951.

Swan, Maureen. *Gandhi: The South African Experience.* New History of Southern Africa Series. Johannesburg: Ravan Press, 1985.

"Ideology in Organized Indian Politics, 1891–1948." Pages 182–208 in *The Politics of Race, Class and Nationalism in Twentieth-Century South Africa,* edited by Shula Marks and Stanley Trapido. London: Longman, 1987.

Ta Chen. *Chinese Migration, with Special Reference to Labor Conditions.* Bulletin of the United States Bureau of Labor Statistics, no. 340 (July 1923). Washington, D.C.: Government Printing Office, 1923.

Takaki, Ronald. *Pau Hana: Plantation Life and Labor in Hawaii, 1835–1920.* Honolulu: University of Hawaii Press, 1983.

Tayal, Maureen. "Indian Indentured Labour in Natal, 1890–1911." *Indian Economic and Social History Review* 14.4 (1977): 519–47.

Thomas, Brinley. *International Migration and Economic Development: A Trend Report and Bibliography.* Paris: UNESCO, 1961.

ed. *Economics of International Migration.* London, 1958.

Thomas, Mary Elizabeth. *Jamaica and Voluntary Laborers from Africa, 1840–1865.* Gainesville: University Presses of Florida, 1974.

Thompson, Leonard. "Co-operation and Conflict,: The Zulu Kingdom and Natal." Chapter 8 in *Oxford History of South Africa,* volume 1, edited by Monica Wilson and Leonard Thompson. Oxford: Oxford University Press, 1971.

Tinker, Hugh. *A New System of Slavery: The Export of Indian Labour Overseas, 1830–1920.* London: Oxford University Press, 1974.

Toussaint, Auguste. *Histoire des îles Mascareignes.* Paris: Berger-Levrault, 1972.

Tsai, Shih-shan Henry. *China and the Overseas Chinese in the United States, 1868–1911.* Fayetteville: University of Arkansas Press, 1983.

Van den Boogaart, E., and P. C. Emmer. "Colonialism and Migration: An Overview." Pages 3–15 in Emmer, *Colonialism and Migration (see above).*

Vandercock, John W. *King Sugar: The Story of Sugar in Hawaii.* New York: Harper & Brothers, 1939.

Visaria, Leena, and Pravin Visaria "Population (1757 1947)." Pages 463–532 in *Cambridge Economic History of India,* volume 2: c. 1757-c. 1970, edited by Kumar Dharma and Meghnad Desai. Cambridge: Cambridge University Press, 1983.

Wallerstein, Immanuel. *The Modern World System III: The Second Era of Great Expansion of the Capitalist World-Economy.* San Diego: Academic Press, 1989.

Welch, David. "The Growth of Towns." *Chapter 4 in Oxford History of South Africa,* volume 2, edited by Monica Wilson and Leonard Thompson. Oxford: Oxford University Press, 1971.

Weller, Judith Ann. *The East Indian Indenture in Trinidad.* Rio Padres, Puerto Rico: Institute of Caribbean Studies, 1968.

Wilkinson, Alec. *Big Sugar: Seasons in the Cane Fields of Florida.* New York: Alfred A. Knopf, 1989.

Willcox, Walter F., ed. *International Migrations.* 2 volumes. New York: National Bureau of Economic Research, 1929, 1931.

Williams, Eric. *Capitalism and Slavery.* Charlotte: University of North Carolina Press, 1944.

From Columbus to Castro: The History of the Caribbean, 1492–1969. London: Andre
    Deutsch, 1970. Reprint New York: Vintage Books, 1984.
Willson, Margaret, Clive Moore, and Doug Munro. "Asian Workers in the Pacific."
    Pages 78–107 in *Labour in the South Pacific*, edited by Clive Moore, Jacqueline
    Leckie, and Doug Munro. Townsville, Queensland: Department of History
    and Politics, and Melanesian Studies Centre, James Cook University of North
    Queensland, 1990.
Wolf, Eric. *Europe and the People without History.* Berkeley: University of California
    Press, 1982.
Wood, Donald. *Trinidad in Transition: The Years after Slavery.* London: Oxford
    University Press for the Institute of Race Relations, 1968.
Woodruff, William. *Impact of Western Man: A Study of Europe's Role in the World
    Economy, 1750–1960.* New York: St. Martin's Press, 1967.
Woon, Yuen-fong. "The Voluntary Sojourner among the Overseas Chinese: Myth
    or Reality?" *Pacific Affairs* 56.4 (1983–84): 673–90.
Wright, Harrison M., ed. *The "New Imperialism": Analysis of Late-Nineteenth-Century
    Expansion.* 2 ed. Lexington, Mass.: D. C. Heath, 1976.
Yamamoto Ichihashi. "International Migration of the Japanese." Pages 613–36 in
    International Migrations, volume 2, edited by Walter F. Willcox. New York:
    National Bureau of Economic Research, 1929.
Yamin, Gill M. "The Character and Origins of Labour Migration from Ratnagiri
    District, 1840–1920." *South Asian Research* 9.1 (1989): 33–53.
Yang, Anand. "Peasants on the Move: A Study of Internal Migration in India."
    Journal of Interdisciplinary History 10.1 (1979): 37–58.
Yen, Ching-Hwang. *Coolies and Mandarins: China's Protection of Overseas Chinese
    during the Late Ch'ing Period (1851–1911).* Singapore: Singapore University
    Press, 1985.

Index